Early Wynn, the Go-Go White Sox
and the 1959 World Series

Early Wynn, the Go-Go White Sox and the 1959 World Series

LEW FREEDMAN

McFarland & Company, Inc., Publishers
Jefferson, North Carolina, and London

LIBRARY OF CONGRESS CATALOGUING-IN-PUBLICATION DATA

Freedman, Lew.
  Early Wynn, the go-go White Sox and the 1959 World Series /
Lew Freedman.
       p.   cm.
  Includes bibliographical references and index.

  ISBN 978-0-7864-4442-7
  softcover : 50# alkaline paper ∞

  1. Wynn, Early.   2. Pitchers (Baseball) — United States —
Biography.   3. Baseball players — United States — Biography.
4. Chicago White Sox (Baseball team)   5. World Series (Baseball)
1959.   I. Title.
GV865.W96F74   2009
796.357092 — dc22   2009033376
[B]

British Library cataloguing data are available

On the cover: Early Wynn carried the White Sox staff and team to
the pennant, winning 22 games and the Cy Young Award, 1959 (Baseball Hall of Fame Library)

Manufactured in the United States of America

McFarland & Company, Inc., Publishers
  Box 611, Jefferson, North Carolina 28640
  www.mcfarlandpub.com

Table of Contents

Preface   1

Introduction   5

1. The Little Left-Hander   11
2. The Deal Maker   19
3. Early Early Wynn   29
4. The Barrier Breaker   37
5. Looking for Keepers   46
6. The Chief and His Indians   55
7. More Than Just Names   65
8. The Guy They Called Little Nell   75
9. Magician with a Glove   84
10. Wynn Joins the White Sox   92
11. Becoming a Contender   100
12. Filling in the Holes   110
13. The New Guy Is Different   118
14. Going for It All   129
15. Erasing 40 Years of Bad Luck   139
16. Veeck — As in What the Heck   147
17. Taking a Run at First Place   156

Table of Contents

18. The Promised Land at Last   165

19. Welcome to the World Series   175

20. Too Late for Early and the Sox   187

Epilogue: Fifty Years Later   195

Chapter Notes   197

Bibliography   205

Index   211

Preface

During the 1959 baseball season an aging, coming-to-the-end-of-the-line pitcher with the winsome name of Early Wynn was the most important player in the game. In an unlikely turn of events that culminated a major-league career that had begun in 1939, the hard-nosed, determined right-hander who had delivered excellence against the odds with a terrible Washington Senators franchise and been a featured performer on one of the best teams in American League history in Cleveland, put an entire baseball team on his broad shoulders and carried it to a pennant.

The Chicago White Sox had not appeared in a World Series in 40 years, since the infamous Black Sox scandal of 1919, when the Sox fixed the Series and threw games, and plunged the franchise into a decades-long dark period. The ripple effect of losing eight top players from the team ransacked the club and left it floundering for more than two decades. Wynn, with a remarkable 22-win season, and a group of popular players who have endured in White Sox lore and as favorites among fans, including the Hall of Fame keystone combination of Luis Aparicio and Nellie Fox, and amiable southpaw Billy Pierce, who had a statue unveiled in his honor at U.S. Cellular Field in 2007, were the cornerstones of the 1959 resurgence.

It was one of the most memorable baseball seasons in Chicago of all time. Shortly before the beginning of the 1959 season the team's ownership passed out of the hands of the Comiskey family for the first time since the franchise's founding. Colorful Hall of Fame owner Bill Veeck, the best friend the baseball fan ever had, bought a controlling share of the team, though throughout the spring and into the season Veeck had to withstand court challenges from a disgruntled family member to gain fully recognized ownership. That was the backdrop to the baseball, but when Veeck got the green light to run things his way, he made his mark. Veeck introduced the exploding scoreboard to Comiskey Park and baseball, held wildly popular fan events like Ladies Day and introduced other promotions. Veeck's philosophy was to make sure fans had a good time whether their team won or lost. He wanted them to remember their ballpark experience and talk about it. Chicago fans are still talking about some of Veeck's stunts a half-century later.

On the baseball side, the 1950s represented a resurrection of the White Sox. The club was repeatedly frustrated by the New York Yankees dynasty during the decade, but in spring training of 1959 manager Al Lopez brashly declared that the Yankees were beatable — and he was correct. Lopez, Wynn, Aparicio, Veeck, and Fox were all on their way to the Hall of Fame and the stars aligned neatly. The 1959 season was the culmination of a 1950s-long rise of the Sox from perpetual losers to perennial contender. All of the pieces seemed in place by 1958, but the Sox kept falling a tiny bit short until Wynn joined the rotation and showed in his last-gasp quest for 300 victories that he had enough left in the tank to uplift a team one more time.

In 1959, when Wynn, at age 39, won 22 games and the Cy Young Award in leading the Chicago White Sox to their first pennant in 40 years, it was also the team's last pennant until 2005. White Sox fans celebrated in '59 as if it was the end of the millenium, not merely the end of a decade. Wynn was the elder statesman on a team of dashing base runners, hit-and-run experts, and slick fielders. Day after day all summer Wynn won the important games, uplifted a solid pitching staff, and was the pitching glue that ended a decade's worth of frustration for a team that had been constructed to beat the hated New York Yankees.

In White Sox legend and in fans' hearts the 1959 team was as good as a Series champ. Several of the most beloved players in team history performed on that team. By all accounts, Wynn was the world's grouchiest opponent facing enemy batters whom he strived to intimidate. He uttered one of the most famous lines in pitching history, saying he would throw at his mother if she dug in at the plate against him. Al Lopez, one of the first prominent Hispanics in major-league baseball, was known as El Señor because he was just about the only Hispanic around when he played in earlier decades. A sage and respected leader, Lopez somehow contrived to live until just a few days after the White Sox won their World Series crown in 2005. Lopez was revered in Tampa, where he grew up, and after the Sox played in the World Series in 1959 he was thrown a parade in that town.

The 1959 season had it all. Bill Veeck, the greatest showman in baseball history taking over the team, the departure of one of the most historic names in the sport's annals from team leadership, a wizened and wise team leader, colorful players, a morale-building trade, and Hall of Fame players. And all of that was before the White Sox won their only pennant in 40 years and played in the first World Series ever staged in California. The Dodgers were still newcomers in Los Angeles and still playing in the antiquated Los Angeles Coliseum when they faced off against the White Sox for the championship.

The White Sox won with pure baseball style. Their speedy hitters ran the bases superbly — Aparicio always led the league in stolen bases (nine years in a row). Their sharp fielders were godsends to the pitchers, chasing down fly balls and plucking grounders off the Comiskey Park infield with ease. During this time period, Ty Cobb, whom many consider the greatest baseball player of all time, and one who disdained the changed emphasis on the long ball, wrote a fan letter to Nellie Fox complimenting him for his prowess playing the game the old fashioned way. Cobb also injected himself into the public eye by predicting a White Sox triumph in the World Series.

So many special things surrounded the season. Although the White Sox did not win the championship, they participated in the first Hollywood World Series. This was the Dodgers' first World Series after abandoning Brooklyn and their devoted fans in the East; it was also soon enough after the franchise transfer that their new ballpark was not yet constructed. The Los Angeles Coliseum is a football stadium that was quirkily shaped for baseball, but was so large the Series games attracted more than 92,000 people a game and set still-standing Series attendance records.

Pitching the White Sox to a pennant in 1959 to end a long drought when no one thought he could do it remained a highlight of Early Wynn's career and made him a legend in team history. It was a super nova of a performance from a man whose athletic career was in eclipse and it remains one of the most memorable aspects of a very sweet baseball season for the White Sox.

Introduction

The old man stood on the mound with more than 48,000 pairs of eyes on him, waiting. Nothing could happen until Early Wynn said "go" by inching into the pitching windup that over a lifetime had been his favorite body language. They were long seconds, but meaningful. It was a heck of a day for October, the sun high in the sky and warming the field. The countdown to action was on Wynn's pace. He was 39 years old, a few months shy of 40, and for a few years now there were whispers that he might be washed up, that his right arm was more noodle than muscle.

The entire 1959 season had been a last laugh for Wynn, a gigantic smirk in the faces of the armchair scouts with their two-bit analysis. Wynn had come to the big leagues in 1939 with the Washington Senators as a young and feisty know-it-all, so concerns about his age were true. But 20 years into a career that withstood the test of everything from Joe DiMaggio's swing and World War II's violence to smart guys' barbs, he did know it all.

Wynn's face was as leathery as an old hiking boot and he did not have the same whiplash arm as he had when he was a boy scrambling to throw his way out of the cotton fields of Alabama. He rode his baseball skill to freedom, escaping from poverty into a life of luxury, prominence and respect. He had lived hard and didn't like the taste. He had enjoyed the spoils and developed a taste for it. There had been times along the way when Wynn had to be mean, to whiz that hardball under the chin of a batter who was trying to steal the hard-won earnings from him, to grab that filet mignon right off the four-star restaurant table and return him to eating corned beef hash from a can. Sure, Early Wynn said he would brush his own mother back if she crowded the plate. But the scribes laughed and misunderstood that. It didn't mean he didn't love his mother.

It meant that no one was going to take away from him the life he had built from scratch.

He was in no way ready or willing to go quietly into that good night, to fade from the baseball scene after the Cleveland Indians gave up on him and shipped him to the Chicago White Sox in 1958. Granted, things didn't look so good then and they didn't really snap into place completely all season with that darned 14–16 record. But you had to give it to El Señor. He knew his baseball and he knew how to coax the best out of Wynn. That was the best thing for Wynn about coming to Chicago, being managed by Al Lopez again. Lopez was the mentor of that great Indians team of '54, the year when Wynn won 23 games.

In Chicago, they had something going. The Yankees owned the decade, but that didn't stop Lopez from telling people that his White Sox were going to do something special. In spring training he predicted that this time those infuriating Yankees, winning pennant after pennant under Casey Stengel, with Mickey Mantle and Whitey Ford, were ripe to be taken. Throughout the 1950s, the White Sox, after long years of suffering, had been building and building, adding a piece there, subtracting a piece here, throwing a fresh arm in there, getting a new set of wheels there. Neither Lopez, nor Wynn, nor anyone else who followed the team knew in March that the missing piece after all of those years of trying, after all of those years of searching, would be Wynn himself.

In 1959, Wynn became the most important player in the American League, maybe in all of baseball. Never before had anyone's right arm shut more mouths without delivering a punch on the kisser. He won 22 regular-season games and woke up on a fine autumn day assigned to pitch the first game of the World Series.

It had been some ride, 1959, all of it, going on seven months of magic. When Lopez gathered the news guys around him in Tampa back in the spring, they accepted his prediction of White Sox supremacy with a "yeah, yeah" attitude. The Yankees had won nine pennants in the last 10 years. What made Lopez think that suddenly New York was vulnerable?

But Lopez out-thought most people. When a guy catches 1,950 major-league games something rubs off. You can't play that long, especially in the intimacy of the position calling games and coddling pitchers, without picking up wisdom. So Lopez knew. He was Mr. Baseball in the city, a favorite native son who was the town's No. 1 baseball connection. They might have laughed in New York, but fans hung on his every word in Tampa as if he were Nostradamus.

Speculative or not, they were comforting words for White Sox fans. And in 1959 the White Sox were a franchise sorely in need of a pick-me-up and just another Schlitz wouldn't cut it. The season was the 40-year anniversary of the worst scandal in professional sports. In 1919, the heavily favored White Sox that manager Kid Gleason had called one of the greatest ball teams of all time, under the influence of gamblers fixed the World Series and lost to the Cincinnati Reds.

The dismaying doings led directly to the appointment of an all-powerful commissioner, Judge Kenesaw Mountain Landis, a man with about as much compassion in his heart as there are calories in a celery stalk. Although eight White Sox players were acquitted of any crimes in a Chicago courtroom, Landis suspended them from Organized Baseball for life. Among them was "Shoeless" Joe Jackson, a man whose hitting stroke was swifter than his feet.

Baseball survived, and quickly thrived again, because of the timely arrival of a fantastic larger-than-life figure named Babe Ruth. Although the White Sox survived, they did not thrive. They became like Moses wandering in the desert, on their own 40-year trek to nowhere, though they had grass rather than sand beneath their feet. Forty years of nothing for the White Sox — a lost era. Wynn had been part of none of it, though he had been pitching on a nearly parallel course for 20 years, missing out on American League pennants for all but one year.

At last things began to tilt the White Sox way, starting in 1949 when general manager Frank Lane acquired southpaw Billy Pierce. That was only the start for "Trader" Lane, but he couldn't trade the Sox to a pennant. In 1957, team vice presidents Charles Comiskey II and John Rigney felt the White Sox needed more oomph. Doing their best Lane imitation, they swung a deal with Cleveland bringing outfielder Al Smith and pitcher Early Wynn to Chicago. It changed the course of Wynn's career and he knew it. Otherwise, Wynn never would have seen another World Series except on TV.

The fastball, which once had so much zip on it that batters flailed helplessly, had lost a mile per hour or two, something potentially fatal for a hurler. Wynn made up for it with his demeanor, a scowl meant to frighten a smidgeon of bat speed from the hitter's wrists. And he had an eager willingness to throw at a man's head, back, or knees, whatever it took to make that player retreat in the batter's box. Wynn employed the intimidation of facial expressions at least as effectively as heavyweight boxer Sonny Liston, who was on his way to his own crown at the time.

By 1959, the baseball world suspected that Early Wynn was a fading athlete, past his prime, working for just another payday. The baseball world thought the White Sox were on track for the same four-decades-in-the-making heartache. And the baseball world at large scoffed at Al Lopez's pennant premonition.

They were all wrong.

Hints emerged early that 1959 would not be just another run-of-the-mill season of disappointment in White Sox World. Wynn did his part. He paraded to the mound every fourth day, taking his starting turn 37 times during the year. And if Wynn always brought his game face, focused, intense, with the glower that made edgy batters nervous and kept them light on their toes waiting for the fastball that might rearrange their brain cells, he did so with inner peace. And although it was not his way to show pleasure on the mound outwardly, he could at least smile inwardly.

The team proved Lopez correct. The White Sox finished 94–60 and won the American League pennant for the first time since the Black Sox scandal had tarnished the national pastime. When the White Sox clinched it in Cleveland, the players jumped on a flight home that night, guzzling champagne on the plane in celebration.

That little private party, the satisfaction permeating the cabin, was something to remember. But it was no more than a lonely star in the sky overshadowed by a constellation compared to what was going on in Chicago. When the Sox defeated the Indians, the joy erupted, sending fans into the streets to dance and shout. Forty years of pent-up frustration spilled into spontaneous noisemaking and unrestrained excitement as thousands of fans turned out at Midway Airport in the middle of the night.

Comiskey Park was transformed for the World Series. It didn't take much. The draping red, white and blue bunting was outerwear that had long been missing from the old ballpark's wardrobe. It was plain, simple, patriotic, and yet meant so much. The World Series was back in town.

Right-handed pitcher Early Wynn was acquired from the Cleveland Indians in 1958 and was supposedly washed up. Instead, in 1959, Wynn carried the White Sox staff and team to the pennant, winning 22 games and the Cy Young Award. (National Baseball Hall of Fame Library, Cooperstown, New York.)

The White Sox watched with curiosity as the Los Angeles Dodgers and the Milwaukee Braves slugged it out in the National League. The Braves had been in the Series two years in a row. The Dodgers were trying to make it back for the first time since the team abandoned Brooklyn after the 1957 season. Darned if the Braves and Dodgers didn't tie at the end of the regular season. They had to go right into a three-game playoff for the right to play the White Sox while the Sox sat around and watched. No big deal. The couple of extra days off might do old White Sox legs good.

Finally, the Dodgers won the playoff. That was OK. The weather was mighty fine in Los Angeles and the beautiful people, all well-tanned, would be sure to come out for the first World Series to take place in California. Not that it mattered much to the White Sox. That stuff was all for show and going West would be a business trip. It didn't make any difference how well-known someone at the park was, they only counted if they were wearing numbers on their backs.

Now it fell to "Burly" Early to improve on the season in Game 1 of the World Series. Dodger third baseman Jim Gilliam stepped into the batter's box and Early Wynn went into his big windup, ball in glove, standing straight up, both arms held high above his head for a moment. Then he turned his body to the side, brought his right arm back and fired the fastball of his recaptured youth toward home plate.

1

The Little Left-Hander

The true rehabilitation of the Chicago White Sox began in 1949 after three decades of wandering aimlessly in the wilderness like Moses when general manager Frank "Trader" Lane targeted a young southpaw with the Detroit Tigers for his starting rotation.

Billy Pierce, who grew up in Michigan and was thrilled to be signed by his hometown team, sat in the Tigers' bullpen as an 18-year-old in 1945 marveling at the sights and sounds of being part of a World Series team. Wide-eyed after appearing in five major-league games over the summer, Pierce, who had made his mark in amateur ball around Michigan, was as much a spectator as a ticket-buyer, enjoying the feats of Hal Newhouser and Dizzy Trout as the Tigers defeated the Chicago Cubs in seven games to capture the World Series crown. At 5-foot-10 and 160 pounds, Pierce was never going to contend for the heavyweight championship of the world, nor was he going to exhibit the same type of blinding speed on his fastball that a blink-and-you-missed-it fireball from Bob Feller could engender. But for a little guy he was fast enough and he always seemed to get guys out.

Pierce was fresh out of high school when he was an up-close eyewitness to the Tigers' triumph. The team knew he needed more seasoning and Pierce's next appearance in a major-league uniform was not until 1948 when he finished 3–0. Pierce never entertained the thought of playing for any club besides the one he watched at Briggs Stadium with his dad while growing up in the Detroit area.

That was out of his control, however. The White Sox had been nonentities in the American League essentially since 1919 when the Black Sox scandal came to light after the team blew the World Series to the Cincinnati Reds and the subsequent banishment of eight players from the team.

Once a mighty team that had to be reckoned with annually in the pennant chase, the White Sox had been relegated to the second division, seemingly permanently, throughout the 1920s, 1930s and 1940s.

Now the task fell to Lane to rebuild and retool, to elevate the once-fearsome White Sox into pennant contention again. Lane was baseball's leading craps player, a gambler who shuffled players around like pieces on a board game. He would try anything, take chances on anybody, and had no sacred cows on his roster. Lane didn't care if a player had the words "White Sox" tattooed on his chest (not a common occurrence in that era), as a sign of devotion, he would trade him in a heartbeat if he felt the return would benefit the franchise.

During the 1948 season, Pierce got his first look at several of the American League cities. At the time teams were stationed in Detroit, New

Southpaw Billy Pierce was the first key component in the rebuilding of the White Sox when Trader Frank Lane became general manager in the late 1940s. Pierce won 211 games in the majors and still makes periodic appearances for the team. (National Baseball Hall of Fame Library, Cooperstown, New York.)

York, Boston, Philadelphia, Chicago, St. Louis, Washington, D.C., and Cleveland. Perfectly happy playing for Detroit, nonetheless Pierce catalogued his first impressions of the opposing cities. "We visited all of the towns and there were two towns where I said, 'Gee, I wouldn't want to play there,'" Pierce said. "One was Philadelphia because the ballpark, Connie Mack Stadium, was old and not too clean. And the fans were a little unfriendly for their home team. And then there was Chicago. When we came in for a night game the aroma of the stockyards was brutal."[1]

Comiskey Park is located on the South Side of Chicago and the stockyards were close enough that on a breezy day the smells from the processing centers could waft over to the crowd attending a ballgame. And the spectators did inhale. The Union Stock Yard, dating to 1848, was once the only shipping point of livestock from the West by train to the rest of the nation; while in the mid–Twentieth century that was no longer true there was still a lot of mooing going on and a lot of deep breathing.

On November 10, 1948, the White Sox traded catcher Aaron Robinson (lifetime .260 hitter in eight major-league seasons) to the Tigers for $100,000 and Pierce, who became one of the cornerstones of the reviving franchise. Pierce did not immediately hoist a beer in celebration or turn cartwheels with joy upon hearing the news. His first thoughts about his new employer's prospects were universally disappointing. Pierce was not happy about moving away from home. He knew the Tigers were a better team than the White Sox. And his olfactory senses were offended. His outlook was candidly negative. "Very dismal," he said.[2]

Objectively, Pierce could not be blamed. He had the right stink, but the wrong smell. Although 30 years had passed since the greatest sin committed in the course of major-league baseball play, the White Sox were still haunted by the crimes of the Black Sox scandal. The revelations that a team favored to win the World Series, to be anointed kings of America's National Pastime, would toy with the feelings of fans, would desecrate the image of sportsmanship, would eschew a chance to be the best for filthy lucre, and would tamper with the integrity of the game, served as a permanent stain on the team. Even worse, for those White Sox fans who might try to forgive and forget, pray for a fresh start, or simply hope for a good team again, the quicksand the club seemed stuck in made it appear as if the Sox would be punished forever.

The doom-and-gloom of the atmosphere surrounding the late 1940s White Sox that Frank Lane was charged with fixing had its roots in the Black Sox scandal and those roots were difficult to eradicate. Thirty years later the Sox were still paying for the mistakes of another era.

What an inglorious mess it was, the entire plot to throw the World Series in favor of the Reds. It is generally acknowledged that the entire story has never been exposed to bright sunlight, but it is believed that most of the tale has been told. Impressions of the accuracy of what has been described has been coupled, however, with mythology and doubt in other areas, so the public perception of the Black Sox scandal is tinted with shades of gray in some quarters.

The White Sox did not run away with the 1919 American League pennant. Their record was 88–52 and they finished three and a half games ahead of the Cleveland Indians. The National League champion Reds finished 96–44. Still, the White Sox personnel were deemed superior and the team was heavily favored to take the title. Manager Kid Gleason uttered several statements indicating how strongly he believed in his team, but no manager on the cusp of the Series would speak differently.

Right-hander Ed Cicotte, who compiled a 29–7 record that season, was the dominant pitcher. Cicotte was nicknamed "Knuckles" because he had mastered a new devastating pitching weapon called the knuckle-ball. The Sox also had "Shoeless" Joe Jackson, the marvelous hitter who batted .408 in 1911, in the outfield, future Hall of Famer Eddie Collins at second base, and the league's best fielding third baseman in Buck Weaver.

Amidst a frenzy of whispering about how gamblers had influenced the Series, Cincinnati toppled Chicago in eight games as part of a best-of-nine format. Ultimately, investigative newspaper work by Hugh Fullerton led to indictments of White Sox players accused of fixing the Series. Confessions were uttered by Cicotte and Jackson, but disappeared before trial.

Though likely false in its details, but truthful in its implications, one of baseball's most famous incidents was said to occur outside the Chicago courthouse while the players were on trial. As Shoeless Joe exited, a young boy accosted him and said, "Say it ain't so, Joe." Jackson hung his head and replied, "It's so." Proof of any such encounter is sketchy at best, though future novelist James Farrell said he witnessed it.

The way the story is spun, tough guys Swede Risberg and Chick Gandil were at the core of the conspiracy. Jackson, who was illiterate, was said to be taken in by more sophisticated teammates (though he always said he played his hardest, hit well and fielded cleanly during the games). Weaver said the only thing he did wrong was not squeal on his teammates. Cicotte, the linchpin of the scheme, who was paid $10,000 when most of his teammates didn't get their money promised, supposedly sent the sign the fix was in by hitting a Reds batter with a pitch in the first inning. Later, it was said that powerful gambling figure Arnold Rothstein was the key figure behind the scandal.

The players were acquitted, but new baseball commissioner Kenesaw Mountain Landis, given unprecedented powers by owners saddened and fearful about how their game had been besmirched, banned eight White Sox players for life. In a strong statement leveled at the players and all of baseball, Landis ruled that anyone who even discussed a plot to throw a game would be treated harshly. Landis suspended Jackson, Weaver, Cicotte, Gandil, Risberg, Happy Felsch, Lefty Williams and Fred McMullin forever, although by the time he passed sentence the 1920 season had passed. They would not be allowed to play in Organized Baseball again. This decree not only kept them out of the major-leagues, but the minors, too.

Most of the players faded from the scene, living out their lives in private. Public sentiment flared up on Jackson's behalf periodically. There was a feeling a babe had been misled into agreeing to actions he never took. Jackson returned to his home in South Carolina and there were occasional reports that he continued to play ball in lesser leagues in the shadows under an assumed name for years. At the time of his death from a heart attack at age 63 in Greenville, South Carolina in December of 1951, Jackson was operating a liquor store. Upon his death, stories carried some of Jackson's comments about his role in the Black Sox scandal. "Regardless of what anybody says," Jackson said, "I was innocent of any wrongdoing. I gave baseball all I had."[3]

Also seen as more of a tragic figure than a vilified one as the years passed was Weaver. Unlike the others, Weaver refused to fade into the woodwork after his suspension. He wrote a letter appealing to Landis for his reinstatement, saying he broke no rules and deserved to have his name cleared. Weaver kept up his letter writing campaign until Landis died in 1944, still in office. Then, even though he was then too old to play, Weaver sent additional appeals to future commissioners. After a career working at horse racing tracks, Weaver died in 1956, his quest unfulfilled. Even as relatives who knew Weaver personally also passed away, they maintained an effort to clear him for a half century. No one in major-league baseball officialdom has looked favorably on the petitions, however.

White Sox owner Charles Comiskey, the team's founder in 1901, was initially out of the loop while his players were plotting. There are contradictory reports about just when Comiskey was informed his players might not compete on the up-and-up. Like an aggrieved parent, Comiskey passed through stages of disbelief, protest, defense of his lads, and verbal assault of them.

By the time the players played out their trial and were kicked off the White Sox roster Comiskey was left with a far diminished team. He had to cope with the wreckage of a once-championship-caliber club. In an era without minor-league farm systems, with very limited scouting, with no formal talent draft and smaller rosters, the White Sox, albeit through their own fault, had been pillaged.

The Dark Ages of White Sox history swiftly followed. Landis, his fiery eyes, white hair and imperial bearing had the appearance of an avenging angel and in this case his deeds had the same effect. With a few slashes of his sword Landis cut down all White Sox hopes. In 1921, the White Sox finished 62–92. That was just a hint of things to come. Year-by-year team records for the rest of the 1920s were 77–77, 69–85, 66–87, 79–75, 81–72, 70–83, 72–82, 59–93. The year-by-year toils during the first half of the 1930s were similar: 62–92, 56–97, 49–102, 67–83, 53–99, 74–78.

Star White Sox players were as rare as Republican voters within the Chicago city limits. Stalwart pitcher Red Faber, who had helped the White Sox to the world title in 1917, but was injured during the 1919 Series, was like a solo trumpeter trying to play great music on his own. He won 254 games in 20 seasons ending in 1933. Ted Lyons, who pitched 21 years, ending in 1946, and won 260 games, was Faber's front-of-the-rotation successor. Shortstop Luke Appling broke into the lineup in 1930, stayed until 1950, and had a .310 lifetime batting average. All three were elected to the Hall of Fame, yet they almost always had a weak supporting cast.

Charles Comiskey, "The Old Roman," did not live long enough to see any resurrection. He died in 1931, though the team stayed in family hands. Comiskey could not dust off the corruption that enfolded his team during his lifetime and left his descendents with the continuous task of trying to rebuild. Comiskey son John Louis Comiskey, who was known by many as "Uncle Lou," took the reigns in 1931. It was Lou Comiskey who made what seemed to be the promising and crucial hire of Jimmy Dykes as manager during the 1934 season.

Dykes brought fresh optimism to the job. An all-star player who spent 22 seasons in the big leagues starting in 1918 with a .280 average, Dykes considered long-time A's manager Connie Mack his mentor. He dreamed of replacing Mack as head of the Athletics, but brought a solid baseball background and a sound sense of humor to his assignment in Chicago.

Dykes' wit made him popular with newspapermen, but he had loud and running feuds with umpires. Combining those two facets of his baseball life, Dykes once wrote an article in which he explained how he was only offering good advice to his close, personal umpiring friends when he engaged them in dialogue, you know, just to help them out. Dykes ran the White Sox ship from 1934 to part-way through the 1946 season. Four times his teams won more than half of their games, but the White Sox never finished higher than fourth in the standings either.

There was a simple reason why the White Sox couldn't do better on Dykes' watch despite his wealth of baseball knowledge and handy baseball temperament: they just didn't have many good players. Dykes knew talent when he saw it and he recognized talent when it was owned by someone else. Dykes did pick up White Sox players who were other teams' discards, but he was not above using sarcasm applied to his players when he saw hitting and fielding deficiencies, sometimes speaking with his teeth crunching on a large cigar.

When he hired Dykes, Lou Comiskey felt he was getting a bargain. "I got the best manager in baseball, didn't I?" he said.[4] Maybe so, but Dykes didn't have the tools to prove it. And Comiskey didn't have the health to see through the rejuvenation of the team. Overweight at 300 pounds and weakened by scarlet fever, Charles Comiskey's only son died at age 54 on July 18, 1939. For Comiskey and the White Sox it was a case of unfinished business. Control of the team passed to Grace Reidy Comiskey, Louis' widow.

This was a perilous time for the White Sox. Not doing well on the field or at the box office at the close of the Great Depression and leaderless as far as someone with expertise in baseball, Grace Comiskey had to fight off bank maneuvers to keep the franchise in the family. She did so, but the battle diverted resources that might have been used to make the team a winner.

Harry Grabiner had been the behind-the-scenes power and voice of continuity with the White Sox since 1915. He was Charles Comiskey's right-hand man and remained general manager until 1946, two years before dying of brain cancer. His replacement, Les O'Connor, had spent his entire baseball career working in the commissioner's office. O'Connor sought to improve the White Sox at the same time Grace Comiskey was trying to save money, and their partnership ran out of gas by 1948.

That set the stage for the arrival of Frank Lane. Three decades had passed since the Black Sox scandal. The White Sox had been spinning their wheels on ice seemingly forever. There was little promise in the farm system, there was minimal talent on the big-league roster, and there was little reason to believe that the 1950s would be distinguished from the 1920s, 1930s, or 1940s.

America was optimistic. World War II was over. The new decade hinted of prosperity. A new-fangled gadget called the television was revolutionizing family entertainment habits. Baseball was on the cusp of perhaps its greatest era with the color line broken and the biggest pool of talent ever at the disposal of a hungry, determined major-league team official.

Just because the White Sox had been buried under the fumes from both the Black Sox and the stockyards for so long, why couldn't they become something special? It was time for Frank Lane to get to work.

2

The Deal Maker

The White Sox needed saving when Frank Lane was appointed general manager on November 1, 1948 and given that assignment. Lane was the Donald Trump of baseball's front offices, a wheeler dealer who was hard to satisfy and felt he had an eye for talent that went beyond spotting a young prospect on "The Apprentice."

Some people called Lane "Frantic Frank" because he seemed never to rest. Others called him "The Man in Motion." And still others described him as "Baseball's Human Hurricane." Those were the catchy phrases that followed Lane around in the media like *Sport* magazine, the *Saturday Evening Post*, the *Chicago Tribune* and the *Chicago American*, all of whom found him to be an irresistible topic.

Lane was born February 1, 1896, and before turning to baseball actually played for professional football teams in Ohio for $100 a game before the creation of the National Football League. A playground umpire who was not as smooth a baseball player himself, Lane became the Cincinnati Reds' traveling secretary in 1933, forging a friendship with owner Larry MacPhail. Lane proved to be sharper at spotting future players than making train arrangements and ended up running the Reds' entire farm system. During World War II, Lane served in the U.S. Navy and when he returned to baseball he went to work for MacPhail again. By then MacPhail was operating the New York Yankees and Lane became general manager of the team's AAA affiliate in Kansas City. In 1946, Lane took over as president of the American Association.

Lane grew up in a struggling family. His father was a druggist, but died when the boy was four. His mother took in sewing. As a youth Frank Lane did chores at a drug store, including washing the windows. He had no athletic background and was flabby. When bullies made him a target of jokes and called him "Fatty Lane" the boy decided to change his image. He began doing push-ups and other calisthenics with the vigor of Jack LaLanne and maintained the athletic routine as a habit well into middle age. After he had reshaped his body, Lane gained confidence and beat up his primary antagonist. "I think that changed my whole life," Lane said. "Up to then I'd just been a big, fat sissy."[1]

Lane not only played football and graduated to umpiring baseball games in the Big Ten and Southeastern Conference, he became sports editor of a Cincinnati newspaper and after high school attended two years of law school. And he did much of that more or less simultaneously. If in later years Lane employees awakened by late-night phone calls wondered if he ever slept the answer was pretty much no. He was getting by on three or four hours of sleep as a young man and even if he eventually trimmed his schedule to one job at a time Lane seemed to keep the same hours as Dracula.

That type of energy was sorely needed around the White Sox. The franchise had been moribund in the standings for so long that the feeling grew and became accepted around baseball that a hired executive couldn't succeed in Chicago. The Comiskey heirs, it was said, were too cheap to spend the necessary money to revive the White Sox. After he had been with the team for a while, Lane publicly addressed the issue.

"When I was offered the job," Lane said, "people told me, 'Don't take it. That's a graveyard. The Comiskeys won't let you spend any money. You'll never be able to get anywhere up there.' But it hasn't been that way at all. The Comiskeys have given me all the cooperation and support a man could ask for and they've let me keep plowing most of our profits back into the ball club."[2]

Chuck Comiskey, the grandson of team founder Charles, met Lane at the 1948 All-Star game. The Sox' then–GM Les O'Connor introduced them. Not long after, Comiskey, then 22, was promoted to the position of vice president by his owner-mother Grace. At the end of that same summer he approached Lane to offer him the general manager's title. Lane accepted. Always energetic, with a thick head of sandy hair that gave him a youthful appearance, trim and fit after a lifetime of exercise, Lane looked younger than his age most of his life. His arrival in the front office of the White Sox was like a fresh electrical charge being shot through the workers. It was as if someone had turned on the lights.

Less than 10 days after assuming his new job, Lane made the trade for Billy Pierce that amounted to a shot across the bow of the American League. Frank Lane was open for business and he was not going to simply sit around behind his desk shuffling paper and twiddling his thumbs. His goal was to bring Chicago an AL pennant, to propel the White Sox into the World Series. Lane was about to break the world record for phone bills and for baseball trading, too. The never-satisfied Lane, still in hot pursuit of a pennant, spent parts of seven years as the White Sox general manager. During that time, from late 1948 to early 1955, he oversaw 241 trades involving 355 players. If you came to the White Sox you needed to consider renting an apartment rather than buying a house. You were also wise to wear a name tag.

Pierce, fresh from Detroit, could barely keep the transactions straight as teammates came and went with the regularity and frequency of birds flying south for the winter. The departure of some players bothered him not at all, but trading some others seemed unlikely to improve the team. "I won't mention any names," Pierce said, "but they had a right-fielder who I saw just take two steps back and catch the ball on the bounce. He just stood there. That didn't impress me too much. I guess I was Frank Lane's first trade, but by the time spring training started, with the exception of about four guys, it was a completely new team."[3]

The turnaround wasn't actually as swift as Pierce remembered it being, but change did follow at a dizzying pace. In October of 1949 Lane made another significant trade with long-term implications. He swapped catcher Joe Tipton to the Philadelphia A's for second baseman Nellie Fox. Fox emerged as a Hall of Fame infielder. Lane called the trades for Pierce and Fox — his first two major deals — the best trades of his career.[4]

When new management assumes control of a sports franchise, whether it is the owner, team president or general manager, and a multitude of changes in personnel follow it is often called housecleaning. It is unlikely that any one in sports history can match Lane's enthusiasm for sweeping, scrubbing, polishing or vacuuming when it came to cleaning out the White Sox player inventory after the 1948 season. He studied the 40-man major-league roster and promptly put the entire team on waivers.

Whether other GMs felt Lane was just kidding, or if he was sincere in his low estimate of the talent level of a ball club that had finished 51–101, claims for only two players were made. Before the end of the calendar year, after about seven weeks as general manager, Lane had engaged in 12 transactions. A year later the White Sox won 63 games, a mere 12-game improvement, and during 1949 Lane concluded an amazing 42 deals involving White Sox players. Some were sales. Some were purchases. Some were player-for-player trades. Some players were acquired one month and traded away the next. Most of them barely made a ripple in the majors.

Still, after a few years of hectic trading, Lane got some negative feedback about his ways. The "Trader" label followed him from Chicago to the St. Louis Cardinals, where he turned that roster upside-down, too. "I do not claim to work miracles," Lane said, "but I apparently was expected, in some quarters, to perform one this year by winning the pennant without making any changes in a ball club that finished seventh last year. Does that make sense to you? I thought not. It doesn't to me, either."[5]

Lane appeared to be counting on miracles early on in his tenure with the White Sox. No one was a more fanatic fan than Lane while watching the team perform on the diamond. If a bunt went awry, if a pitcher missed the strike zone, and Lord forbid if an umpire missed a call, Lane was up on his feet yelling, foaming at the mouth, spewing profanities. He was like a Little League father watching his son play and believing that everything Little Johnny did was perfect, or else the world was in a conspiracy against him. Lane could not control his emotions and behavior at such times. Speaking anonymously to a reporter, a Lane friend said he would not attend White Sox games with the general manager unless Lane's wife and daughter were present. If they were, Lane could keep his emotions sufficiently under wraps. "Otherwise," the friend said, "it's too embarrassing. Everybody can hear him for 25 rows around."[6]

Lane was single-minded, even obsessed, about his White Sox makeover. Outside of spending time with his family, he had no other hobbies. He had been a golf player, but gave up the sport because it was no longer relaxing and so he could devote just about all of his waking hours to the Sox challenge.

Once, outfielder Bob Nieman had to leave the first game of a White Sox doubleheader with an injured wrist. After initial treatment in the clubhouse he decided to watch the rest of the game in the Comiskey Park press box. Nieman found an open seat next to Lane. This happened to be a game where the fates seemed to be against his White Sox, so Lane was ranting and raving, skewering his players for their failure to make the right play. Nieman was abashed and astonished. It didn't take long for Nieman to slip out of his seat and approach a sports writer elsewhere in the box to ask, "Is he like this all the time?" The reply was straightforward: "This is one of his quiet days. If we blow this first game, stick around for the next. Then you'll really hear something." Nieman allegedly considered that option for a moment, but suddenly recalled that he was supposed to get an X-ray on that darned wrist, and disappeared.[7]

Lane was an equal-opportunity trader. If another general manager picked up the phone, Lane felt the courtesy was worthy of a deal. In January of 1949, Lane bought pitcher Floyd Bevans from the New York Yankees — and on March 28, before the season even began, he returned Bevans to the Yankees. In September of 1949 (also in one of Lane's finest deals), he traded infielder Fred Hancock (along with pitcher Charles Eisenmann and cash) to Montreal for shortstop Chico Carrasquel. On April 12, 1950, Hancock was returned to the White Sox from Montreal. On April 14, Hancock was sold to Buffalo.

In July of 1951, Lane bought outfielder Jim Rivera from Seattle. In November of 1951 he traded Rivera to the St. Louis Browns in a multiplayer deal. Then in July of 1952, Lane bought Rivera back from St. Louis. Rivera became a White Sox regular. For a time, however, Rivera was like the ball spinning on a roulette wheel, not knowing whether he was going to land on odd or even when it stopped.

Rivera was with Seattle of the Pacific Coast League, playing for the Hall of Fame second baseman Rogers Hornsby when Lane made the first deal. Soon, Hornsby became manager of the Browns and wanted Rivera back. Thinking big, Lane and Browns owner Bill Veeck — at least as interested in producing a tall headline in the morning paper as Lane was — put together an eight-player deal. The White Sox sent five players to St. Louis and the key figure in the other half of the trade was catcher Sherman Lollar, a major acquisition for Lane and Chicago. But Lane liked the swift-footed Rivera and he paid cash to bring Rivera back to Chicago. The move made Rivera quite happy. "Hell yeah," he said. "I was going from the depths of the cellar to near the top. Wouldn't you be happy? The White Sox were building and the Browns were down on their knees."[8]

In fact, the Browns were soon on their way to becoming the Baltimore Orioles. Rivera was on his way to being a notable building block for the 1950s White Sox. He was so glad Lane reacquired him that he could have kissed him. "Good old, Trader Frank Lane," Rivera said. "He was a very entertaining guy. Everybody loved him."[9]

Except perhaps shortstop Willie Miranda, who was probably baffled by Lane's likes and dislikes. Miranda was traded back and forth between the White Sox and the Browns three times between 1951 and 1952. All deals were consummated between Lane and Veeck. If there was ever to be a series of such transactions between two clubs it made sense that Lane and Veeck were involved. Just like Lane, Veeck did without much sleep. Just like Lane, Veeck loved to swap players to create excitement and hopefully jump-start his team. Just like Lane, Veeck was addicted to the telephone. It was no accident that the White Sox and Browns made so many deals. There had to be times when Lane and Veeck were the only two baseball authority figures awake in America. They probably had no one else to talk to so talked to each other and couldn't hang up until they made a trade.

After the back-and-forth series of trades with Miranda, who could have piled up frequent driver miles on Interstate 55, Veeck joked to Lane that the White Sox should put one of their minor-league affiliates in Mattoon, Illinois, about halfway between Chicago and St. Louis. That way, Veeck said, Miranda would have a place to stop for coffee each time he drove past.[10]

There was an irony in all that bartering between the two kindred spirits. By the end of the 1950s, Lane would be out as White Sox general manager and in as Cleveland Indians GM. Veeck would become owner of the White Sox and in some ways benefit from Lane's incessant trading. Of course, in the early 1950s, neither man could foresee such a thing happening. Veeck was trying to save the hapless Browns from going bankrupt or moving to another city without his approval or ownership and Lane was frantically trying to win the White Sox a pennant.

As the first one on the scene — and as someone who wasn't shipped out before he could unpack his suitcase — Pierce watched the trading circus while busy trying to establish himself as a major-league pitcher. While Lane was viewed as a chatterbox who wove humorous yarns to the press,

Pierce said Lane rarely talked to the players and did not specifically chat them up, except perhaps to say hello or goodbye.

Pierce said it took a couple of years as the revolving door spun ever faster before he realized that Lane's quirky trading habits were definitely benefiting the team. Nellie Fox came over in the fine deal with the A's — and stayed. Minnie Minoso was acquired from the Cleveland Indians — and became a star. Once he stopped passing Willie Miranda on the highway between Chicago and St. Louis, Rivera became a fixture. "It was probably two years before I had a sense that Chicago was really working to turn things around," Pierce said. "By 1951 you could see that this was a ball club that was going to be better, that we would be in competition among the better ball clubs in the American League. Everything really started in 1951. Frank Lane definitely earned the nickname 'Trader.' He turned the franchise around. Chuck Comiskey helped a lot, too. He signed a lot of fellows for the minor leagues who developed to help our ball club. Chuck was kind of instrumental in the changes, too." Maybe Lane never bantered with the players because he didn't want to get too cozy with them and then send them down the Mississippi River to St. Louis, or somewhere else, in a trade. Whenever he did talk to you, though, Pierce said, you could believe what Lane said. "If he told you something," Pierce said, "it was gospel. In my estimation, he was very truthful in the statements he made. He lived up to them, whatever it was."[11]

At the same time, even Pierce did not know if he was throwing off a mound made of quicksand or not. Lane had made it abundantly clear that there were no sacred cows on the White Sox roster. It probably wouldn't have mattered if you were a cousin, not even that would protect you if Lane felt that you were an important ingredient in a trade that could improve the team. He didn't care if you were South Side Irish, if you had had season tickets since Ought-Six, or if you were Mayor Richard J. Daley and had been a Sox fan since the womb, once Lane developed the notion he could get equal value, you were out of there.

One season in the early 1950s at the June 15 trading deadline, the White Sox had an off day and several players joined coach Ray Berres at his Wisconsin cottage. To Lane, June 15 was like a high-holy-day religious holiday and had to be observed. The players went off to frolic in the north woods, but they couldn't stop talking about what might be happening in

Chicago in their absence. Sure enough, when they drove back to town a couple of the players who had been on their little excursion were ear-marked for another team.

"You never knew what Frank was going to do," Pierce said. "But he did always seem to improve the ball club. I don't know how many ballplayers we got rid of that stayed somewhere and did a lot. Not that many."[12]

It was obvious from the first moment Lane did a pushup in Chicago that no one on the roster was going to be safe. It was equally apparent that Lane was going to be hiring his own man to take care of business in the dugout. If Lane was going to remake the team in his own image he did not want to be stuck with a manager who thought differently.

Unfortunately, that was the case with Jack Onslow. Jimmy Dykes had performed his yeoman service between 1934 and 1946 and provided White Sox fans with their first pleasing seasons in years. But when Dykes departed, his successors presided over a return to the ugly days of yester-year. George Haas was manager for about 10 minutes in 1946, finishing with a 5–7 record. He was followed by local hero Ted Lyons, the stalwart pitcher who had achieved when the team around him didn't. Lyons completed the 1946 season in charge and managed in 1947 and partway through 1948 with little luck and poor results. Lane was in place as general manager when the White Sox shopped for a new manager. Lane did not have much input into the decision. Chuck Comiskey had his heart set on hiring Onslow, who was known as "Honest Jack." He convinced his mother, Grace, to go along. So Onslow was in, whether Lane wanted him or not. It was "or not."

Onslow was a baseball lifer with good credentials as a coach, minor league manager, player and scout. It was unclear if anyone could have been a winner with the White Sox in 1949, but when the club slumped, Lane began sniping at Onslow. He called him "a lousy manager" and second-guessed him. Onslow lost his temper over that and the two men were not going to be seen downing beers together at any South Side saloons. Facing off with broken beer bottles in their hands, maybe.[13]

Onslow survived a 63–91 season in 1949, and since he had a two-year contract the White Sox kept him on for 1950 as Lane steamed. An 8–20 start to the 1950 season doomed Onslow's career in Chicago. John "Red" Corriden, at 62 another baseball lifer, shepherded the White Sox through a 52–72 mark over the rest of the season. And then Lane could finally hire the man he wanted for the job.

Paul Richards was as quiet as Lane was flamboyant, but he had a reputation as a very sound baseball man. Richards was unflappable and cared only about what happened on the field. He didn't care what Lane said to newspapermen as long as he gave him the type of players Richards felt he could win with. Born in 1908 in Waxahachie, Texas, Richards was a catcher who played his first big-league game with the Brooklyn Dodgers in 1932. He was not an accomplished player, but after an eight-season major-league career he turned to coaching and managing. Before taking over the White Sox, Richards won three pennants in the high minors. He was viewed as a whiz at teaching pitching techniques and was also a creative strategist.

Lane was constructing a young team that could fly around the base paths and he felt Richards was an up-and-coming manager well suited to supervise a blossoming team. Lane always jealously guarded his prerogative to hire and fire and juggle personnel, but he admitted that while he did not consult with his manager in advance of making his trades he was trying to tailor a team to Richards' strengths. "I wouldn't get a man I knew Paul wouldn't want, or give away one I knew he wanted to keep," Lane said. For his part, Richards displayed a mostly placid demeanor and bemusedly referred to Lane as "Frantic" in casual conversation.[14]

Richards always seemed confident and never seemed like a man who cared too much about public appearances, at least in terms of trying to appease public opinion. He knew baseball and did his best to transfer his knowledge to the youthful players on his team. He let Lane entertain the writers and he talked to them in a businesslike fashion. "Satisfy yourself as to what you are doing and at the same time satisfy your men that you're getting the most out of them," Richards said.[15]

Pierce, the first key player acquired by Lane, stayed with the White Sox long enough to play for Richards and Al Lopez, the Hall of Fame manager who carried the team the final step in the late 1950s, but decades later he said he preferred playing for Richards, that Richards was his favorite White Sox manager. "Richards was more of a teaching manager," Pierce said. "Richards was more about instructing guys what to do. There were a lot of fellows he improved upon their pitches and he developed Nellie Fox, without question. He convinced him to use a different bat. He worked with Nellie an awful lot, bunting, on double plays, on so many different things."[16]

Richards seemed to be the right man at the right time for the young White Sox. Lane was sure of it. He just kept hustling to give his man the type of material that would end the White Sox pennant drought. Lane never rested in his pursuit of making the pennant dream into reality.

3

Early Early Wynn

Summers in Southeast Alabama featured undiluted sun that baked the land and humidity that sweated the energy out of the inhabitants. Hartford, Alabama, where Early Wynn was born on January 6, 1920, was scorched by the same type of heat as Dothan, the nearby city.

The teenager who soon would be rescued by baseball from a harder life working the fields was the only son of Early Wynn Sr. and his wife Blanche in a small community that had only the spelling of its name in common with the much larger Hartford, Connecticut. Even today, Hartford, Alabama, has a population of only slightly more than 2,000 people.

Hartford, Alabama, was neither a metropolis nor a locale where people flocked to chase their dreams. Early Wynn Sr. was an automobile mechanic, operator of his own shop, and a proficient semi-pro baseball pitcher. His son was much more fascinated with the game than he was with the cars and by the time he entered Geneva County High he was an exceptional athlete capable of being a standout on the baseball and football teams.

By then, the younger Wynn had enough experience with the area's main cotton crop that he knew he did not want to make a career out of hard labor. Wynn spent a summer earning 10 cents an hour lifting 500-pound bales of cotton. It was dirty and sweaty work and while it may have helped build his physique at a time when kids who played sports did not yet dream of lifting weights, it was mentally wearing.

Wynn's heart belonged to baseball, but he also seemed likely to become his school's top running back as a sophomore. Right at the start of the season, in practice, as he returned a punt, Wynn was clobbered by a tackle and broke a leg. "My best break ever," he said much later. "It sort of forced me into baseball."[1] Football was more of an amusement than a passion for Wynn, who was an only child, and favored baseball because of his father's play anyway. However, at least one hometown observer believed that Wynn had it in him to become a better football player than baseball player. "Ole Early was quite a football player," said Hartford physician Dr. Hubert Strickland. "He was big and strong and would have been a much better football player, probably professional, if he hadn't broken that leg."[2] Of course, Wynn was more than just a mere professional in baseball. He became a Hall of Famer.

Over the years, Wynn explained that he was of Indian-Scottish-Irish heritage, but in the big leagues he was often casually described as being from Indian stock. He was part Cherokee and that stood out for many who wanted to label Wynn, but he may have had no more than one-eighth Indian blood.

When he was 17, and still in high school, Wynn took a flyer on a try-out camp held at a baseball school in Sanford, Florida. He had little money for such an undertaking, but he had a place to stay at the other end with an aunt. Strickland said that he loaned Wynn $2 for the 1937 trip.[3]

Wynn, who was six feet tall and weighed more than 200 pounds during his major-league career after he filled out, combined natural talent with a baseball education gained from watching his dad play. He had a good fastball and an assortment of other tricks he was still developing. Early Sr. had been a good role model. "We used to throw a lot by the shop when Early was young," his father said. "I had it all. I had a fastball, curve, slider, and a pretty good knuckler, too. I used to travel around quite a bit playing baseball — almost turned pro myself, but decided to open an automobile repair shop."[4]

The younger Wynn didn't cotton to picking cotton and if he wanted to spend his adulthood with his head under the hood of an engine he could always come back and work for his father. But he aspired to more than the limited lifestyle offered in Hartford and he believed pitching was his best talent. He was right. Wynn was noticed in Sanford, making a good impression as a pitcher with potential.

Clyde Milan, who had spent his entire 16-year major-league career as a .285-hitting outfielder for the Washington Senators, liked the way Wynn threw. Retired from the playing field since 1922, Milan was scouting for the forlorn American League club that was hungry to find new talent for a team rapidly disintegrating into a perennial loser. Milan signed Wynn to a $100-a-month contract and the teenager never returned to high school.

Conveniently, the Senators had a low level minor-league club right there in Sanford, playing in the Florida State League. Wynn spent the 1937 season hurling for Sanford and compiled a promising 16–11 record. It was a lot more fun than picking cotton. Wynn's next minor-league outpost was Charlotte in the Piedmont League, where he met his first wife, Mabel. The couple married in 1939 and had a son, whom they named Joe.

As the season of 1939 waned, the Senators brought Wynn to the majors for the first time. He played in three games, starting all of them, and finished 0–2. Although it could hardly be foreseen, those appearances later meant that Wynn would be a rare four-decade major-league player. Wynn did not spend a minute in the majors in 1940, but went 3–1 in 1941 during a late-season call-up after putting together a 16–12 record in the Eastern League for Springfield (Massachusetts). His first full season was 1942 when Wynn took his place in the starting rotation, but finished 10–16. That was not a very good year for Wynn. Mabel was killed in an automobile accident.

Wynn's first solid, winning year with the Senators was 1943, when he finished 18–12. However, 1944 was a nightmare. Wynn's record was 8–17. And before the year was over, he was in the U.S. Army. Wynn met his second wife, Lorraine, while he was a soldier and the two were married for a half century, from 1944 to 1994, when she died. The couple had one daughter, named Sherry.

Wynn missed all of the 1945 season serving in the Army and was discharged after being in uniform for about two years. At the time he was a corporal. If there was any doubt about where Wynn's interest lay, he approached the Washington Senators the day before his discharge to inform them he was ready to pitch — the next day. Without practice and even without bothering with a minor-league warm-up. Wynn was aching to get back into the majors. Wynn told the Senators, "They'll let me out tomorrow morning. I'll be ready to pitch tomorrow afternoon." The ball club asked Wynn if swapping uniforms so quickly would not be overdoing it. "No, sir," said Wynn. "After 23 months in the Army at $65 a month, I'm not rushing a thing."[5]

31

Washington did not take Wynn up on the offer and did not use him again against major-league competition until the next season. It was only in 1946 that Wynn's life began getting back to normal. While pitching in just 17 games Wynn put up an 8–5 record. In 1947, Wynn emerged as one of the workhorses of the Senators' staff. He pitched 247 innings in 33 starts and finished 17–15.

During the early years of Early Wynn's career, the Washington Senators were one of the weakest teams in the American League. Every once in a while the team would put up a mediocre record, usually something like 75–76, that provided some optimism among fans from the Oval Office on down. Usually, though, the team would plod through summer with a record like 64–90 (a surprisingly consistent statistic during the decade). If anything, the Senators would get worse in the coming years, spawning the sarcastic phrase, "Washington, first in war, first in peace, and last in the American League." For a player who would ultimately land in the Hall of Fame, Wynn was not as much help as might be thought. He was not yet good enough to lead a team on his own. The Senators had less talent than the U.S. Congress, and given popular opinion, that wasn't a compliment.

Wynn showed hints of greatness, but was bothered by lack of consistency. He could fire his fastball past any hitter, but might have a mental lapse and surrender a home run soon after. He was an innings eater, but at his best on a lousy team could not nudge his won-loss record much over .500. Still, Wynn did develop a reputation for fierceness on the mound, a description and label that followed him for the rest of his career. It became obvious to baseball men that you didn't mess with Early Wynn. That term meant a number of different things. Any batter who crowded the plate was asking for a fastball aimed at his ear to brush him back. A batter who deigned to bunt and made Wynn field it was asking for trouble. Wynn took such actions personally and was likely to retaliate with a brush-back fastball the next time the fellow came up. Similarly, if a batter stroked a line drive up the middle that Wynn had to duck to avoid, that was grounds for payback.

Mickey Vernon, the slugger who was the Senators' best hitter while Wynn was with the team, and who also made his debut in 1939, said the bunting or even the accidental line drive through the box really got on

Wynn's nerves and he believed in making his feelings known. "He hated to have anybody bunt on him or hit one up through the middle," Vernon said of Wynn. "If you did that, he'd knock you down the next time up."[6]

Wynn was supremely territorial and he owned a terrifying scowl. He could contort his face into expressions of anger and resentment that would send a shiver up a batter's back. When Early looked at you with fire in his eyes there was a good chance that you were going to see fire in his fastball coming at you at more than 90 miles per hour. Occasionally, Wynn did not have the patience to wade through the batting order for nine hitters to wait for an offending batsman to come back up. "That SOB is so mean he would $#&ing knock you down in the dugout," Yankees star Mickey Mantle said once.[7] Mantle had good reason to be frosted. Once, Wynn threw a ball at him while he was standing on first base, trying to hit Mantle in the foot.

The word "mean" came up a lot when opposing hitters talked about Wynn. Umpires were more liberal in the 1930s and 1940s. They didn't warn pitchers or eject them from games very often for throwing at batters. It was understood that pitching inside was part of the game. A bench-clearing brawl because a pitcher threw inside to a hitter, knocking him on his keister and forcing him to dust himself off, too, was also rarer. In more recent decades, those activities are not tolerated to the same degree. Batters now threaten hurlers even when a pitch is only inside, never mind making contact. And umpires warn pitchers at the slightest sign of loss of control. If a pitcher is having a wild day, walking many or hitting batters with pitches, there is an equal chance an umpire will throw him out of the game before his manager can replace him with a reliever.

Wynn did all he could to cultivate an image of a pitcher who was an avenging angel. He had left a life of potential poverty behind him, was starting to make the type of salary that would allow his family to be comfortable, and he knew that the people who could take that all away from him were hitters wielding big sticks. "A pitcher has to look at a hitter as his mortal enemy," Wynn said.[8]

So there was no mystery about where Wynn was coming from in his thought process when he reared back on the mound and fired to the plate. He spelled it out for hitters too dense to figure it out by themselves without the Clif Notes. And if they didn't get the message from a forthright statement like that, Wynn gladly explained his philosophy again and again to newspapermen. He wanted to scare batters, to have them think that just maybe he was a little bit crazy, that maybe he was daft enough to hit them with a fastball for no apparent reason.

"A pitcher will never be a big winner until he hates hitters," Wynn said.[9] Wynn was free with this type of intimidating talk. He wasn't going to pal around with opposing hitters at the batting cage before a game. He wasn't going to go out to dinner on road trips with members of the other team as a friendly gesture (at least not until much later in his career). No. Wynn's friends were his teammates and his best friends of all were the fastball, curve and knuckler. In a sense he was like a gunslinger that relied on his six-gun for protection and enforcement.

Wynn did not really hate hitters as much as he viewed them as obstacles standing in the way of his own success. To him it was just business. A base hit might lead to a run, which might lead to more runs, which would lead to a loss, which would lead to other losses, which would lead to him being cut from the team and forced out of baseball, losing his livelihood and the good life baseball allowed him to live. Pretty simple, really. "That space between the white lines, that's my office," Wynn said. "That's where I conduct my business."[10]

Wynn's most memorable comment on his style of pitching was uttered more than once, in more than one way, and has been repeated in so many forums that it's not just clear exactly what he said, how he said it, or how many different ways he said it. In essence, Wynn said, "I would hit my own mother if she was crowding the plate." Point made. At other times, however, Wynn was quoted as saying his "own grandmother" or his "own son." He may have said the same thing to different reporters at different times, only varying the relatives. It could be that the sports writers knew they had a good thing going and just wanted to hear the pronouncement from Wynn's own lips. Once, Wynn was asked if he would throw at his own mother on Mother's Day. "I would if she were crowding the plate," Wynn said.[11] Another time that Wynn was asked if he would throw at his mother he said, "I would if she was digging in."[12] Certainly, there is a touch of whimsy in Wynn's replies, especially as he carried on the running conversation.

Several years into his career, when Wynn's reputation as a hard-nosed thrower was established, he was asked just why he felt so much apparent enmity for hitters. Not denying that some of the fiery persona came naturally to him, Wynn explained that Bucky Harris, his first manager with the Senators, made him in that image with threats. When he was 19 and breaking in with Washington, Wynn said Harris ordered him to send into the dirt any batter that he got two strikes on. If Wynn did not do so, Harris said he would be fined $25. With as much money as present-day ballplayers make, $25 doesn't even cover their bubblegum budget. But in 1939, just after the end of the Great Depression, $25 seemed like a fair chunk of change to throw away, especially for a rookie. "I was making $350 a month," Wynn said. "I couldn't afford giving up $25."[13]

Still, another story told about Wynn harkening back to his cameo appearances for Washington as a rookie made it seem as if the knockdown pitch was hard-wired into his psyche before he ever had a conversation with Harris. Ben Chapman, a feisty outfielder for the Cleveland Indians, and who like Wynn made his off-season home in Alabama, supposedly stuck his head in the Senators' dugout on the day of Wynn's debut to ask who was pitching that day. Harris pointed to the unknown Wynn and Chapman, typical of his demeanor, figured the rookie would be dead meat and announced, "I'll get five hits." Wynn said, "If you get five hits, the last three will be from the prone position."[14] A witty retort, to be sure, but did young Early Wynn from Alabama talk like that? Regardless of accuracy, by a few years into his career, baseball people told stories like that about Wynn.

Wynn may have inspired wariness in batters, but after bouncing up and down from the Senators to the minors and back, and enduring an interrupted career because of World War II, he was still an inconsistent pitcher by the late 1940s. After posting an 8–19 season in 1948, Washington gave up on him. At 28, Wynn was no longer a young prospect. Despite being capable of making batters shake in their spikes, enough of them had mastered his pitching repertoire to put him in the losers' column more often than the winners' column.

Although nothing they had seen gave the Senators long-term faith in Wynn's ability to become a big winner, their trading of the hard-throwing righty turned into a terrible deal. On December 14, 1948, Washington sent Wynn and Vernon, who had won a batting championship for the

Senators and made two All-Star teams, to the Indians. In return, they received Eddie Robinson, Ed Kielman and Joe Haynes.

It was a fresh start for Wynn at the right time. Fortunately for him the trade moved him to a team with a pitching coach who was a perfect match and who could teach him the type of things he needed to harness his great talent and exploit it.

4

The Barrier Breaker

Trader Lane never rested, it seemed. He worked the phones, the waiver wire, and his contacts with equal fervor. He was like a mad scientist, always tinkering, always trying to improve on his patent, always try to find something better.

In 1950, Lane supervised 18 trades involving White Sox players. In 1951, he had a hand in 26 barters. He bought players. He sold players. It was as if Lane was using Monopoly money, tossing it here and there, raking in a couple of hundred when he passed "Go." All of the action was being done in the interests of building hotels on Boardwalk and Park Place.

On April 30, 1951, Lane pulled off another of his coups, acquiring Sam Zoldak, Ray Murray, and a sizzling young player nicknamed "Minnie" for Lou Brissie. The given name of the player some sportswriter had labeled Minnie was Saturnino Orestes Armas Arieta Minoso.

Minoso, who has said he has no idea who bestowed the nickname Minnie on him, or why, grew up in Cuba. He dreamed of playing baseball in the United States, but because he was dark-skinned he was treated the same as American blacks were until 1947. Baseball's unwritten color barrier was in place, consigning talented black athletes to the Negro Leagues. There was no room in the majors for Satchel Paige, Josh Gibson, or Buck Leonard, and there was no room for a Minnie Minoso, either.

Minoso was a slick ballplayer. He had exceptional speed and daring on the base paths, and also possessed a degree of power that enabled him to slug doubles routinely and home runs occasionally. Growing up in Cuba's sugarcane country, Minoso lived in poverty. His parents divorced when he was a child and then his mother, who was raising him, died when he was 10. Minoso then moved to Havana where he was raised by two sisters. Minoso's baseball ability got him noticed and he did get the chance to come to the United States to play ball, albeit at first with the New York Cubans in the Negro Leagues in 1945.

Minoso's first language was Spanish, but he slowly and effectively picked up English. Perhaps because of misunderstandings with American journalists, his age was never pinpointed with birth-certificate accuracy. The *Baseball Encyclopedia* lists Minoso's year of birth as 1922. The Baseball Almanac website says he was born in 1925. Minoso has publicly said that the 1925 date is correct.

After the Brooklyn Dodgers promoted Jackie Robinson to the majors in 1947, and then added such black all-stars as Roy Campanella and Don Newcombe under the aggressive policies of general manager Branch Rickey, other teams gradually became receptive to signing black men to contracts. Minoso became property of the Cleveland Indians and made his major-league debut in 1949, appearing in nine games. He did not make the big club in 1950, but when spring training ended in 1951, Minoso was on the Indians' roster. Not for long, however. After hitting .429 in eight games, Minoso was pried away from the Indians by Lane. Minoso said that Sox manager Paul Richards was the man in his corner because he watched him play in the Pacific Coast League and told Lane about him. "Paul Richards, he was the guy who wanted me," Minoso said.[1]

On May 1, 1951, a day after joining the team, Minoso became the first black White Sox player. The White Sox were playing the Yankees and Minoso hit a home run that prodded the Comiskey Park fans to give him a rousing welcome. Another young player was making his debut in Chicago that day, though for the opposition. Mickey Mantle was a rookie and Minoso likes to point out that he hit a home run before the switch-hitting slugger did.

In later years, Minoso's role as a barrier breaker, the man who cracked the color line for the White Sox, has earned attention and praise. He experienced discrimination because of his skin color and also because he spoke Spanish at a time when Americans were more likely to make fun of those who relied on a foreign language than embrace it. Minoso has always remained proud, but low-key about being the White Sox' first black player, and he thinks his 439-foot home run didn't hurt any in making friends in the Windy City.

"I have a good memory and I always remember that date," Minoso said. "I made a good impression on the fans. White Sox fans always liked me after that. I never heard any boos. I am the first black player for the White Sox, but it had to be somebody. It is a good thing, but I am not a special person because of that. I paid my price, just like Jackie."[2]

It was easy for fans of the White Sox to like Minnie Minoso. Not only was he a cheerful, easy-going presence in the clubhouse, he was electrifying on the field. He could run, hit, field and throw. He brought a new dimension to a moribund franchise. Some baseball people might have wondered if Lane knew what he was doing, but he did always have a vision for the roster's end product. Lane was not averse to populating his team with good hitters, but he wanted a club that was speedy on the field.

Minoso was the perfect match. He hit a league-leading 14 triples, batted .326 and made the American League All-Star team. Minoso stole 42 bases and showed he would do just about anything to get on base, including risking his health. Minoso stepped into the batter's box with no fear and he never let a pitcher see him worried. Slow to bail out, Minoso also led the league in being hit by pitches with 16. In the coming years he was hit so often, so hard, and sometimes so dangerously in the head, that he was transported directly from the field to the hospital.

In 1951, though, Minoso was able to stay in the lineup, and it was he who made people jittery by employing daring leads off base and his unpredictable steals. That year, the phrase "Go-Go White Sox" made its debut. The label was applied by fans energized by a fresh breed of player collected by Lane and personified by Minoso. "The Go-Go White Sox really started in 1951," said pitcher Billy Pierce of the appellation that is still used to describe the team. "That was because of Minnie at first and Jim Busby. And then Jim Rivera was part of that when he rejoined the team."[3]

Busby spent parts of three seasons with the White Sox between 1950 and 1952. An excellent fielder, Busby hit .283, made the All-Star team, and stole 26 bases in 1951. Like Minoso, he was sparkplug-type player and he looked to have a long future with the team. Although Busby was only 25 and coming off an All-Star campaign, Lane traded him to the Washington Senators early in the 1952 season, along with infielder Mel Hoderlein for outfielder Sam Mele. It was not a popular or successful swap and only when Lane went after Rivera and brought him back to Chicago did he correct his mistake.

Minnie Minoso grew up in Cuba and became the White Sox' first black player when he joined the team in 1951. Minoso's daring on the base paths helped to create the image of the "Go-Go White Sox" of the 1950s. Long identified with the team, Minoso was traded away before the 1959 pennant run and then reacquired. (National Baseball Hall of Fame Library, Cooperstown, New York.)

"I was faster than I was powerful," said Rivera years later, reflecting on his 1953 league-leading 16 triples that represented more than the number of dingers he hit in any season. "I wasn't a home-run hitter. I thought I was one of the fast guys."[4] Rivera stole 21 bases combined between the Browns and White Sox in 1952 and he stole 22 bases for the White Sox in 1953. Rivera was born in 1922 and grew up in New York. He was a good, all-around athlete, boxing when he was in the Army, though neither have anything to do with his nickname.

In his first spring training with the White Sox, Rivera reached first base with a base hit off Dodger pitcher Don Newcombe during an exhibition game at Vero Beach. "I always had the steal sign (from Richards and the coaches)," Rivera recalled. "Me and Minnie, and later, Aparicio. They let us go. We didn't have to wait for the sign."[5] As he led off first base, Rivera began swinging his arms in a manner that might distract the pitcher. Back and forth he swung. Sox radio announcer Bob Elson took note of the activity and said, "He looks like he's in a jungle." The arm swinging didn't help Rivera on his attempted steal of second because he was thrown out despite a head-first slide. Elson's comment made the rounds and in the next day's paper a perplexed *Chicago Sun–Times* sportswriter commented on Rivera's arm waving. He nicknamed Rivera "Jungle Jim." The name stuck for the rest of the outfielder's career. In an era where nearly everyone was slapped with a nickname and not all of them flattering, Rivera didn't mind. "It's better than some of the names," he said.[6]

From outside the front office, it was never easy to tell which ones of Lane's acquisitions were keepers and which ones were going to be sold or traded for fresh meat. One of Lane's earlier deals that was quieter than most was a seemingly innocuous purchase of a young Venezuelan shortstop from the Brooklyn Dodgers in October of 1949. Perhaps the most unlikely aspect of Lane's pickup was that he talked Brooklyn's otherwise one-step-ahead-of-the-world personnel genius Branch Rickey out of Chico Carrasquel for $45,000.

Few foresaw that in 1950 Carrasquel would be the White Sox's starting shortstop and that by 1951 he would be an All-Star. In fact, Carrasquel became a hero to his country's baseball fans and he was nationally emulated in a nation that came to view the position of shortstop as part of its birthright. Carrasquel was the first Latin American member of a major-league All-Star team and he was the first in a line of dazzling star Venezuelan shortstops, many of whom also played for the White Sox. This included Luis Aparicio and later Ozzie Guillen, who also became manager of the team.

For two decades, the White Sox shortstop was Hall of Famer Luke Appling. Appling not only hit .388 for an American League batting championship, he dropped anchor at short, never to be budged after 1930. He was planning to coax one more starting season out of his aging body, but Carrasquel did what no one had been able to do before — relegated Appling to the bench.

"He said he wanted to play one or two more years," Carrasquel said of Appling in 1994. "But because I looked so good in spring training, the sports writers asked management of the ball club who was going to be the starting shortstop. When the answer was 'Chico Carrasquel,' it surprised everybody, including Luke. Appling was told that he could play some first base."[7]

Consistent with Lane's aspiration to build a younger, faster, slicker fielding team, Carrasquel won the job and hit .282 in 141 games. Carrasquel had a 24-game hitting streak at one point, but his season was cut short because of a knee injury. The next year he was even better, stealing 14 bases and playing 147 games while creating a buzz with his glove. That season, Carrasquel handled 297 chances over 53 games without making an error, a league record at the time. "The kid from Caracas is indisputably one of the game's nimblest glove men," a Chicago sports writer observed. "Miracle plays are a daily occurrence for Carrasquel, and there are baseball men with practiced eyes who proclaim him the most instinctive player they have ever seen."[8]

When Carrasquel joined the White Sox he needed an interpreter to make his thoughts known in English. Billy Pierce said Carrasquel's limited English had particularly hampered him in the minors before joining the White Sox and he conveyed a story to his major-league teammates saying that he ordered apple pie with every meal he had in Fort Worth in 1949 because that was all he could say.[9] He became more and more fluent as time passed and later made his warm feelings known for manager Paul Richards. "To me, Paul Richards was one of the best managers I ever played for," Carrasquel said. "I remember one day he said, 'Chico, I love you. I treat you like my son. If you don't do what I say, I'll trade you because I love my family. If you do what I say, you'll stay with me.'"[10]

Carrasquel was a four-time All-Star for the White Sox and his teammates appreciated his acrobatic fielding play. "He was a hell of a shortstop," said 1950s Sox pitcher Jack Harshman. "And a tough hitter. More than people realize. He'd get that big hit. I enjoyed having him play behind me, I'll tell you that."[11]

It actually did not take very long for the rest of the American League to take notice of Carrasquel's smooth fielding, either. Even before the end of Carrasquel's rookie year Yankee manager Casey Stengel singled him out before an upcoming series with the White Sox as someone to watch out for. "I get butterflies in my stomach when I think of him at short gobbling up base hits," Stengel said. "He'll be the best in the game in a year or two."[12]

Of course, the guy Carrasquel had to worry about when it came to trades was not Richards, but Lane. Eventually, the arrival of Luis Aparicio, one of Carrasquel's protégés, pushed him out the door in 1955. Carrasquel landed in Cleveland, but after retiring he returned to Chicago to handle Spanish-language broadcasts of White Sox games.

Despite being sandwiched between two Hall of Fame White Sox shortstops — Appling and Aparicio — Carrasquel is fondly remembered in Chicago. "I was glad to be able to call him a friend," said Harshman.[13]

Throughout baseball Carrasquel is credited with spawning a coterie of Venezuelan shortstops who wanted to be just like him — from Aparicio to Davey Concepcion, from Omar Vizquel to Guillen.

When Carrasquel died at age 77 in a hospital from a heart attack that was a by-product of a long battle with diabetes in 2005, Guillen, one of those devoted followers, could not go to Venezuela for the funeral because he was busy piloting the White Sox to their first World Series championship in 88 years. "I don't think he was the greatest player ever to come from the country," Guillen said. "But to me, he was the greatest man to come from Venezuela." Venezuelan President Hugo Chavez did not go quite that far, but in a nationally televised speech he yelled, "Viva Carrasquel" and proclaimed a two-day period of mourning.[14]

Minoso was wounded when he was traded from Cleveland to Chicago, but he adapted to his new home quickly and just as quickly established himself as one of the most exciting players in the American League. By 1956, Minoso, who answered to "Minnie," but was called "Orestes" by his closest friends, had led the league in triples three times, and was a regular .300 hitter. He patrolled the outfield with aplomb and always was dancing off first base trying to ruin opposing pitchers' concentration.

What fans saw in Minoso was a player who competed with joy in his heart and a reckless abandonment of good sense in keeping his body in one piece. A pitch from the Yankees' Bob Grim struck Minoso in the head and after suffering dizzy spells he was hospitalized. Another time he crashed into a wall chasing a fly ball and incurred a fractured skull. Ten different times Minoso led the American League in being hit by pitches, several times reaching the mid-teens for a total and one season accumulating 23 bruisings. Yet he always crowded the plate and refused to change his batting stance.

"Nobody hit me on purpose," Minoso said in 1955 after his beaning by Grim, who visited him in the hospital. He said he received between 500 and 600 get-well cards from around the country while he was convalescing and missing a month's worth of play. "I won't change my stance. I don't care if I die."[15]

Minoso did not change his stance and did not die on the field. In fact, in an off-and-on bit of public relations hullabaloo stretched over decades, Minoso and his old friend owner Bill Veeck, and then Veeck's son Mike, collaborated to allow the player to establish an unusual longevity record. The Veecks kept bringing an aging Minoso back for one more appearance on their major-league and minor-league teams. Minoso was in his seventies the last time he batted and he set the mark of playing professional baseball in seven different decades. He wears a special ring commemorating the achievement.

In the early 1950s, Minoso was not participating in a stunt. He was doing everything he could to make the White Sox a better team and his play was symbolic of the franchise's new look. The Go-Go White Sox were created by Frank Lane and players like Minoso, Carrasquel and Pierce were putting them on the map.

The irony for Minoso is that in 1957, when he was certain he would be a White Sox player forever, he was traded back to the Cleveland Indians. Frank Lane was out as White Sox general manager as of September 1955, replaced by a personnel team of Chuck Comiskey, the young team vice president, and John Rigney. Lane moved on to the St. Louis Cardinals as GM for two seasons and by late 1957 he was handling that task for the Indians. So it was Lane who traded for Minoso, bringing him back to Cleveland along with Fred Hatfield. Minoso was at least 35 years old, depending who you believed.

Minoso was very upset at being traded from the White Sox. He was disconsolate. "When I first heard that I was traded to the Cleveland Indians, I felt that I had fallen into the ocean," Minoso wrote in his autobiography. "In those days you developed a real emotional attachment to a club and the fans. We didn't sell our bat to the highest bidder."[16] The one thing that Minoso did feel good about was that Lane had sought him out. The two men had a good relationship and the fact that Lane had come after him with his first trade in Cleveland was soothing.

And who did Lane trade to the White Sox to get one of his favorite players? Outfielder Al Smith, who hit .247 in 1957, and pitcher Early Wynn, then age 37. His 1957 record was 14–17 and his earned run average was an unruly and unpromising 4.31. Just about everybody in baseball felt Wynn was probably over the hill and close to retirement.

5

Looking for Keepers

Trader Frank Lane was running the world's largest swap meet out of his Chicago office. It was as if he was a general, deploying the troops, with pins stuck in a map. I want Joe Outfielder from Boston. I want Sam Pitcher from New York. I'll send Billy Catcher to Detroit so I can get Eddie Infielder from Cleveland.

When it came to minor leaguers, it was now-you-see-him, now-you-don't. When it came to major leaguers, it was here-today, gone-tomorrow. The real question was whether or not all of Lane's player juggling would work out, or if the White Sox were all smoke and no substance. Lane was a newsmaker. Of that there was little doubt. He knew how to create headlines in the morning paper. But would the acquisitions pay dividends? Could the White Sox threaten for the pennant? Could the White Sox win a pennant?

At first, in the earliest days and years of Lane's tenure, nobody could be sure whether Lane was just a bigger noise-maker than his predecessors, or if he was really improving the team and fan interest. But gradually, it seemed as if Lane was winning the war with his personnel maneuvering.

The White Sox were as awful as they ever had been in 1948, finishing with a 51–93 record, eighth and last in the American League. They weren't so hot in 1949, either, but won 12 more games. In 1950, when people might have started to wonder if Lane was on the right track, the Sox won only 60 games. But finally, in 1951, the moves seemed to be nudging the long dreary White Sox towards prosperity. Under Paul Richards that year, the White Sox went 81–73. They posted the same record the next year and finished third. That equaled the team's highest placement in the standings since 1920. In 1954, while still third, Chicago finished 94–60. The last time the White Sox won more games was also 1920.

The season before Lane became the general manager, the White Sox attracted 777,844 fans to Comiskey Park. In 1952, they drew 1,231,675 fans. The South Siders apparently liked what was going on with the team more than they had before. Lane searched out-of-the-way small towns, the minors, and major-league rosters to find players and Richards had provided a winner.

Sometimes it seemed as if Lane merely borrowed big-name players to use in additional trades. Some of the players had done great things with other teams and when they came to Chicago the fans couldn't help but be impressed by their resumes. However, pitcher Billy Pierce said that occasionally the arrival of a well-known guy was a bit misleading. "Most of them were past their primes," Pierce said. "A lot of them had their best years behind them."[1]

In some cases, Lane was taking a chance. He thought he could squeeze just one more good year out of an aging player. And often he was right. If the player then showed any sign of deteriorating, Lane would trade him away just as fast as he obtained him.

For the most part, when Lane latched on to a good player, especially if he seemed likely to be successful for several years, he held on to him. Pierce was Exhibit A. When the southpaw first appeared in the majors in 1945 he was very raw, a schoolboy still trying to earn a degree in major-league pitching. Lane spotted the talent hiding behind the inexperience and gave Pierce every chance to grow.

By 1951, Pierce was a 15-game winner. He also won 15 games in 1952 and won 18 games in 1953. After an off-year in 1954, Pierce won 15 games again in 1955 and then in 1956 and 1957 he won 20 games each season. He evolved into one of the team's most popular players of the era.

Not that Pierce was confident Lane's apparent faith in him would keep him in Chicago. Just like anyone else on the team, even when he was going well, he half-expected to be traded at any minute. "Oh yeah, I could have been the next guy out of town," Pierce said later. "It happened that my name came up in trade talks. At one point there was talk of me being traded to New York. There was talk about it, but it just didn't develop. We knew it could happen fast. Trades happened quickly then."[2]

In 1953, Pierce made the first of his seven American League All-Star teams. And in 1955, despite a record of only 15–10, he led the league in earned run average with a miniscule mark of 1.97. In 1954, Pierce battled injuries and missed several turns in the rotation. In 1955, he was at full strength and his stuff baffled AL hitters more than ever.

"Every game you figure you're going out to win," Pierce said. "You thought you were going to pitch nine innings. That was the key thing. That's the difference between nowadays and back then. They gave you the ball when the game started and you figured you weren't going to give it back until the game ended. The game was nine innings and you figured you were going to throw nine innings. I don't understand this business about quality starts where a starting pitcher is praised for going six innings and giving up three runs. That's a 4.50 earned run average."[3]

Pierce had so many teammates that he might not be able to remember them all if forced to make a list. Some of them were good players, too, for the moment.

Minnie Minoso was the first black player to take the field for the White Sox, but later in 1951 a budding African-American slugger named Bob Boyd made a cameo appearance, playing in 12 games. He made more of an impact in 1953 when he hit .297 in 55 games. Boyd was a late bloomer who had his greatest success as a first baseman with the Baltimore Orioles when he hit over .300 several times. A renowned line-drive hitter, Boyd was nicknamed "The Rope" for his propensity to smack those hard liners.

Boyd was from Mississippi and when he was breaking into baseball he gave his date of birth as October 1, 1925. When he died in 2004 from cancer, however, the date of birth in a *Wichita Eagle* story about him gave his birth date as October 1, 1919 and his age as 84.

Although Jackie Robinson broke the major-league baseball color barrier in 1947 and teams throughout the majors were adding African-American players to their rosters, there were still racist obstacles many newcomers faced. In the early 1950s, before the St. Louis Browns became the Orioles, the Missouri city represented the southernmost outpost in the majors. Attitudes were slower to change in St. Louis than they were in northern communities and black players felt the sting of discrimination more keenly there.

The Chase Hotel was a regular stopping point for teams at the time, but it was notorious for black players. They were prohibited from staying in the hotel with their teammates and were farmed out to all-black hotels or to private homes in the still very much segregated city.

Rocky Krsnich, who saw limited action with the White Sox as a third baseman between 1949 and 1953, said that he was naïve. The team bus pulled up to a building after a night game once and Krsnich, who is white, prepared to disembark. "So the bus stops," Krsnich said, "and I remember standing up with the black players to get off and somebody grabs me and tells me to sit down. The black guys got off the bus and we went on to the Chase Hotel. What a sad, sad commentary."[4]

It took some years before major-league teams laid down their own law to hotels in cities that still discriminated and to spring training centers in Florida where their black players were also segregated. Eventually, the threats to take all business elsewhere were rewarded with equal-opportunity housing.

Lane was a tinkerer and he trusted his instincts, but he could not tell the future. One of his pitchers, Lou Kretlow, showed promise and during the 1952 season he pitched two straight two-hitters within the same week. Kretlow was only 4–4 for the season, but those high points kept the White Sox interested in his future. He shut out the Red Sox and Yankees in July, but when he couldn't duplicate his success Lane dispatched him to the St. Louis Browns where he suffered a serious arm injury. "I hurt it like Dizzy Dean," said Kretlow, comparing his situation to the career-ending woes of the star right-hander. "Underneath it hemorrhaged and the blood clotted and I was out for about a month."[5] His career never took off after that, though, and Kretlow's lifetime total was 27 wins.

One of those long-time old-timers that Lane plucked was third baseman George Kell. Kell played 15 years in the majors and was eventually elected to the Hall of Fame. While his best years were with Detroit, after being acquired for Grady Hatton and cash, between 1954 and 1956 Kell did nothing to diminish his reputation with the White Sox. Kell exhibited solid hitting, including a .312 season in 1955.

The White Sox had been searching for a third baseman for the better part of 20 years, so they were happy to obtain Kell. But he had slowed down and injuries kept him out of a number of games. In 1956, Kell was part of a six-player deal with the Baltimore Orioles. The White Sox received Dave Philley and Jim Wilson. Kell was described as "an undemonstrative, no-flare type in and out of uniform" who worked hard and let his performance on the field do his talking.[6]

While the search for a steady third baseman seemed to span continents, Lane possibly probed outer space to obtain pitchers capable of joining Pierce in the rotation. In 1953, he thought he mined gold with an unusual find. Bob Keegan, nicknamed "Smiley," was a 33-year-old rookie when he went 7–5 for the White Sox that season to earn a second look. The 6-foot-2, 207-pound Keegan, who grew up in Rochester, New York, dreaming of becoming a baseball player, was sidetracked by service during World War II and college at Bucknell University in Pennsylvania. The Yankees found him there, where Keegan had spent more time playing the infield than pitching, but he got lost in the New York farm system. In one of Lane's innumerable deals, he bought Keegan's contract from AAA Syracuse. Keegan wasn't a complete secret since he won 20 games in Syracuse, so Lane felt fortunate to grab him.

When Keegan got a full chance to start in 1954, he finished 16–9 and made the All-Star team. "I never expected anything like that," Keegan said. "That was a thrill."[7] The sports writers were shocked by Keegan's fast start. "Big Man of the White Sox' pennant drive so far this season has been Robert Charles Keegan. He has looked like the best pitcher to don a Comiskey uniform since Ted Lyons' heyday."[8]

Keegan was one of the Sox players who enjoyed playing for Richards and felt the older man's advice was extremely helpful. During the off-season before the 1954 campaign Richards spelled out a program for Keegan to follow. "Paul prescribed off-season conditioning which prevented arm soreness this spring," Keegan said.[9] Richards was soft-spoken and often a tough guy, but he showed empathy to young players and he let players know where they stood with him. Keegan appreciated that. "Richards was a hell of a manager and I knew he had confidence in me. And that helps a player."[10]

Keegan did not get along quite as well with Al Lopez, one of Richards' successors and by 1958 he had been replaced in the White Sox rotation by Early Wynn. Lopez and Wynn had a rapport from their days with the Indians and Keegan felt like the odd man out. Keegan had considerable respect for Wynn's record and history, so he did not feel aggrieved being substituted for by Wynn. But he was especially peeved at Lopez because he couldn't find any other way to use him.

During the 1957 season, Keegan finished 10–8. On April 20, 1957, Keegan also threw a no-hitter, shutting out the Washington Senators. He felt that with his recent track record Lopez could have found more work for him than two starts and 14 overall appearances. Keegan's record in 1958 was 0–2 and that was his last year with the White Sox and final year in the majors.

"Wynn was Lopez's pet," Keegan said, suggesting a double standard. "He could go out and get knocked out of a game 10 times in a row and still start. If I got knocked out of a game once, that was it for me. I'll never forgive Lopez for that. I would have liked to gone out battling them, ya know?"[11]

Another pitcher who gave the White Sox even more consistency and solid help during those early 1950s building years was lefty Jack Harshman. Acquired from Nashville after going 23–7 Harshman produced a 14–8 record in 1954, went 11–7 in 1955 and 15–11 in 1956 as the Sox improved into a contender.

"It was a learning experience in a lot of ways," Harshman said. "I was still a young pitcher, although I was not a young player."[12] The remarkable thing about Harshman's career was his abrupt switch from promising power hitter in 1951 in the minors to a steady winner on the mound three seasons later. Property of the New York Giants, Harshman was the regular first baseman for Nashville in the AA Southern League in 1951 and creamed 47 home runs (including six grand slams) and knocked in 141 runs. But he could not develop the consistency he needed to stick in the majors in brief shots with New York. He was an enigma and as unlikely as it seemed Harshman took a bold chance shifting to the mound when he was 25. This came at the suggestion of Larry Gilbert, owner-general manager of the Nashville club who told Harshman that hurling would be a quicker route to the majors for him. It was not clear what this fellow saw in Harshman, but he was right. "People thought that I was crazy back there in 1951 when I insisted that Harshman's only real chance was to be a pitcher," Gilbert said. "I was thinking about all of the 108 times he fanned. And his lousy .251 batting average. Terrible! But the clincher to me was his good, live arm."[13]

At his best, Harshman was a very good pitcher for the White Sox. He bested the Tigers 1–0 in 16 innings and struck out 16 men against the

Red Sox. He also pitched a one-hitter against the Orioles. The K's Harsh-man recorded represented a team mark for the White Sox at the time, though during the game he had no idea how many he was compiling until Minnie Minoso tipped him off. Minoso went to Harshman after the seventh inning and said, "The boy up in the scoreboard tells me you've got 15 strikeouts. Did you know that you had 15 strikeouts?" Harshman said he didn't let the information faze him because his top priority was to win the game. But when it was over he was pleased he set the record.[14] In 1957, the hitter-turned pitcher ruptured a disc in his back and that led to the end of his career. Harshman was part of the White Sox building stages, but wasn't with the team for the payoff.

Although he often tackled bullpen assignments, Sandy Consuegra had one magical season for the Sox. In 1954, coming off a 7–5 season, the Cuban right-hander dazzled the competition. He finished 16–3 and made the All-Star team. His .842 winning percentage was a team single-season record. He could do no wrong and in a May game against the Philadelphia Athletics, Consuegra took a perfect game into the seventh inning. The game concluded as a two-hitter.

Consuegra, another slick pick-up by Lane, who bought his contract from the Washington Senators, was a likeable player who helped keep the clubhouse loose with his joking, this despite not having perfect English. When Consuegra died at age 85 in 2005, his former pitching coach Ray Berres was still alive. Berres recalled an incident between Consuegra, who was bothered by an ailment and wanted to go to the hospital, and then-manager Marty Marion. "Me itch," Berres quoted Consuegra as saying. "Marion says, 'You itch here with us until the end of the season. Then you can go home and itch all winter.'"[15] Consuegra was only a so-so 6–5 the year after his huge season and faded out of the game within a few years of that.

One of the unlikeliest of White Sox players during the building years was Phil Cavaretta. He was the Mr. Cub of the preceding two decades, a player who came right off the sandlots of Chicago as a teenager to move into the Cubs lineup for seven games in 1934. He stuck around for nearly 20 years, but Lane showed that he would accept anybody from anywhere if he thought they could be useful. In 1954, Cavaretta batted .316 for the White Sox. In Chicago, the running joke is that the red line subway is what the Cubs and White Sox have in common because the same train connects Wrigley Field and Comiskey Park. No one would have expected Cavaretta to overlap, even for a minute.

Cavaretta, a four-time National League All-Star who won the league batting title with a .355 average in 1945, was the Cubs' manager entering the 1954 season. He made the mistake of informing management that he did not believe his club had a chance to be a winner. So Cavaretta was fired and was resting on the couch at home in Dallas when Lane came calling with a better offer. If part of his intention was to embarrass the crosstown rivals, so be it. If so, the ploy worked. Cavaretta played 71 games for the Sox that year and retired after playing just a handful more in 1955. "I wanted to stay in baseball," Cavaretta said. "It is my life." Cavaretta said he wrote to every general manager in the majors informing them he was still capable of hitting, playing the field sometimes, and definitely pinch hitting. Lane believed him. "The big idea, of course, was to remain in the game."[16]

Another of Lane's famous "gets" was first baseman Ferris Fain. Fain was feuding with his front-office bosses in Philadelphia. The dispute could not be kept quiet and spilled into the newspapers. Although he seemed like too hot a property to be shuffled away quite so readily, the internecine debate was the explanation offered for the January 27, 1953, deal Lane swung. He shipped Eddie Robinson, Joe DeMaestri and Ed McGhee to the A's for Fain and Bob Wilson. Fain was the reigning American League batting champ with his .344 average in 1952.

One sports writer said, "Strong sentiment following one of the most baffling trades in recent baseball history was that the personality clash between Fain and the A's front office had reached a point where profit was no longer the object compared to the opportunity of getting an adequate replacement for the out-spoken and dissatisfied Fain."[17]

There was considerable speculation that Chicago was only going to be a brief stop for Fain on his way to the New York Yankees, but Lane vehemently denied it while extolling Fain's hitting ability. "We lost 15 or 20 games last year that a timely hit would have won," Lane said. "We are not a farm club of the Yankees. We didn't get Fain to prevent the Yankees from getting him, nor to work a better deal for him with the Yankees."[18] Fain was indeed a regular for the White Sox in 1953, and won the batting title again with a .327 average. This despite breaking a hand in a bar fight in Washington. Fain was a five-time All-Star, twice with the Sox, and he never did play for the Yankees.

One of Fain's nicknames was "Fearless" because of the way he charged toward the plate to field bunts. Twice in the same week, however, while he was playing for Philadelphia, Fain rushed to grab bunts and trying to head off the lead runner overthrew his fielder at third base. Manager Connie Mack addressed a fuming Fain with some advice. "Young man, don't you ever do that again," Mack told Fain. "Don't ever throw any more bunts to third base." A disgruntled Fain replied, "What do you want me to do with the ball, Mr. Mack? Sit on it and hatch it?" Mack, then 87, and not to be outdone by a whippersnapper, retorted, "It might be safer."[19]

Called "Burrhead" by some because of his crewcut, Fain also had less flattering nicknames that fit with the view of the Philadelphia officials who wanted him out of town. Fain was alternately called "The Firebrand," "Fain the Fiery," or "Furious Ferris" because of his temperament. "He's as cocky as they come and so uncompromisingly competitive that he will verbally rip apart his best friend after a bobbled ground ball," a magazine writer noted.[20]

Fain, who got a late start in the majors at 26 because of his military commitment during World War II, had a major-league career that lasted only nine seasons. It was cut short by a 1956 knee injury, the problem that prevented Fain from sticking around as the White Sox' long-term answer at first base.

Long after his retirement from baseball, in 1988, while reportedly suffering from arthritis, diabetes and leukemia, Fain was arrested for growing marijuana at his California home. Living on Social Security at the time, Fain testified during his trial that he was only using the drug for its therapeutic value to cope with the pain and discomfort of his illnesses. Apparently ahead of his time in the medical use of marijuana, Fain convinced the judge he was not deserving of much in the way of punishment. Fain, who could always hit in the clutch, was sentenced to four months of house arrest — and he lived another 13 years.

6

The Chief and
His Indians

In 1954, Lane's plan to win a pennant for the White Sox was coming together. The Yankees, under Casey Stengel, still appeared dominant. New York's lineup featured sluggers like Mickey Mantle and Yogi Berra and the Yankee pitching was anchored by Whitey Ford, Allie Reynolds and Bob Grim.

New York had won five consecutive pennants and didn't seem to be any weaker. White Sox manager Paul Richards was the only one who believed differently — or he was just saying so to hearten his troops. "The Yankees are indisputably on the downgrade," Richards commented.[1]

Richards was both right and wrong in his observation. The Yankees won 103 games, which did not exactly constitute a slump. But they did not win the pennant. That year the Cleveland Indians, managed by Al Lopez, set a new American League record for victories with 111 and advanced to the World Series.

Alfonso Ramon Lopez was born in Tampa, Florida, in 1908 and his family was originally from Spain. His parents moved to Cuba for about eight years and then the United States. The clan lived in the Ybor City area, a cigar-making enclave, and his father was a leaf selector. Although Tampa is now one of the most heavily populated big cities in Florida, Lopez remembered that it had just 40,000 people when he was growing up in what he called "horse and wagon days. There was no traffic when I was a kid. Most of the streets in Ybor were unpaved."[2]

A good baseball player from the time he took up the game, Lopez had an auspicious debut as a 10-year-old catcher minus equipment. "I didn't have a mask, shin guards or chest protector," Lopez said. "But I had plenty of nerve. The first batter swung at the ball and I missed it, but the ball didn't miss me. The pitcher had a lot of arm and the ball hit me on the nose and knocked me cold." Lopez said the other kids thought he was dead and notified the police. An ambulance took him from the ball field to the local hospital. As he regained consciousness, the first thing Lopez said was, "I'll never play baseball again."[3]

Lopez made it through just one year of high school before being signed by the Tampa Smokers of the Florida State League to a $150-a-month deal as a 16-year-old in 1925. "It was good money," he said.[4] Years later, a more mature Lopez described himself as "a dumbbell and a green-horn," at that age.[5]

Within three years Lopez was in the majors. Lopez's catching talents were first identified by the Washington Senators, who used him as a practice player. While still a teenager, he caught Hall of Famer Walter Johnson. Lopez, who was 5-foot-11 and 165 pounds during his playing days, broke into the majors with the Brooklyn Dodgers in 1928. He retired 19 seasons later having caught a then-record 1,918 games out of the 1,950 he

played in. A two-time All-Star who led his league in fielding percentage four times, Lopez hit just .261, but was regarded as a superb glove man and field leader. He was a natural to move into the dugout as a manager.

Lopez was nicknamed "El Señor" because of his Spanish

White Sox manager Al Lopez was the leader of the 1959 team that won the American League pennant. Obsessed with beating the perennial champ Yankees, Lopez, a Hall of Fame catcher, also topped New York when he directed the Indians to the 1954 pennant. (National Baseball Hall of Fame Library, Cooperstown, New York.)

heritage. The appellation was commonly used in newspaper headlines throughout his career and there was no doubt about who was being referred to in the story. That was partially true because there were no Latin American ballplayers around, either, who might be confused with Lopez.

Throughout his long career, Lopez always returned to Tampa in the off-season and he became completely identified with the community and its baseball connections. "He's a baseball icon for the Tampa Bay area," said Tampa Bay Devil Rays chairman Vince Naimoli. When that expansion team began play in 1998, Naimoli had Lopez throw out the first pitch at the team's first home game.[6]

Lou Piniella, the one-time manager of the Seattle Mariners, Tampa Bay and Chicago Cubs, and a native of Tampa, said Lopez was the key figure in Tampa baseball. "He always was an inspiration for a lot of kids in Tampa," Piniella said. "The whole city of Tampa was aware and very proud of him."[7]

Best known in Tampa and in the baseball world during the first half of the twentieth century for his catching, Lopez remained a prominent baseball figure when he became a manager.

In 1948, under the ownership of Bill Veeck and the field generalship of player-manager Lou Boudreau, the Cleveland Indians won the World Series. A couple of years later, however, Boudreau was traded to the Boston Red Sox. In 1951, Lopez was appointed manager of an Indians team still wealthy in talent. By 1954, Lopez was determined to break the Yankees' stranglehold on the American League.

The Indians produced one of the most remarkable seasons in history. Some said their starting pitching was the best of all time. Bob Lemon finished 23–7. Mike Garcia finished 19–8. Art Houtteman finished 15–7. Nearing the end of his career, Bob Feller finished 13–3. And Early Wynn finished 23–11 with an earned run average of 2.73.

After the trade that brought Wynn to Cleveland from Washington he went 11–7 in 1949 and then got better and better. All of the raw talent on display with the Senators was harnessed with the Indians. In 1950, Wynn was 18–8. A year later he had his first 20-victory season, going 20–13. Then, in 1952, he topped that with a 23–12 record. Wynn was 17–12 in 1953 and his 23-win campaign in 1954 led the American League. He was still an innings eater, too. Wynn had blossomed into the pitcher many thought he could become and was on his way to seven All-Star game selections.

When he was a teen and full of the vim and vigor of youthful promise, Wynn knew exactly where he was going in life. He attended school for as long as it was practical, but his mind was always on baseball. Once, he informed one of his Hartford, Alabama, math teachers that "the shortest distance between two points is a fastball," and that "the longest distance known to man is the walk from home plate back to the bench after you've fanned with the bases loaded."[8]

Well before he joined the Indians, Wynn was nicknamed "Gus" by a teammate, though there was no good reason for the choice. Still, "Gus" stuck to Wynn for the rest of his life. Much attention was also paid to Wynn's part-Indian heritage when he was trying to make a name for himself with the Senators. One sports writer said, "Proud of his Indian ancestry, and the mark of race is stamped indelibly upon his features, Wynn hopes to take his place with ... Louis Sockalexie, Chief Bender, Chief John Tortes Meyers, and Jim Thorpe."

Wynn did not actually speak about such aspirations. He was more focused at making the grade as a solid big-leaguer who could escape poverty. "When I signed my Washington contract I felt that I signed an Emancipation Proclamation. I felt emancipated from want and worries in my age. If I am as good a ballplayer as I think I will be, I have nothing in the world to worry about. That is, unless something goes wrong with my arm, or I take on too much weight to be a good pitcher."[9]

But Wynn did not make the type of progress that he and the Senators had expected, so when he was traded to the Indians he did have things to worry about. It was not at all clear that Wynn would ever be a first-tier pitcher and that he would be able to collect a major-league salary for much longer. Unless he took on some advice and made some changes.

In Cleveland the difference-maker for Wynn was Indian's pitching coach Mel Harder. Harder was a hard-throwing right-hander who had a variety of pitches in his repertoire (though his curveball was judged his best). Harder came up to the majors in 1928 with the Indians and spent the next 36 years with the team. He was active for 20 seasons, ending in 1947, and won 223 games; then he was the team's pitching coach for 16 years.

Harder won 20 games in 1934 and a career-high 22 in 1935. He pitched in four All-Star games and in 13 innings spread over those appearances Harder did not surrender a run. While Harder feared no batter, he joked that Ty Cobb "hit me like he owned me. He had a perfect swing."[10]

Harder possessed several qualities that aided him in his role as an instructor, including patience and an even temperament. Even he admitted that it seemed as if he was always in a good mood. The way Harder saw it, life was grand if you could make a living in baseball, so what was there to complain about? "Life was rosy, just right," Harder said. "We play ball for a living and stay in the best hotels."[11]

By contrast, Wynn did not try to present a placid demeanor in public. He wanted to seem like a grouch to competitors, so that they didn't get too close and they didn't take his attitude for weakness. He continued to cultivate his image as a pitcher to be feared, who was unpredictable and might scalp you with a fastball, or at least give you a close shave.

The comment about brushing his mother, or grandmother, back from the plate, was a recurring theme with reporters and Wynn always played along in one way or another. When asked again if he would brush back his grandmother, Wynn said, "Only if she was digging in."[12]

For all of his bluster, though, Wynn was not supremely confident when he joined the Indians. His pitching results with the Senators had been too up-and-down for him to be too cocky. He needed soothing by and attention from Harder — and he got it. Wynn was forever grateful and frequently praised Harder for putting his career on track. Harder, the whiz with the curveball, showed Wynn how to improve his curve. Then he coaxed him into mixing more sliders and knucklers into his pitching selection to complement the curve and his already wicked fastball.

"The biggest thing that ever happened to me in baseball was Mel Harder," Wynn said. "He taught me fundamentals, so I could find the trouble when my curve and slider weren't breaking. Harder made me realize that nothing concerns a pitcher except the player at bat."[13] Wynn gained so much confidence in Harder's opinion that when the hurler made his once-in-every-four-days start he asked the coach to sit in the dugout instead of the bullpen to watch his motion and warn him if he was unconsciously changing his pitching style.

One thing that did not change was Wynn's passion for victory and umbrage taken when any batter purposely or accidentally invaded his space, whether it was in the batter's box or on the mound. After one Indians game that did not go well, a frustrated Wynn threw a tantrum in the clubhouse. His teammates, who followed him into the locker room, either missed most of it or stood aside. When Wynn's rampage ended after the tough loss, fellow pitcher Hal Newhouser bemusedly assessed the situation. Gazing at Wynn's uniform shirt hanging over a rafter after he had tossed it toward the ceiling, Newhouser said, "My God, old Gus has hung himself!"[14] It was not reported whether or not Wynn laughed, though teammates surely did.

Wynn developed his personal eye-for-an-eye retaliation program early on when batters hit the ball through the box and it didn't matter if he knew you or not, it was a rule he never deviated from — for the sake of consistency, you know. Washington's Jose Valdivielso belted a line drive back at the pitcher and Wynn was unable to dodge in time. The cowhide smashed into Wynn's face and he needed 18 stitches. He eventually needed a dental plate with seven teeth in it. Wynn was not able to hit Valdivielso when he came to the plate next because the infielder dove to the ground before the ball even left Wynn's right hand.

There was an oft-told story about Wynn and Yankee infielder Gil McDougald at Yankee Stadium. When McDougald settled into his stance, Wynn noted that the hitter was not properly positioned in the batter's box. Wynn informed the umpire that one of McDougald's feet was over the white line of the box. "Only the toe is over," the ump said. "I'm not going to move him back." Wynn responded, "Either you do, or I will." On the next pitch, McDougal sprawled in the dirt. After that he adjusted his own stance.[15]

Wynn was a firm believer in his philosophy. In his mind, any pitcher who gave up an inch of territory to a batter was dooming himself to a life outside the sport. It was inevitable that the guys wielding the big sticks would take advantage and run the pitcher out of the game. Wynn had no intention of losing his job for that reason.

"It's just simple economics to keep those hitters away from the plate," Wynn said. "The guy who won't do it might as well go out and get the lunch pail. Now you got little-bitty, 150-pound kids jacking balls 400 feet over the fence and breaking bats and still knocking them in the seats right down the foul line. The ball's so live, you can hear it breathing. (If) you're gonna let that batter stand there and hang over home plate looking hungrily for a pitch he can break a seat with, they should call the law on you for non-support of your wife and children."[16]

It was not true that Wynn did not make friends in baseball — he just had trouble keeping them. Wynn had been traded to the Indians with his old Senators roommate Mickey Vernon, but Vernon, a lifetime hitter of a nearly .300 average, ended up back with Washington and had to face his old pal during a real game. Vernon smacked four hits off of Wynn, but worst of all, the fourth hit was a line drive back at the pitcher that ricocheted off Wynn's glove and knocked the leather to the ground.

Vernon knew what that meant, and if there was any question Wynn put it to him straight. "When I got to first base, he was steaming," Vernon said. "He looked over and said, 'Roommate or not, you've got to go in the dirt the next time I see you.' Sure enough, the next time I faced him, the first pitch was up over my head."[17]

No quarter was shown to any batter. If Wynn could spot a weakness he probed it and tried to seize upon what might be a tiny or major advantage. Joe DiMaggio retired from the Yankees after the 1951 season. Some time later he said he was forced to quit not so much because of the Achilles heel that people blamed, but because of a completely different reason. "Early Wynn did (it)," DiMaggio said. "He found out I was no longer able to hit the high, inside fastball. After I broke my left collarbone I wasn't able to bring my left arm around high enough to be ready for the tight pitch. I didn't tell anybody, not even our trainer, that I couldn't come all the way around. I just hoped I could keep the secret. I knew pitchers wouldn't throw high and inside to me on purpose. Well, Wynn threw one and then another and another. I couldn't just stand there and he saw my grinding swing. I tell you, it didn't take more than a week for the word to get around the American League. They all had me pegged and I was dead."[18]

There was not a lot of compromise in Early Wynn. That mother or grandmother line kept circling his life like a school of sharks. He did a humorous job of deflecting it when given the opportunity, though. Would you really hit your own grandmother, Early, if she crowded the plate? "I would," he said. "Grandmother was a pretty good hitter."[19]

Wynn might have been the king of full counts because he wasted so many pitches sending messages to players. The ones that didn't hit a batter were catalogued as balls in the count. *Los Angeles Times* Pulitzer-Prize-winning sports columnist Jim Murray wrote that Wynn "threw well over half a million pitches in his lifetime and it has been estimated that nearly 100,000 of them knocked somebody down."[20]

Looked at that way it's a wonder that Wynn ever got anybody out, but he did and won 20 or more games in a season five times. Hall of Fame outfielder Ted Williams, who some consider the best hitter of all time, had a major-league career that was similar to Wynn's in years and longevity, sticking with the Red Sox from 1939 to 1960. "Early Wynn was the toughest pitcher I ever faced," said Williams, who hit .344 lifetime with 521 home runs.[21]

Wynn was probably never tougher than during the 1954 season when he won his 23 games and the Indians finished 111–43. He started 36 games, appeared in 40, and also earned two saves in relief while throwing more than 270 innings. The Indians were loaded on the mound that year. Wynn, Lemon, and Feller were later elected to the Hall of Fame. So was Newhouser, who had a 7–2 record. The other key starter, Mike Garcia, nicknamed "The Big Bear," won 19 games that season.

Garcia did not have the notoriety of the others, but won 142 games in a 14-year major-league career, four times at least 18 in a season, and made two All-Star teams. Besides keeping batters off-balance with his good fastball, Garcia fooled people because he was agile on the mound, able to field his position well despite a comparatively rotund appearance. "From the beginning, Mike was a sneaky quick pitcher," said Feller. "For a big guy, he was certainly mobile."[22]

It was an unusual collection of pitching talent on one roster and the Indians also had the hitters to back up the mound work with third baseman Al Rosen, first baseman Vic Wertz, second baseman Bobby Avila (who won the batting title with a .341 average) and outfielder Larry Doby.

Doby was a pioneer who broke the American League color barrier as its first black player when Bill Veeck brought him to the majors with the Indians in 1947 just a few months after Jackie Robinson's Dodger debut. Doby cracked a league-leading 32 homers during the Indians' charge to the pennant and complemented that crown by also leading the league in RBIs with 126.

Wynn may have been a southerner from Alabama, but in his first season with the Indians in 1949 he made it clear on where he stood on Doby as a man and as a teammate. A Detroit pitcher knocked Doby down twice during the same game with inside pitches. Wynn determined that was no coincidence, so when that pitcher took his turn at bat Wynn knocked him into the dirt four straight times. "Doby is on my team," Wynn said. "If they hurt him, they hurt me. I've got to teach them manners."[23]

For all of their regular-season greatness, however, the Indians were upset in the World Series by the New York Giants. The Series is best remembered for a stupendous catch by New York center fielder Willie Mays in the eighth inning of the first game. After Larry Doby and Al Rosen reached base, Vic Wertz caught hold of a pitch that he drove to deep center in the Polo Grounds.

Mays turned and sprinted toward the wall. After a long run, Mays reached up his glove, speared the ball over his shoulder well over 400 feet from home plate, and in one motion, with his cap flying off, spun around and fired the ball back to the infield. The runners, who were going because it seemed a lock that the ball would land safely, had to dash back to their bases. The catch prevented the Indians from taking control of the game. The Giants won the game in extra innings and took the Series in four straight games, a shocking upset that spoiled the Indians' otherwise glorious season. "I had it the whole time," Mays said. "[24] And the Giants had the Indians the whole time. The season of 1948 remains the last time the Cleveland Indians have won the World Series. Al Lopez had beaten out the Yankees, but he still lost out on the big prize.

After the 1955 season, Frank Lane left the White Sox and became the general manager of the St. Louis Cardinals. By the time Lane joined the Indians, Cleveland had traded Wynn to his old team in Chicago. Once, however, the two men crossed paths and Wynn jocularly said to Lane, "You're my favorite general manager." Lane at first smiled about the compliment and then realized Wynn had played on teams he ran, but never when Lane was there. "But you never pitched for me," Lane said. Wynn smiled and said, "That's why you're my favorite general manager."[25]

In 1954, the White Sox had put together their best season since 1920, before Shoeless Joe Jackson and his compatriots were banned from the game for life. While Early Wynn's Indians looked like a powerhouse that could sweep to another pennant the next season, Frank Lane's work had borne fruit, with 94 wins. Just maybe 1955 would finally be the year the White Sox took the pennant.

7

More Than Just Names

During his eight seasons in the major leagues, spread out between 1932 and 1946 and wrapped around World War II, Paul Richards was a catcher. So it was no surprise that Richards considered it a high priority to upgrade White Sox catching from a hodge-podge group in 1951 when no one really owned the first-string job.

Catcher is a take-charge position, a cornerstone of a club, and the man who is the number one guy should be a first-rate fielder and a great communicator with pitchers. Given how swiftly players were coming and going on the White Sox roster in the early 1950s, it was possible that not every pitcher knew each catcher's name.

The remedy for any such confusion arrived with the trade for veteran Sherm Lollar in 1952. Once in a while, Frank Lane had a keeper and was wise enough to hold onto that player. Lollar staked out the territory behind the plate as if he was claiming gold mining land in the Yukon. He caught 132 games his first season with the Sox and introduced stability to the position at a time when most other slots on the team were changing by the month.

Lollar, who grew up in Fayetteville, Arkansas, was 6-foot-1 and weighed a sturdy 185 pounds. The family owned a grocery store, but Lollar's father died when the boy was eight. John Sherman Lollar, Sr., had been a semi-pro baseball player and Sherm took to the game as a youngster. When Lollar was 12 he became the bat boy for the Class D team in Fayetteville. Lollar honed his catching skills with the older players by warming up pitchers. Then he played three years of American Legion ball. "It seems like I was born with a catcher's mitt on my hand," Lollar joked many years later. "I can remember playing pepper and catching when my arm was still sore from a vaccination. That must have been before I was six years old."[1]

A young high school graduate at 16, Lollar began drifting to find work. He worked in a grocery store and was an assistant to a mule skinner in Kansas, but clung to baseball with various semi-pro teams. A pitcher for the International League team in Baltimore saw him play and recommended that the short-handed team sign him. Lollar was exempt from military service during World War II because he had a cyst on his throat.

After a couple of years in AAA, Lollar had matured into a big-time player, who was in demand. The Cleveland Indians bought his rights, but traded him to the Yankees. The Yankees had a bit of a log-jam at catcher with Bill Dickey and Yogi Berra rating ahead of any new prospects. Lollar was shipped to the St. Louis Browns and ultimately Trader Lane found him and brought him to Chicago. That became Lollar's home for most of his 18-year major-league career. "It was one of the best trades I ever made," Lane said. "Sherm turned out to be one of the best catchers in the American League."[2]

White Sox managers all appreciated Lollar's know-how. He was a solid hitter, clouting 155 home runs, driving in 808 and batting .264 over his career, but his glove work and behind-the-plate savvy won him the most praise. Lollar was fortunate to be managed by two White Sox leaders who had been catchers. Al Lopez also understood that he had a gem calling the games. "He had tremendous ability with young pitchers," Lopez said of Lollar. "I think he shows great ability at handling men, which is the most important part of managing in this game."[3]

Lollar was a seven-time All-Star and hit a career-high 22 home runs in 1959 the year after hitting 20. It was 1957, though, that brought frustration. On pace for a career year, Lollar broke his wrist when he was hit by a pitch and caught just 101 games that season. While Lollar was healthy, they led the American League pennant race by six games. But the margin disappeared to the Yankees in just two weeks.

Billy Pierce, like Lollar a building block of the franchise, was kept around throughout the Lane administration once he had been acquired. He was very fond of his catcher and greatly respected his judgment. Lollar had the arm to throw out potential base stealers, but he almost never stole bases, going through entire seasons with zero swiped.

"I pitched to him for many years," Pierce said. "He called good pitches, called the game well, knew the batters well. He was the type of man you'd like to have catching for you. He wasn't the fastest guy on the base paths, though that was true of many catchers. They're down in that crouch all the time and that certainly isn't going to help your legs for running. I knew if I ever had a running race with him I could beat him."[4]

Lollar played for four teams in seven seasons at the beginning of his career, but once he joined the White Sox he never played for another in 11 more seasons. Not all of the fielders being counted on were so reliable. Any time a player was acquired in a deal it represented a chance taken. Some players looked better from a distance than they did up close. Some players seemed to have incredible potential and they never lived up to it. Some players performed better in one city than another. Not every trade was going to be a winner and not every trade was going to be a mistake. Deals were risky business, but Lane never shied away from making one if he thought he could benefit the team.

Ron Northey had been in the majors since 1942 and was a reliable hitter who ended up with a .276 lifetime batting average. He was not a star, but by the time the White Sox obtained him in 1955 in a trade for Gil Coan they knew he could be relied upon to fill in for starters when they needed a rest.

In 1955, Northey played just 14 games for the Sox after joining the club in August, but he hit .357. His on-base percentage was .471. In 1956, Northey played in 53 games and hit .354. Now that was the kind of fill-in every team could use and loved to have for pinch-hitting assignments. In 1956, Northey was the best pinch-hitter in the majors, scoring a hit at a .406 percentage. Northey was neither fleet afoot, nor a fabulous glove man, but he had a terrific batting eye. He struck out only once in his 51 pinch-hitting chances in 1956 and often swatted a hit with two strikes. A year later, Northey couldn't remember the name of the pitcher who struck him out, but he could remember the circumstances. The pitch came right down the middle, he said, and he just swung and missed. "I was the most surprised guy in the world," said the hitter who always make contact.[5]

In the off-season, Northey was a toy manufacturer who ran his own company. In season, he toyed with pitchers, coming into games off the bench without warming up, but routinely reaching them for safeties, anyway. "I just wait for a pitch I like, then cut at it," he said, "and the balls have been falling for me. He (the pitcher) has to get it over or walk you, so you just wait till you get your pitch. If you're in a hitting streak and it comes in, you get wood on it. I like pinch-hitting. I can always bear down more when there are men on base."[6]

In his mid–30s at the time, Northey had passed his prime as an outfielder. His weight was up to 210 on his 5-foot-10 frame and he had a weak knee that could buckle at any time. That meant running down to first base was about the extent of Northey's sprinting. His 1956 manager, Marty Marion, lamented being unable to use Northey more often in order to bring him to the plate four times a game. "He's as good at coming off the bench cold for one swing as anyone I've ever seen," Marion said.[7]

Marion and Northey had been roommates when they both played for the Cardinals in the 1940s and Marion had had plenty of first-hand views of the destruction Northey could wreak with his bat. Most players perform better when they get a chance to take batting practice and loosen up in the field. By the time Northey got the call he had been sitting around in the dugout for an hour or so more or less as a spectator with a vested interest. Going back decades, there has always been a one-liner tossed about the game concerning hitters like Northey. Players who marveled at the type of swinger who could hit so well without warming up, often say, "He can hit falling out of bed."

That was Northey. However, he did have one superstition when called upon to bat. He was a tobacco-chewing man and he refused to take his cuts without a chaw in his mouth — and not just any chaw. "I'd grab my bat, put a fresh chew in my mouth, and go to work," he said. "Even if I bite off a slice a few minutes before going to bat, I get rid of it and take a new one."[8] And some people think the secret to hitting is hand-eye coordination. Apparently, it is teeth-eye coordination.

Northey was a valuable addition, but was too old to build around. Ron Jackson was another story. He was not yet 21 when he broke in with the White Sox in 1954. He was a magnificent power specimen, standing 6-foot-7 and weighing 225 pounds. There was hope he would blossom into the next great American League slugger. There were deep sighs over Jackson's potential.

For the next six seasons, through 1959, Jackson made appearances in a White Sox uniform. But he never developed the necessary consistency to stay with the team for a whole season and play more than 61 games in any one year. Jackson had some artistry around the first base bag and whenever he went down to AAA and played regularly he hit well, often more than .300. He won the American Association batting crown, hitting .330, in 1954. Another year he hit .304 in Vancouver. But every time he came back to the White Sox, he fizzled. Eventually, the White Sox ran out of patience and sent Jackson to the Boston Red Sox.

Jackson's problem was that he couldn't beat out veteran Walt Dropo. Dropo had been the Rookie of the Year in 1950 with the Red Sox and he still had some juice in his bat when he joined the White Sox in 1955 when he hit 19 home runs. But he was fading a bit and his playing time dipped somewhat the next year. A combination of Dropo's extra-large size at 6-foot-5 and 220 pounds, and his home town of Moosup, Connecticut, conspired against him to provide the nickname "Moose." In college, at the University of Connecticut, Dropo was a star in football (the Chicago Bears were after him), basketball, and baseball.

In a singles-hitting lineup, Dropo was one of the White Sox most likely to hit a home run. But ironically, when he was reminiscing about an uncharacteristic White Sox 29–6 destruction of the Philadelphia Athletics in 1955, he said he actually enjoyed baseball more when it was played trying to scratch out runs rather than waiting for the long ball. "With Chicago, every game we played seemed to be close, low-scoring," he said. "And I liked that because every play meant something. Every pitch meant something."[9] Not during the 29–6 game, however, and on that day Dropo went 3-for-7 with three runs scored and three RBIs.

When Lane was trying bluster to convince other general managers into giving up their best players for little return, either by talking so fast they had trouble pinning down his true intentions, or by confusing them with his mention of so many different players, he always kept his eyes on the prize. He was willing to take a chance on a player with a track record if he thought the player had some tread left on his tracks. Some teams were more cautious about dealing with Lane than others. Some like the St. Louis Browns were generous because they were the worst team around and also needed money. Browns owner Bill Veeck was not so much an easy mark as someone who was open to suggestions and also in desperate need of player assistance and financial help. Time and again this worked well for Lane.

Virgil Trucks was a mainstay of the Detroit Tigers' pitching staff, but when they inexplicably tired of his services they traded Trucks, Hal White and Johnny Groth to the Browns for Owen Friend, Bob Nieman and J.W. Porter. The exchange turned out to be of more benefit to the White Sox than the Tigers. That's because the always friendly Browns were used to wheeling and dealing with Lane. The Browns sent Trucks and Bob Elliott to Chicago for Darrell Johnson and Lou Kretlow and an important $100,000 in mid-season of 1953. This was another winner for Lane, hoodwinking the other guys once again.

In less than half a season, the right-handed Trucks went 15–6 for the White Sox for a 20–10 overall record, and lived up to his nickname of "Fire." As in Fire Trucks. Trucks was not happy to leave Detroit and never thought the team would trade him. But once he was suiting up for the enemy, Trucks took full advantage of anything he knew about his ex-teammates' foibles and beat them four times in 1953. "Heck, if I could have faced them in every one of my starts that year I might have been 33–0!" Trucks wrote in his autobiography.[10]

Trucks said he was sorry to leave the Browns because he had become good friends with Satchel Paige and other players and said that Veeck told him the only reason he was letting him go was because he needed the cash to meet the payroll. Trucks was greeted in Chicago by newspaper stories saying how much the White Sox needed him and although the team did a surprisingly strong job of scoring runs for him, they were more adept at carving out one-run wins by working for runs one base at a time. "They were more of a hustling type team that manufactured a run and then held the lead with good pitching and defense," Trucks said. "Having a defense like they had behind you made all the difference in the world."[11]

At one point, the White Sox were 58–38 — with the Yankees still in sight — and Trucks thought he might have lucked into a pennant winner as he compiled an eight-game personal winning streak. Trucks ended up winning his 20th game of the season in his last start and had to beat his old friends on the Browns to do it. The White Sox did not keep up the same pace as Trucks, though. They finished with 89 wins and placed third in the American League.

Trucks said that one of the most enjoyable parts of the season for him was playing for Paul Richards. Richards, he said, acted as his own pitching coach and was extremely knowledgeable. "One edge that Richards had over other pitching coaches was that, like my dad, he could throw equally well with both hands," Trucks said. "If he was working with a lefty he could turn around and show him just as well as he could show a right-hander."[12]

Trucks was just as good the next season, going 19–12 for the White Sox. "I was hoping for another 20-win season as we went through spring training, as were all the writers in the Chicago papers, but I came up just a little short," Trucks said. "Going to the White Sox was like going to the Yankees after where I'd been. My increased success with Chicago just shows you what you can do with a good defense."[13]

Trucks was thriving, but Richards did not make it through the 1954 campaign. He was Lane's hand-picked guy and the manager Lane felt sure would lead the White Sox to a pennant, but they were no longer as close as they had been. Richards' contract was running out and he wanted security. He asked the team to give him $40,000 a year for three years. Grace Comiskey refused to pay the price and in late August, Lane allowed Richards to discuss a new job as general manager with the Baltimore Orioles. On September 10, despite the White Sox being on their way to 94 wins and theoretically still in a pennant race (though the Indians were realistically running away with things), Richards traded employers.[14]

The new manager installed immediately was Marty Marion, the old Cardinals shortstop who had been such a good fielder he was nicknamed "Octopus" or "Mr. Shortstop." Marion was an eight-time National League All-Star, the 1944 Most Valuable Player, and was part of three Cardinals championship teams. He was the manager of the Browns as the team disintegrated through the dispersal of players and loss of money because of lousy attendance.

Marion hooked on with the White Sox as a coach at the right time. It was only months before Richards' and Lane's relationship deteriorated to the point where Lane allowed Richards to leave before the end of the season. Four days after Richards' departure, Marion was named the new field boss. By 1956, Lane was gone, too, and it wasn't clear if the White Sox were still going to be willing to invest in the type of players they needed to progress to the point where they could finally claim that elusive pennant.

The White Sox won 91 games under Marion in 1955 and 85 in 1956, but one not terribly appreciated public faux pas was his commitment to going home to St. Louis on Sox days off. After the 1956 season ended, Marion heard that the team was trying to lure Al Lopez to town as the new manager, so he quit before he could be fired. "In my heart I know I did a good job," Marion said. "Other people didn't think so and that is why I resigned."[15]

Larry Doby was a seven-time All-Star by the time he joined the White Sox in 1956 and was not yet acknowledged as the historic figure he was later appreciated as. History has well chronicled all of the racism, grief and obstacles Jackie Robinson endured when he broke into the majors in 1947 with the Brooklyn Dodgers as the first African-American player in the twentieth century. Out-spoken, combative, determined, and proud of being a pioneer, Robinson is well-established as a legend for his courage and his baseball ability.

When Bill Veeck, then the owner of the Indians, brought Doby to the majors as the first African-American player in the American League only a few months after Robinson smashed the color barrier, his heart was in the right place. Years before, Veeck had made an aborted attempt to bring black players into the majors from the Negro Leagues, but was thwarted. Unlike Branch Rickey, Veeck did not have an elaborate game plan for easing Doby's way, other than to say his door was always open to talk and offer counsel.

Veeck was not naïve, however. He knew what he was doing by signing the league's first black ballplayer. "Lawrence," he said, "you are going to be part of history." Doby's reply was indicative of his low-key demeanor. "Part of history? I have no notions about that. I just want to play baseball. I mean, I was young. I didn't quite realize then what this all meant."

Like Robinson, Doby was warned not to get into physical altercations or battles with umpires. He was supposed to turn the other cheek if he felt wronged. What was feared by Rickey and Veeck and to the extent that they thought about it, Robinson and Doby, was that a slip-up might give opponents of integration ammunition to try to ban blacks all over again. "This was something that both Jack and I took seriously," Doby said. "We knew that if we didn't succeed, it might hinder opportunities for other African-Americans."[16]

The quieter, more retiring Doby, put up with the same amount of racism and unfair criticism as Robinson did, though his struggle was a bit less publicized. He was not the instant sensation in the game as Robinson was, either, participating in just 29 games with 32 at-bats and hitting only .159 during his debut season.

Doby was uneasy in the Indians' locker room. Veeck introduced him to manager Lou Boudreau, but Boudreau was the boss on the other side of the clubhouse door and Doby said the team did not exactly make him feel welcome on his first day at the office. "Some of the players shook my hand," Doby said, "but most of them didn't. It was one of the most embarrassing moments of my life."[17]

After the slow start the first season, Doby became a star. He led the American League in runs scored, RBIs, and home runs twice in the early 1950s. Doby commanded a pretty hefty price when the White Sox went after him. Chicago had to give up All-Star shortstop Chico Carrasquel (which it was willing to do because Luis Aparicio was on hand) and outfielder Jim Busby.

Manager Marion predicted that Doby's power would be a boost for a team that had difficulty scoring runs and lost a fair number of close ball-games. "The guy used to murder us when we played Cleveland," Marion said. "He'll make a big difference in the number of one-run and two-run decisions we might lose."[18]

Marion was correct. The 6-foot-1, 182-pound outfielder was 32 when he joined the White Sox and Doby hit 24 home runs with 102 RBIs for Chicago in 1956. The next year he hit 14 home runs with 79 RBIs, and batted .288. Doby did good work for the Sox. Also, nearly a decade after taking Veeck's words to heart, the rules governing his behavior were long extinct. When a pitch came in too close to his head, Doby had no hesitation about blowing off steam or helping instigate a bench-clearing brawl such as the one between the White Sox and Yankees in 1957.

American League president Will Harridge liberally sprinkled around fines to Doby and Walt Dropo of the White Sox and Enos Slaughter, Billy Martin and pitcher Art Ditmar of the Yankees after a fight when Doby (slapped with a $150 fine) threw the first punch. Doby dove in the dirt to avoid a Ditmar inside fastball, then sprung to his feet, charged the mound, and decked Ditmar with a punch. Slaughter and Dropo squared off against one another. Then after Ditmar was stretched out, Martin jumped in to fight Doby.

Those with a good memory probably thought Doby deserved at least one free shot for all he put up with back in the 1940s when he said he was called "nigger," "coon," and "jigaboo." Those insults stay with a man. "There's something in the Bible that says you should forgive and forget," Doby said. "Well, you might forgive, but boy, it is tough to forget."[19] Doby said the slights made him play more aggressively and sometimes he just swung too hard at a pitch. The pitch, not the punch.

In 1978, long after he retired, Doby returned to the White Sox to become the second African American manager in major-league history. Once again the owner was Bill Veeck. And in 1998, five years before he died of cancer, Doby was elected to the Hall of Fame. At the time, Chicago baseball writer Jerome Holtzman wrote, "Hurrah!"

Doby was elated that his moment had come. "You look back 51 years ago and you never thought this type of situation would come about," Doby said, reflecting back to his rookie season. "You think about some of the changes that have happened in baseball. It's a feeling of struggle in the past. It's a feeling of a certain amount of relief. It's a great feeling."[20]

8

The Guy They
Called Little Nell

Trader Frank Lane's deal for Nellie Fox in October of 1949 scored points for him on the genius scale. Nobody touted Fox as the White Sox' second baseman of the future. Nobody was even convinced that he would make a big-league roster for a minute.

Fox was acquired from the Philadelphia Athletics for White Sox catcher Joe Tipton. Tipton had to go because he and manager Jack Onslow had engaged in a fist fight. It was a clearing-the-air and clearing-the-bench move for Lane. He did not count on Nellie Fox becoming a Hall of Famer. The biggest rap on Fox was that he did not make a good first impression on talent scouts and sports writers who were swayed less by his abilities than his appearance. Fox stood about 5-foot-9 and his listed weight was 150 pounds. People tended to think that he would shatter on contact, though they learned over time he was too tough to break.

Fox was born in tiny St. Thomas, Pennsylvania, on Christmas Day 1927 and his true love growing up in the rural town was baseball. His primary interests were baseball, baseball and baseball. Fox was just 16 when his mother delivered him to legendary A's manager Connie Mack for a try-out in 1943. Mack liked the boy's spunk and spark. It was the middle of World War II and there was a manpower shortage, so Mack decided to keep Fox around. "This boy has baseball in his blood," Mack said.[1] Plans were made for Fox to drop out of high school during his current sophomore year and join the A's organization. Confident or not as a young player, Fox was still starry-eyed. "He was so excited at shaking hands with Connie Mack, that he wouldn't wash his right hand," Fox' mother said.[2]

The funny thing was that Fox could act so boyishly one minute, but in the next minute still enjoy a cigar. That was his one grown-up activity as a 16-year-old. Mack went from being polite to being impressed, even though Fox' primary background was playing first base. The shrimp-like Fox was not a natural match to that position where in the big leagues the infielders like to throw to a big target after they scoop up their grounders. Fox spent part of 1944 in Class B, then Class D, hitting over .300 in both locales. Assigned to the International League in the spring of 1945, Fox was drafted. He spent two years in the Army and returned to the A's organization in 1947. Before the end of the season, Fox appeared in seven major-league games. He spent a chunk of 1948 in Nebraska in Class A ball, but played in three more games for Philadelphia. Coming out of spring training in 1949, Fox stuck with the big club and that season he got into 88 games.

Fox had made the big leagues for good, though he had no idea that his future lay in Chicago. Watching from afar as Fox hit .255, Lane liked what he saw. Lane said that Fox was the type of youthful player his team needed and he appealed to him because "he was young and aggressive."[3]

The White Sox second baseman was Cass Michaels, who had hit .308, and neutral observers didn't see a place for Fox with the Sox. Soon enough, Lane shipped Michaels out of town and manager Paul Richards and coach Marty Marion developed Fox into a smooth-fielding second sacker, helping him to learn a silky double-play pivot.

If anyone harbored doubts about Fox's durability because of his small stature, those thoughts were misplaced. He played through injuries that would sideline someone with a lower pain threshold and became visibly agitated any time his name was not penciled into the starting lineup. Once, in a spring training game, Fox was smashed in the mouth when a ball took a bad hop. The impact knocked out one tooth and broke another, but Fox didn't even tell anyone he was wounded. After shortstop Chico Carrasquel told Richards, the manager at last persuaded Fox to come out of the game. But he wouldn't take days off to see a dentist and heal up.

Fox' jaw always seemed to be working overtime. Not talking, but chewing. No player in baseball history was more identified with chewing tobacco. Fox always played with a plug of chaw in his mouth and was often photographed with a bulge in his cheek so large that it made people wonder if he had swallowed a baseball. Fox appeared to have a kinship with snakes that ingest their prey, only to have a huge bulge in their bodies until the meal is digested.

Fox was one of those humans, though, who did not gain weight or body fat no matter what they ate. His favorite food was ice cream and he did not often push back from the dinner table without eating dessert. Fox married his childhood sweetheart while he was playing in the minors and Joanne Fox, the cook around the house, admitted Fox' dietary preference was heavily weighted to sweets. "Dessert is really the most important part of his meal," she said.[4]

However, chocolate cake was not the secret of Fox' success on the diamond. A fierce work ethic, a willingness to practice extra hours, and an awareness of self contributed to a career that included All-Star selections in 12 seasons. Fox recognized that he was not going to be a power hitter, so he concentrated on working hard to make other contributions at the plate. Fox struck out only 13 or 14 times a season in nearly 600 at-bats. He swung a large bat and wasn't shy about choking up on the handle. He was happy with singles instead of home runs and understood he was making a contribution to the offense when he got on base any way at all.

The more he fielded ground balls at second, the better he got. Fox led the American League in fielding percentage at his position six times and won four Gold Glove Awards. Before he retired, Fox set several fielding records, including leading AL second baseman in putouts 10 times and in overall chances nine times. That meant that not only did Fox get to a lot of balls with his excellent range, his ability to reach the ball translated to outs for his team. "Of all of the stars now in the game," Richards said in 1957, "he's the greatest example to young players and even to players yet unborn. In fact, he's baseball to all of Young America. Here is a man who ... pulled himself up by his own bootstraps."[5]

One thing that never changed — Fox did not enjoy a growth spurt. He remained one of the smallest star players in baseball throughout his career. Wherever he traveled, sportswriters routinely called attention to his size, calling him "Little Nel." It sounded as if he was a character in "Little House on the Prairie," but Fox couldn't shake the nickname. His physical measurements were not something he could easily alter, so he forgot about that and put his energy into becoming a better player.

Even Richards remembered not being very impressed by Fox at first, but when he realized he did not have much choice but to use him at second, the manager enlisted a tag-team group of coaches to drill Fox in the field and at bat. In the end, it was Fox who out-lasted everyone else on the diamond and begged for more. "He was so eager to learn and to improve himself that he wore everybody out," Richards said. "He was the first on the field and the last to leave. But it paid off."[6]

By 1951, also through the diligence of repetition, Fox had made himself into a .300 hitter, finishing with a .313 mark. How Fox ended up with that figure is a story in itself. He had been hitting well all season, but fell into a slump in September. The White Sox' position was pretty much fixed in the standings and Richards, knowing that it meant a lot to his second baseman to complete the year over .300, approached him when he dropped to .302 and asked if he wanted to sit out the final games. Fox was inwardly indignant. When Richards saw that Fox was taking the news poorly, he brought the subject up again. "I'd like to hit .300," Fox said, "but I'd like to hit it playing." Richards reinserted Fox into the lineup and he went on a hitting tear, raising his average 11 more points before season's end.[7]

Fox was a self–effacing ballplayer, not given to braggadocio. He did not move away from his childhood home area, instead preferring to maintain his Pennsylvania roots in the off-season. He opened a bowling alley and took advantage of the abundance of deer in order to indulge his passion for hunting. He once noted that he did not plan to move because he enjoyed escaping into the woods with his shotguns in pursuit of venison too much. Fox was more accurate with his throws to first than he was in shooting deer, though, nailing just three in a 13-year period. It was just being out in the wild that counted the most to him.

The White Sox honored Fox with a special day and gave him presents that included a trip to Hawaii, a television set, record player, a freezer, a fur stole for his wife, a set of silverware and a car. There was just one miscalculation. The Sox gave Fox a boat, but he had no place to put it and confided in owner Bill Veeck that he actually would have preferred some mountain land near home. "We would have given him the land," said Veeck, always the showman who wanted to make a big splash with the fans as witnesses, "but you can't row a piece of land into a ballpark."[8] An oft-quoted comment made by Ralph Kiner, the Pittsburgh Pirate slugger who led the National League in home runs seven times, was that home-run hitters, not singles hitters, drove Cadillacs. As it so happened, Fox did have a Cadillac and singles bought it.

Praise like Richards' accumulated for Fox. He was a perfect fit for a White Sox team that emphasized sound defense, the hit-and-run, playing intelligent, taking the extra base, and collected its runs one at a time rather than on three-run homers. To some, Fox was a throwback player, the type who would have succeeded and excelled in baseball's deadball era before 1920. A bit slowed down from his heyday of nearly a half-century earlier, but still keenly following the game, was one fan whose opinion was significant.

One day, unexpectedly, Fox received a fan letter from an unusual source. The mail came from Ty Cobb, the Detroit Tigers great whose .367 average is the highest lifetime mark in history. Cobb was the truest embodiment of the style of game the Go-Go White Sox played. He was always a bit contemptuous of the prevalence of slugging and a proponent of the so-called "thinking man's game" that he played. In his hand-written letter to Fox that is preserved in the Baseball Hall of Fame, Cobb essentially says the younger man was one of them.

"As you know, I also played baseball...," Cobb began in an exceptionally understated manner. Having seen Fox play, he said, he "feels an impulse now to write you to extend congratulations (for) the honors you have recently received and in particular to relate my admiration of your ability and play. Your play is along the lines of the boys of yesteryear." Cobb, who stole 892 of them, extolled the value of the stolen base, something the White Sox duly recognized and said that Fox should take notes because "you will someday be sought as a manager" and predicted he would be able to stay in the game past his playing days because "You are strictly managerial material. Much luck and success. Sincerely, Ty Cobb."[9]

Ty Cobb might have been the most hard-nosed ballplayer who ever lived. He has been described as a mean-spirited man that came into the next base with spikes sharpened and aimed at the fielder. Fox was more good-humored, but he played the game hard and it was noticed. Esteemed baseball writer Roger Kahn said of Fox, "He plays the game as if the manager were standing by with a bus ticket to South Grand Forks marked, 'One Way: N. Fox.'"[10]

They called him "Little Nell" because Nellie Fox stood just 5-foot-9 and weighed 160 pounds, but he played an outsized second base. Fox was the Most Valuable Player in 1959 as the White Sox captured the American League pennant. Fox was later elected to the Hall of Fame. (National Baseball Hall of Fame Library, Cooperstown, New York.)

Al Lopez, who eventually inherited the managerial job of the White Sox after Richards and Marion took their turns, also inherited Fox. He had seen him from across the diamond when manning the dugout for the Cleveland Indians, but once he worked with Fox on a daily basis, he fell in love. "You have to say that Nellie is the hustlingest player in the league," Lopez said.[11]

Fox said he needed all the instruction he could get during his first couple of years with the White Sox. He was still learning how to hit and make that critical pivot on the double play. And he was grateful that Richards and the other Sox coaches provided that help. "By '51, I'd been up for two years," Fox said. "Suppose I'd gotten smart and told myself I didn't need coaching. You know where I'd be? I'd be out of the big leagues by now, that's where."[12]

Instead, Fox was an in-demand baseball player, not only on the field. He began writing a column for the *Chicago Sun–Times* called "Nellie Fox Reports," and loaned his name to numerous product endorsements. He was in ads for Louisville Slugger baseball bats, Wilson baseball gloves, Viceroy cigarettes and Crosman Pellguns, which he used for target practice. Of course, Fox also had an endorsement deal with a chewing tobacco company. His brand was Favorite.

One Fox trait that was surely admired by Ty Cobb and was noted on many occasions by pitcher Billy Pierce, who roomed with Fox on the road for 11 years, was the second baseman's competitiveness. That showed through not only on the field, but in other endeavors.

"Nellie was probably as good a competitor as anybody," Pierce said. "He would go for any ball when he was on defense and you didn't strike him out. He'd get a piece of the ball all of the time. I don't care what he was doing, bowling or gin rummy, it was always a competitive thing to him. If Nellie won three hands in a row and he lost one, you could hear him screaming all over the place. He was just all heart, giving everything he had. When we played the Indians and they had Herb Score in his first couple of years before he got hurt, Nellie would go up to the plate and come back to the dugout and we would ask, 'What does he have?' Nellie would say, 'He doesn't have a thing.' The guy was throwing 100 mph. He was certainly not ever going to give in."[13]

That was one of Fox's intangibles. Glen Rosenbaum, who spent 43 years in the White Sox organization starting in 1955, as a minor-league pitcher, and then as a batting practice pitcher, and eventually as traveling secretary, said everyone looked up to Fox. "I always said that Nellie Fox was the manager on the field," Rosenbaum said. "He was just that type of guy. He always knew what was going on in the field. Nellie was just a special type of person. He didn't have any ego. He's still my all-time favorite. He'd battle you and he was always full of life, always up."[14]

Rosenbaum, who thought he would make the big club more than once when he won 16 or so games in the minors, was a raw 19-year-old in spring training in 1955 after growing up in rural Indiana. Rookies might become the butt of jokes, or at the least be left on their own to absorb lessons, but more than 50 years later, Rosenbaum recalled a Fox kindness.

Rosenbaum took the mound for his turn of 15 minutes of throwing batting practice. All around him infielders were handling grounders and taking care of their own business. This was in an era before screens were put in place in front of the mound to protect pitchers from line drives. Rosenbaum had thrown to a couple of guys and Minnie Minoso was stepping into the batting cage. Minoso was notorious for slashing line drives through the box, the type that would make pitchers dance out of the way or throw up their gloves to protect their heads. Rosenbaum didn't know that. Fox trotted over from second base and spoke to Rosenbaum.

"All of a sudden, here's Nellie on the mound," Rosenbaum said. "He goes, 'Be alive. He'll take your head off. Be alive. He comes back through the middle.' A veteran like that comes running in to a 19-year-old kid, a nobody, and warns me. I think that describes Nellie Fox about as well as anything could. A lot of other guys would stand around and go, 'Hey, watch this.' A lot of them would do that and let you learn the hard way."[15]

Fox had learned his own lessons through hard work and had developed consistency on a very high level. He led the American League in fielding percentage six times, including one season where he recorded a remarkable .990 average. The only thing Fox did more consistently than field ground balls was chew tobacco. He never went out on the field without that hunk of tobacco wedged in his cheek.

Although Fox was a cigar smoker when he was quite young, he came to chewing tobacco rather by accident. When he was playing for Lancaster in the minors under manager Lena Blackburne, the boss suggested that he chew on something to stay calm. "What should I chew?" Fox asked. "Try licorice," Blackburne urged. After just two innings, Fox began to feel sick to his stomach. That was the end of the licorice experiment. "My dad chews tobacco," Fox told Blackburne. "I think that's what I'll start chewing, too."[16] So that's how it began in the late 1940s.

Not all White Sox fans realized that Fox was a habitual chewer. One day in the late 1950s a woman telephoned the sports department of the *Chicago Sun–Times* with a question. Was there something wrong with Fox' head? she asked. The woman said he seemed to have a deformity because one cheek was perpetually swollen. Could it be a permanent case of the mumps? she queried. Informed about Fox' commitment to chewing tobacco the woman apologized, but said that she thought it was a bad habit and she very much hoped that Little Leaguers did not follow in his footsteps.[17]

In the 1950s, Fox grew up with the White Sox, grew and improved, even as the White Sox were growing and improving. He was part of something exciting, part of the turnaround putting years of drudgery to rest. And Fox was one of the main reasons why losing was now in the past.

9

Magician with a Glove

There were times that Jim Landis just plain forgot to do his job because he was virtually hypnotized by Luis Aparicio's fielding. The White Sox shortstop was a ballet dancer on a baseball field, a wizard with leather, and he made so many brilliant plays that the Sox center fielder was stunned into immobility because of his admiration for the Venezuelan's skills.

"Luis made every play possible," Landis said. "I don't care, going in, going back, going sideways, either way, and he had one of the strongest arms you could have for a shortstop. I was supposed to back him up on certain plays, but I was mesmerized, no joke."[1]

The White Sox, and Lane, thought they were set for years once Chico Carrasquel took over the shortstop role. After all, he was an All-Star. No one in Chicago imagined that within a few seasons the team would come up with someone who was even better.

Aparicio was born in Maracaibo, Venezuela, in 1934 and he was born into a baseball family. His father, Luis, Sr., who had been offered a contract by the Washington Senators in 1939, played the game, and so did his uncle Ernesto. Aparicio was 16 when he became the starting shortstop on the team his dad operated. Family members tutored "Little Looie," as he came to be called in Chicago. Aparicio and Nellie Fox bonded immediately and created one of the finest double-play combinations of all time. Ironically, they were both small men. Aparicio stood 5-foot-9 and his listed playing weight was 160 pounds. He and Fox were roughly the same size. The press dubbed Fox "Little Nell," and Aparicio was stuck with "Little Looie." They may have been physically little, but their impact was huge.

There are conflicting stories about some of the details of how the White Sox got young Luis in their clutches. Aparicio was playing ball at home on a team his father owned when he was managed by Red Kress, at the time a coach for the Cleveland Indians. Kress' employers were interested enough to send a scout to check out Aparicio. The Aparicios asked for more than $10,000. Indians general manager Hank Greenberg said no. He offered a ticket to spring training and a willingness to pay $5,250 if Aparicio showed well. Behind-the-scenes comments were made that the Indians had actually concluded that Aparicio was too small for the majors. Lane was more intrigued than Greenberg. He obtained Aparicio's rights from the Caracas team for $6,000 and promised $4,000 to the player as a minor-league salary. Deal. By today's standards, the dollar figures are puny, but by such maneuverings are fortunes changed in the standings. By 1956, Aparicio was the White Sox' starting shortstop and Carrasquel was playing for Cleveland.

Carrasquel was revered in Venezuela and the many accomplished shortstops who followed him from that Latin American country to the U.S. credit him for paving the way for future players to be noticed. Aparicio felt the same way, as a youngster hanging around the ballpark at home trying to catch Carrasquel for an autograph. "Chico was my idol," Aparicio said. "He's a tremendous guy and he helped me a lot. If he hadn't played in the big leagues, I don't know if other (Venezuelans) would have had an opportunity. He's so likeable and back home everyone idolizes him."[2]

Aparicio was 19 when he came to the United States, and although he had studied English, his language skills were not fully formed. He was quiet in the 1955 spring training camp and Glen Rosenbaum, also a rookie and also pretty quiet, became friendly with the newcomer. "I clicked with him," Rosenbaum said. "He was just a rookie and so was I. I had come from a farm and I was not an aggressive type of person. I was pretty much in awe about everything and I'd go out every day and kept my mouth shut. I never said anything and whatever we were supposed to do, I did it. So did Luis."[3]

If home-run hitters followed the Teddy Roosevelt advice of talking softly and carrying a big stick, then a superb fielder like Aparicio spoke softly and carried a big glove. "Luis was unbelievable," Rosenbaum said. "I can still see him in my first exhibition game. I turned around on the mound when a batter hit one of those little toppers. He was just fluid motion going into the hole. He was something. You don't see that fluidity and efficiency. He made everything look easy and it wasn't that easy."[4]

Aparicio's glove work immediately brought him attention, but what was not initially envisioned was how devastating a weapon he would be as a base stealer. Aparicio was a perfect fit with the Go-Go White Sox. More than that, he became the ring leader, taunting opposing pitchers with his big leads, and his ability to jump-start the Sox offense by swiping second base (and sometimes third) after reaching on a walk.

Baseball was in one of its hitters eras in the 1950s, where teams counted on the long ball, but Aparicio was playing a different game. He led the American League in stolen bases an astonishing nine straight seasons beginning in 1956. He was money in the bank on the basepaths, four times stealing more than 50 bases in a season.

Despite playing high-level ball in Venezuela for four years and gaining seasoning in the minors for two more before the Sox installed him as their shortstop, Aparicio still had doubts about whether or not he belonged. He made his major-league debut on April 17, 1956, against the Indians, but said he might not have made it that far if not for the advice, counsel and kindness of catcher Sherm Lollar and his soon-to-be keystone sack partner Fox. "Especially Sherman," Aparicio said. "He really helped me in showing me the attitude I should have for the game. When I broke in I got a lot of help from him and Fox. I don't think I would have made it if it wasn't for them. Their attitude to me was great."[5]

No one enjoyed watching Aparicio swipe bases more than White Sox owner Bill Veeck. There was just something about Aparicio's lead-off style that tickled him. "He's a delight to watch," Veeck said, "particularly when he dangles off first base like a yo-yo, a yo-yo that might spin out to second base on any pitch."[6]

Pitchers went on high alert when an Aparicio got on base. They have to pitch from a stretch with men on base and they have to watch the first base area out of one eye, even as they ready to throw to the plate. A runner who jumps around a lot can make them edgy. This is especially true if it is a runner who has a track record of success and a reputation for stealing whenever the mood strikes him.

Aparicio once offered a sports writer an analysis of what he was looking for when he was leading off to make stealing easier, but it's possible

Hall of Fame shortstop Luis Aparicio was a terror on the base paths, stealing almost at will as he led the American League in stolen bases for nine straight years. Here Aparicio is sliding easily into third as Yankees third baseman Andy Carey stretches for a high throw from catcher Yogi Berra. (National Baseball Hall of Fame Library, Cooperstown, New York.)

that some of the explanation was lost in translation. "Almost every right-hand pitcher, I watch the left shoulder, 95 percent," Aparicio said. "I've got the best jump. I got a real good quickest start. Help me 75 percent. I think I have the real good reflexes. I'm not very fast. But when I decide to go, I just go. If I don't get a real good jump, I come right back. I try to steal relaxed, real loose, relaxed, loose. I don't say to myself, 'I'm going to steal,' but they give me a chance, I go. I go. I go."[7]

Reading between the lines, trying to glean meaning, it sounds as if Aparicio stole bases when it felt right to him. That would put the endeavor more into the realm of instinct rather than science. And if so, perhaps there was no way he could thoroughly explain the process so anyone not in his shoes could completely understand what it took. To the casual observer, Aparicio's protest that he was not fast seemed specious. But what made his start special was that he could be at full speed by his second step.

Once established in the White Sox lineup and as a star, the Aparicio of the 1950s came across as a very happy guy. He had a wife and several children. In his free time he went fishing and watched television westerns. He loved to dress well, buying suits that had his initials sewn into them. He often greeted opposing players at the batting cage with banter, once teasingly calling Yogi Berra of the Yankees "Shorty." It turned out Berra had been calling Aparicio by that nickname and Aparicio discovered that Berra was no taller than he was. Maybe Berra shrunk from squatting down behind the plate all of the time.

"I'm a happy person, I guess," Aparicio said of his feelings about life as a major leaguer. "I get along with people. I think I'm lucky. I'm a nice guy? Everybody's a nice guy."[8] One thing that made Aparicio happy was his status in the sport. It was not long before he was recognized as the best shortstop in baseball. He led the American League in fielding percentage eight times and was a 10-time All-Star. "I think you need three things to be a good shortstop," Aparicio said long after his retirement. "Good hands, quick reflexes and smarts. And I think I had them all, so I guess I turned out to be a good shortstop."[9]

Some in the American League might have looked askance at the White Sox for shedding Carrasquel in favor of the untried Aparicio. Carrasquel was an All-Star. So there was some pressure on Aparicio to perform. He never seemed to notice it, however, and it was not long before everyone in baseball comprehended what pushed the White Sox to make such a drastic move. Aparicio shone so brightly on so many occasions his star power eclipsed not only Carrasquel's, but also that of all other shortstops in the league.

Yankees manager Casey Stengel essentially said that playing against Aparicio gave him heartburn because he got to so many grounders that even Carrasquel would never have reached. Paul Richards, the former Sox manager then leading the Orioles, said Aparicio was on his way to becoming the best shortstop he had ever seen. "He's so quick getting the ball to second base that he often saves Fox from being blocked out on double plays. And some of his stops make you blink."[10]

In only a few seasons, Aparicio had gone from being unknown outside of Venezuela, to breathlessly being discussed as possibly the greatest shortstop of all time. In Al Lopez, Aparicio had a manager who was on board with the White Sox' Go-Go style and who appreciated his talent with the glove on a team where fielding in general was regularly praised. Lopez held an infielding philosophy that described how he felt about Aparicio's skill. "A good chest helps a third baseman," Lopez said. "A second baseman can knock down a ball and still nail the runner. But a shortstop is on his own."[11]

Shortstops have more territory to cover and that means they usually must be faster than the other infielders. The second baseman has that margin for making a mistake and still recovering to throw out a runner because he is situated so much closer to first base. Aparicio's quickness and range set him apart from other shortstops. That capability of covering vast areas of ground contributed to Aparicio leading the league in assists for six years in a row.

The Yankees' Stengel so marveled at Aparicio's continuing improvement that he suggested he might not even have to throw the ball to first to obtain an out. "One of these days, that little feller's going to field a ball and beat the runner to first base," Stengel said. "[12]

Seeing with your own eyes was believing during the 1950s and 1960s because not every team's games were on TV locally and national exposure in an era without cable TV was limited. So even if a player had been in the league for a few years his skills were not as widely known unless seen in the All-Star Game, the World Series, or first-hand.

It just so happened that during a double header at Comiskey Park that pitted the White Sox against the Kansas City Athletics, Aparicio reached new heights of magic with an all-around performance that even surprised him. At the plate, he drove in six runs. He stole two bases. And in the field, he made a catch that defied belief.

Kansas City's Whitey Herzog lifted a short fly ball that swerved towards the left-field foul line and seemed certain to land beyond the grasp of Sox left fielder Minnie Minoso, third baseman Gene Freese, and Aparicio. The quick analysis was that the ball would drop in for a double. Aparicio kept his eye on the ball, ran full out for about 100 feet and speared the ball as it was about to hit the turf by thrusting out his bare, right hand. Out. Former White Sox pitcher Hollis Thurston was an eye-witness and said, "That's the greatest catch I've ever seen any shortstop make."

He wasn't alone in that appraisal. Ralph Kiner, the former slugger, was present in his capacity as general manager of the Pacific Coast League's San Diego franchise. "With Luis making those kind of catches in left field, Minoso should be good till he's 50," Kiner said.[13]

A grinning Aparico was in accord with the outside commentary. "It was the greatest day in my life," he said. "I don't think I knock in six runs in one day even in winter league. The catch was the best I ever make."[14]

In the early 1950s, it appeared that the White Sox would be set for years with the superb double-play combination of Nellie Fox and Chico Carrasquel. Finding a new shortstop was not one of the team's great needs to advance in the standings. It was difficult to upgrade from an All-Star. But when an even better All-Star presented himself, the Sox were flexible enough to react and take advantage. As good as Carrasquel was, Aparicio was better.

Also, as good as Fox and Carrasquel were together, Fox and Aparicio were better together. After a few years of watching them work in tandem, sportswriters were comparing the Fox-Aparicio duo to the best of all time. There was mention of Eddie Collins and Buck Weaver on the White Sox of 1919. Nominations included the Yankees' Phil Rizzuto and Joe Gordon and the Dodgers' Pee Wee Reese and Jackie Robinson. "Aparicio and Fox are so good that they doubtless not only form the finest second-base combination in White Sox annals, but deserve to be ranked among the great middle-of-the-diamond duos of all time," a Chicago sports writer said.[15]

Some players just click. Fox said although Carrasquel and Aparicio were both great for him to play with, the fact that Aparicio's English was better than Carrasquel's helped their communication. Also, the fact that Aparicio released the ball so quickly to him on the double play kept him out of harm's way when runners were trying to take him out. "He gives it to me in time for me to avoid my getting clobbered," Fox said.[16]

White Sox pitcher Billy Pierce was a long-time teammate of Fox and Aparicio and he benefited greatly from their smoothness in the field. Having that twosome behind him gave Pierce great confidence every time he was on the mound. It was like an insurance policy. Pierce might have been hit hard with sharp grounders, but Aparicio and Fox could rectify the mistake with a neat pickup and throw, or rescue him with a double play. "They were great," Pierce said. "Just knowing that they were out there was a great help to a pitcher. We didn't always score a lot of runs, so to have those two guys in the field meant that we were not going to give up a lot of runs."[17]

Aparicio always gave credit to Fox for taking him under his wing and helping him develop as a major leaguer and Pierce said Aparicio paid close attention to what Fox did on and off the field to the point that he began to mimic one of Fox's superstitions.

"Nellie had a thing that every time at the end of an inning when he was coming to the dugout, he stepped on third base," Pierce said. "A superstition. And after a couple of months you noticed that Luis was doing the same thing. Luis respected Nellie as much as anybody who he ever played with. There was a great respect there. Luis was young at the time, just a rookie coming up, and Luis had as much respect for Nellie as any ballplayer could have for another one."[18]

Proof of that feeling was evident when Aparicio named one of his sons after Fox.

10

Wynn Joins the White Sox

Whether he was a young pitcher, a middle-aged pitcher, or an aging pitcher, Early Wynn's fierceness never flagged. He once explained his incredible intensity and ferocity mixing it up with hitters by making it sound as if the emotions were almost beyond his control.

"You can't get enjoyment out of hate," Wynn said. "I wish I could live by this 100 percent, but every fourth or fifth day in the summer I go into a Jekyll and Hyde act. Every time a player gets a hit or a home run off me I get strange notions and ideas of things I would like to do to him. Then after the game I feel ashamed and think to myself, 'This guy is a nice fellow and I wonder what's happening to you, Early?' So I'll call him up and invite him to be my guest at dinner and spend the evening talking shop."[1]

If anything, that reflective statement represented Wynn mellowing. In his earlier days he would never think of making amends with a social evening. Maybe that was Early talking. Gus would never think that way.

The reality was that Wynn changed his personal policy for nobody when it came to the rule against hitting the ball through the box and jeopardizing his safety. It didn't matter if the smash up the middle occurred in a regular-season game, an exhibition game, or in batting practice when the hitter was a teammate. After fellow Indian 20-game-winner Bob Lemon stroked a shot through the middle, sure enough Wynn brushed him back.

Since that's how Wynn reacted to close calls, it was no surprise that he blew a gasket when a pitcher had the audacity to throw at his head. In a game against the Yankees, after Wynn joined the White Sox, he was sent sprawling by Jim Coates. Wynn hit the dirt and his batting helmet flew in another direction. Although Coates went through the standard who-me routine, Wynn did not for a moment believe the pitch near his noggin was an accidental heave and he promised immediately to obtain revenge. "Some day I may get all nine of them," Wynn said. "I know he threw at me. He hit me last year. He had no trouble with control in the rest of the inning. He is a bush-leaguer, anyway."[2]

The Senators and Indians had watched Wynn at his angriest for years. Now the White Sox got to see him up close, throwing at opposing batters on their behalf. When Wynn was pitching, they knew they would be protected. Wynn took personally any perceived slights to his teammates. "What a temper he had," White Sox pitching coach Ray Berres said.[3]

Early Wynn had spent nine years with the Cleveland Indians after his start in the majors with the Washington Senators. He won 20 games four times with Cleveland and made three All-Star teams for the Indians.

But during Wynn's last season in Cleveland he finished with a 14–17 record and he was going to be 38 prior to the 1958 season. Besides, Al Lopez, one of Wynn's biggest fans, was out as Cleveland manager and had become the new manager of the Chicago White Sox. If anyone knew Wynn's strengths and what he still might have left, it was Lopez.

A few months after the 1957 season ended, Wynn became convinced he was going to be traded. He was suspicious of Frank Lane's motives as soon as he came to Cleveland and any player watching from afar who studied Lane's trading habits wouldn't be buying a new home or taking out a long-term lease on an apartment. Wynn wrote a baseball column for the Cleveland News, and when he caught the rumors of his impending exile, he shared his thoughts with readers in an off-season column.

"They're talking about trading me again," Wynn wrote under a dateline from his winter home in Nokomis, Florida. "Well, I want everyone concerned to know that I'm sick and tired of sitting around all winter listening to this talk and wondering what team I'll be playing with next spring. If they want to trade me why don't they quit talking about it and go ahead and make a deal?"[4]

Whether Lane already had his mind made up, or Wynn gave the deal just the nudge it needed, by the next week, he was an ex–Indian and writing a farewell column. "Well, they quit talking about it, didn't they?" Wynn wrote. "That's the shortest time I ever worked for a new general manager. I'm sorry to leave Cleveland. I have a lot of friends there and the fans have always been very fair to me. But I can't squawk about being traded."[5]

This was the trade that moved Minnie Minoso back to Cleveland for a second time, along with Fred Hatfield, and added outfielder Al Smith to the White Sox roster, too. Minoso suggested periodically in the following years that manager Al Lopez just didn't like him because he traded him twice, from Cleveland to Chicago, and back to Cleveland when Lopez came to Chicago. "Perhaps it was just a bit coincidental," Minoso wrote gently in his autobiography, "but both times the manager of the club that traded me happened to be Al Lopez."[6]

Despite his somewhat wistful comments about leaving Cleveland, Wynn did not sound terribly broken up about the shift to the White Sox. "So it's back with Al Lopez now and I can truthfully say that I will be very happy in Chicago," Wynn wrote. "I feel very fortunate to be back with Lopez. There's one angle to this trade I don't like. I'd rather have that Minnie Minoso on my side."[7]

When Wynn joined the White Sox he had 235 big-league wins. At his age, neither he nor baseball experts thought of him as a potential 300-game winner. He was busy making a fresh start in Chicago and connecting with new teammates. He still thought he could pitch, but he was not as speedy as he had been in his youth. There were no radar guns measuring fastball velocity. The best guess anyone might have was that Wynn's fastball in his prime came across the plate at 90-plus mph. No one could know for sure, though.

However, Wynn was long past the point of relying just on his fastball. Mel Harder cured him of that when he joined the Indians. "He wasn't as fast as he had been because he was getting up there in age," said fellow hurler Billy Pierce. "With the White Sox he couldn't throw that hard any more, but he had a good slider and he put it in the right places all the time. I don't believe that anyone thought he still had a 20-game season in him. Of course, that wasn't his first year with us. He had very good control. He was throwing the ball well. He got people out, but he was a very slow, deliberate worker on the mound." Pierce added, "No question that intimidation was part of his game. I think the only one else in our time who was like that was Bob Gibson of the Cardinals and I didn't see too much of him because he was in the other league. Early was just that way and it helped his game. Home plate and a couple of inches around it were his. Don't get in the way."[8]

Wynn was such a slow worker that Pierce felt like any game the big guy started was going to last four hours. Wynn did not always get ahead in the count and blow hitters away. He worked them and they waited him out, often forcing a full count. "He could drive you nuts," Lopez said. "He could get ahead two strikes, but then he tried to finesse the batter. He had a lot of 3-and-2 counts. It wasn't unusual for Early to throw 150 pitches in a game."[9]

Wynn would have found it difficult to adapt to the modern game where starting pitches are often yanked after six innings even when they are going well and complete games are rarer than healthy newspapers. In one game with the Sox after Wynn surrendered five runs, Lopez trudged to the mound to relieve him. Wynn didn't want to leave the scene of the crime and said, "I'm not coming out. I can get this next guy." Lopez did not change his mind and said, "You've had enough." A furious Wynn took a couple of steps backward and threw the ball into Lopez's gut, then stomped off the mound. Back in the dugout, a fuming Lopez said, "Don't you ever do that again." Wynn still may have resented what he saw as a quick hook on future occasions, but he did not repeat the action.[10]

Jim Landis was trying to solidify his standing as an outfielder with the White Sox when Wynn began his term with the team. In spring training of 1958, Landis was playing center field, next to the newly acquired Al Smith in right, who watched Wynn operate in Cleveland. Landis was not familiar with Wynn's ways and his regular use of the brush-back pitch even if a guy was just swinging hard.

That was one Wynn's peeves, too. He thought if a slugger was winding up with a big swing that was showing him up, even if he didn't connect with a shot. One day Joe Cunningham, the hard-hitting first baseman who would later play for the White Sox, but then was with the Cardinals, took one of those huge cuts that created a 50 mph wind. "Hey, Jim, watch this next pitch," Smith yelled to Landis. "I didn't know what the heck he was talking about," Landis said. "And Wynn drills Cunningham. It was

Early Wynn, the king of brushback pitchers, was famous for saying he would deck his own mother if she dug into the batter's box too close to the plate. (National Baseball Hall of Fame Library, Cooperstown, New York.)

only a swing and it was only spring training. That's how ferocious he was."[11]

Landis said he struggled with his own attitude on the days Wynn pitched. Knowing the game was going to take a long time because Wynn took his time could affect concentration. Yet knowing how much Wynn hungered to win could infuse fielders with the same desire.

"There were two ways you could look at playing behind him," Landis said. "One was knowing how badly he wanted to win — and that made you play harder. But the other thing was — don't laugh at this — I had a certain habit I developed over time because he took so long to pitch a ball. As he was standing on the mound I'd look up at the sky and start singing to myself, and then I'd look down and think he was ready to throw the ball. It was hard to get set playing defense for him. Landis added, "When Billy Pierce pitched the game took maybe an hour and 45 minutes. If Early Wynn was pitching it was at least a three-hour ballgame. You got used to it in a certain way."[12]

As a craggy-faced veteran with a reputation for being ornery, the young White Sox players had a certain fear of Wynn if they crossed him. And since they didn't know exactly what would count as crossing him, they often stayed clear of his corner of the locker room. Landis was an exceptional fielder and he did not make many mistakes in the outfield, but one day he made an error when Wynn was pitching.

Nervous that Wynn was going to blast him, Landis tried to sneak into the clubhouse and hurry up and dress and get out of there before Wynn had a chance to berate him. Landis was quietly going into the clubhouse with his head down and Nellie Fox by his side. Fox said, "Here comes Gus over here." Wynn tapped Landis on the shoulder and Landis thought, "Oh, god, what's going to happen?" Landis was afraid that Wynn was going to tell him off, or Lord knows, even pop him one out of anger over his miscue. Instead, Wynn firmly told him that he was going to take him out to dinner. A surprised Landis dined on Wynn's ticket that night. The old pitcher wanted to beef up his confidence, not tear it down. "Hey, that's gone now," Wynn said of Landis' error. "There's another day tomorrow." Landis and Wynn had a pleasant dinner and then went home. "It was very nice of him," Landis said, "but I was scared at first."[13]

So Wynn could be generous to a young player. He wasn't a meanie all of the time. And he could be witty with newspapermen when he wanted to be. After Wynn retired as an active player and became a pitching coach, a journalist asked him what was more important to a young man, a good IQ or a good arm. "How good a curve could Einstein throw?" he said.[14]

Wynn was always a high ball pitcher. That was part of his makeup on the mound. Throwing purpose pitches just fit in with his style and the way he operated. Glen Rosenbaum was a minor leaguer seeking to secure a spot on the major-league roster when Wynn first came to the White Sox, and he said Wynn was never a talkative guy, usually reserved, and let his pitching speak for him.

"He always pitched above the belt," Rosenbaum said. "The guys who hit the ball up the middle, he would make them pay. I guess that was just his persona, or maybe he just wanted to uphold his image. I heard him say that he threw at his kid's head when he hit one back through the middle, too."[15]

For all of the times Wynn was quoted as saying he would throw at his mother if she was crowding the plate, or throw at his grandmother if she was taking such liberties, there are only a fraction of times he was quoted as saying that about his son Joe Early. However, Wynn actually did brush his son back in White Sox spring training camp for the very same infraction of his personal code that others violated — the line drive through the middle. If the other statements were jokes, or apocryphal stories, this was the genuine article. There were witnesses, among them Billy Pierce and Jim Landis, who saw Wynn deck his son with a fast pitch.

Joe Early was in spring training and took batting practice against his father. The ball flew out of Wynn's hand toward the plate and at the crack of the bat the ball sailed over the mound, just missing the pitcher. The Early rule kicked in. Next pitch at the batter's head, no exceptions.

"His son hit the ball through the middle, which Early didn't like," Pierce said, "and he knocked him down. I saw him knock his son down."[16] So did Landis. He had heard the old one-liners about Wynn hitting his mother or grandmother if they were crossing the invisible line of demarcation that belonged to the pitcher, but was still amazed when Wynn actually threw at his son. Did that truthfully happen? "Yeah," said Landis. "I saw it. That wasn't just talk."[17]

After all of those years of hearing about Wynn being just crazy enough to hit his grandmother, mother or son at the plate, the White Sox now saw that it was definitely true. "They said it about all of them," Sox outfielder Jim Rivera said with a laugh. "I don't know in what order, either. You believed he would do it. He was all business."[18] It should be noted, however, that Wynn never actually hit his kid, just frightened him a little bit.

11

Becoming a Contender

By 1951, the White Sox were winners. The culture of losing had been eradicated. The team was firmly entrenched in the first division of the American League. Now thoughts were focused more on what it would take to push the White Sox ahead of the Yankees.

Losing records were in the rear-view mirror. Under Paul Richards' field leadership the Sox flirted with pennant contention. In 1951, Chicago finished 81–73, in fourth place. In 1952, Chicago finished 81–73 again, in third place. In 1953, Chicago finished 89–65, in third place. In 1954, Chicago finished 94–60, again in third place. That was the year the Cleveland Indians set the then AL record with 111 wins.

Richards was gone after the 1954 season and he was a tough act to follow for his replacement, Marty Marion. But Chicago went 91–63 to finish third again in 1955. In 1956, Marion's second year, Chicago dipped to 85–69, yet again placing third.

During the first half of the 1950s, the White Sox had repaired their relations with their fan base, had put a team on the field worth rooting for. Now the organization wanted to give the community the greatest gift of all — a championship.

Frank Lane laid a foundation and was off to the St. Louis Cardinals. Chuck Comiskey thought the fastest route to the next level was by hiring a new manager. Not just any manager, but Al Lopez, the only field boss who had cracked Yankee hegemony thus far in the decade.

When Lopez took the reins in spring training of 1957, he said exactly what White Sox management and fans wanted to hear. The Yankees, he said, could be had. Lopez directed the Indians in 1954 when they wrested the pennant from the Yankees. The Indians finished second to the Yankees and ahead of the White Sox in 1955 and 1956. The Yankees had

Mickey Mantle, Yogi Berra, Whitey Ford, Elston Howard, Bobby Richardson, Bill Skowron, Tony Kubek and depth at every position. But Lopez said aloud what everyone else in the American League wished to see evidence of— the Yankees were not perfect.

In mid-season of 1957, Lopez gave an interview to reinforce his position. He noted examples of Yankee mistakes on the field. "I cite these cases to show off that the Yankees have their human frailties," he said, "although writers have built them up as supermen. The idea that the Yankees 'always win the big ones' is a myth, encouraged largely by newspapermen."[1]

Lopez dismissed headlines such as "Break Up the Yankees!" as bunk and said New York's pitching staff didn't begin to match up to the caliber of the starters a few years earlier when the club trotted out Allie Reynolds, Vic Raschi, and Ed Lopat. "The whole business gave me a laugh," Lopez said of the break up the Yankees theme. "The only real outstanding pitcher in the current crop is Whitey Ford."[2]

Lopez, temporarily turning newspaperman, apparently sought to answer any question raised by any sportswriter in the country. He tried to shoot down the notion that teams tensed up (he even used the words "choke up") and didn't play their best when they met the feared Yankees because of New York's tremendous track record. "I can only say that when I was at Cleveland, the Indians always looked forward to meeting the Yankees. So does this present White Sox team."[3]

It is difficult to imagine a manager cooperating on a lengthy essay of several thousand words in a national circulation publication in the middle of a season and uttering such inflammatory statements these days. Reading between the lines, it seems as if Lopez tried to employ the forum to get messages across to his own team more than the Yankees, as if he wanted to keep building the White Sox confidence and to keep reminding them not to listen to anyone outside of the clubhouse.

The story appeared on the eve of a doubleheader with the Yankees and the next day the Sox won the opener 3–1 in a manner that energized the team and frustrated New York. The White Sox trailed the Yankees by three games in the standings. There were 48,244 fans on hand at Comiskey Park and late in the game the score was 1–1. The Sox had the bases loaded in the sixth inning with outfielder "Jungle" Jim Rivera on third base. Bobby Shantz was pitching for the Yankees and given the Go-Go White Sox' reputation he was quite aware that Rivera might be up to something. Chicago third-base coach Tony Cuccinello told Rivera to stay loose because he was sure Lopez would flash a suicide squeeze sign.

Lopez went into the typical hand jive that constituted the signs, usually so confusing the opposition can't tell what is intended. However, Rivera didn't quite grasp the plan, either. Shantz wound up and Rivera, one of Chicago's many speedsters, dashed for the plate. Shantz reacted slowly and Rivera beat the throw for the go-ahead run. The funniest part of the successful play is that it was a bit of an accident. Lopez was calling for the batter to bunt to force Rivera in and instead Rivera simply stole home. "It made it look like, you know, I was a genius," Lopez said. "But, actually, Rivera, by trying to steal home at the same time the squeeze was on, made the play for us."[4]

The clubhouse was gleeful after that result, but the Sox lost the nightcap, 6–4, so the Yankees really lost nothing on the day. The Sox, meanwhile, were playing without catcher Sherm Lollar, who had a broken wrist, and outfielder Larry Doby, who had a pulled muscle. Their prolonged absences over the rest of the summer contributed in a fall-off for the Sox.

Throughout the 1950s, the path to greatness in the American League always led through New York. With Casey Stengel brilliantly manipulating his men and the surfeit of talent eclipsing that of all other teams, the Yankees were dominant. Those were the facts. But Lopez didn't just want to give the pennant to the Yankees every year. He wanted New York to have to fight for it. In 1957, the White Sox did so. They were not mathematically eliminated from the pennant race until September 23.

"We'll bounce back," Lopez said at the end of the season. "They didn't run us out of the park. They can be beaten." Lopez conceded the Yankees their ability to beat the Sox when they had to, but said in the big picture a stronger bullpen might have allowed Chicago to overcome. "If we had had a stopper, we could have won it easily. The games we lost in the late innings were criminal. We dropped nine games in the ninth and seven in the eighth. In extra-inning games we won eight and lost 10."[5]

Billy Pierce, who was at the front of the White Sox rotation for most of the 1950s, still lives in the Chicago area and when he makes public appearances, which he often does, he is frequently asked about playing the Yankees during that era. Pierce had a number of duels with Whitey Ford and the Hall of Famer Ford, like the Yankees, usually edged the White Sox and Pierce. Pierce has developed a one-liner answer to deal with the repeated questions. It was not so much Ford, as great as he was, who beat him, Pierce says, but guys named Mantle, Berra and Howard.

"I highly respected them," Pierce said. "To be truthful, the majority of those years, the Yankees had the best talent, and talent is going to prevail. It was a tough roster. The Yankees never beat themselves. The Yankees didn't give you runs. They didn't make mistakes. They threw to the right bases. They went from first to third on singles. They did everything right and in the long run that prevails."[6]

When Lopez took the White Sox job some baseball experts thought he was making the wrong move, that he was assuming command of a team that might get old on him fast. Although the Sox had moved into the top echelon of the American League, several players, notably Pierce, Rivera, and Fox, had been with the club for years and in baseball terms five years of stability is an eternity. Even without Frank Lane's mind on the premises racing 100 mph, though, the White Sox were not stagnant. There were still pieces to be added, and Lopez, Chuck Comiskey, and John Rigney, Comiskey's right-hand man in evaluating personnel, were on the prowl for the missing pieces that would boost the Sox over the Yankees.

As long as there have been baseball teams the search for strong arms has consumed franchises. The Sox were no different, seeking out and experimenting with young, live arms, hoping one or two would crack the rotation or could anchor the bullpen. In 1957, a 26-year-old pitcher named Don Rudolph was given a look-see in the bullpen after kicking around the minors for seven years. Rudolph appeared in five games, went 1–0, and had an earned run average of 2.25. Rudolph seemed to be a promising find.

Although his numbers were solid, Rudolph received an inordinate amount of publicity, first as a minor leaguer and then as a rookie. That's because his wife, who used the name "Patti Waggin," was a stripper. In 1958, Rudolph started the season in AAA Indianapolis and was used in just seven games with the big club. In 1959, Rudolph made the Sox out of spring training. But after four showings and only three innings pitched, including a save, owner Bill Veeck, believing Rudolph would never provide the answers needed, included him in a trade to the Cincinnati Reds.

Making light of the move and in reference to Rudolph's equally famous wife, Veeck said, "Alas, the wrong Rudolph had the great curves."[7] Even worse for Rudolph, in 1968, four years after his major-league career ended, he was killed in an automobile accident at age 37.

The White Sox placed more faith in a rising, 6-foot-3, 210-pound fireballer named Barry Latman who turned 21 during the 1957 season. When he was a veteran, some years later, Latman recalled his major-league debut quite vividly, as if he was delivering a stand-up comedy monologue. The adventure began, according to Latman, when he was assigned to sit in the White Sox bullpen for a game against the Yankees that did not turn out very well for Chicago.

"By the time the fifth inning rolled around we were behind about 16–1," Latman said. "The phone rang. The voice on the other end said, 'Warm up.' You know, the manager doesn't mean the pitching coach because he's 60 years old. And it can't be the catcher, so it's me. 'Yeah,' the manager continued, 'might as well bring that guy in.'" Latman continued, "You pass the center fielder on your way to the mound, and out of the corner of your mouth you say, 'Move back a little.' You get to the mound and Dick Donovan gives you the fish eye and says, 'You?' with a look of astonishment, and then adds 'Humph,' as he walks off the hill. Manager Al Lopez pats you on the rumble seat and says, 'Good luck,' and I'll swear you feel like following him off the mound."

That was because the bases were loaded. Latman said he glanced to the on-deck circle and saw a No. 7. That would be Mickey Mantle. He went through his warm-ups in less than spectacular fashion. "You throw your curve, and it bounces a little, maybe 20 feet in front of the plate. You throw your fastball and it hits the screen. The next one hits the catcher, so you know you're ready."

Latman decided to rely on his fastball, his bread and butter pitch. With so much adrenaline coursing through his body, he figures the ball was traveling up to the plate at around 180 miles an hour. "Only Mantle hits it and it takes off 360 miles an hour," Latman said. But he got lucky. The line drive is speared by the second baseman, who is knocked so far back by the velocity of the smash HE is caught by the right fielder. But all ends well because Latman has retired the side.

Back in the dugout, he said Lopez quizzed him about what he threw to Mantle and when he proudly said it was his fastball, the manager looked at him and said, "Son, please learn another pitch."[8]

Latman went 1–2 in a brief taste of the majors that year, but it seemed possible that he would claim one of the key spots in the starting rotation in 1958. Not quite. Latman showed hints of belonging when he went 3–0 that season, but in the season-long pursuit of the Yankees there wasn't much wiggle room for Lopez to try out Latman.

Things seemed different in 1959. Latman was still young, going on 23 in May, and in spring training he seemed more sure of himself. The White Sox very much wanted him to succeed. "I don't feel that there is any pressure on me," Latman said. "The pressure was last year. Now the White Sox know what kind of pitcher I am. If I think I'll be good enough, I'll be starting." Catcher Sherm Lollar, who admired Latman's fastball, definitely thought he would be starting.[9]

In the late 1950s, teams relied on four-man rotations rather than five-man rotations that supplanted that pattern in the closing years of the twentieth century. But there was always a need for a spot starter, whether because of injury or a crush in the schedule. Latman got his chances in 1959 and he produced, finishing 8–5.

Another fledgling major-league pitcher for the White Sox in 1956 and 1957 was Bill Fischer. Fischer was born in Wausau, Wisconsin, in 1930, and after attending a tryout camp following high school graduation, was signed by the White Sox as a 17-year-old. That should have given him plenty of seasoning to hit the big leagues by the time he turned 21, but his career did not follow a straight path. Although he promptly won double-figure games repeatedly in the minors, just when he was likely to gain some Sox attention Fischer went off to the Korean War with the Marines.

Back in the United States, working the kinks out of his arm, he had to "re-prove" himself. Fischer did not get a sniff of the majors — with the White Sox — for 10 years and he didn't stick with the club until 1957 when he posted a 7–8 mark. "I never even saw a big-league game until I pitched in one in Tampa, Florida," Fischer said.[10]

Although Fischer did not ever make a huge impact in the White Sox' mound fortunes, his slowly developing career ended up spanning more than a half century. Combining time spent in the minors, nine years spent in the majors (including a 2–3 partial season with Chicago in 1958), and then minor-league and major-league coaching, Fischer never took any time off from the game.

Fischer hit his 50th year in baseball in 1997 and some of his prize pupils he had worked with as a pitching coach, from Tom Seaver to Roger Clemens, offered kudos. Clemens wrote a note to Fischer in which he reminded people that when he twice struck out 20 batters in a game he walked none in either appearance. "That's especially a tribute to you, Fisch," Clemens said. "Being a power pitcher, you always instilled in me the second part of that, being a pitcher. I thank you."[11]

At the time Fischer was considered to have enough potential to become a White Sox starter. Nobody knew in the 1950s, however, that Fischer's true skill was teaching pitching.

There was a certain amount of irony when the man who emerged from the pack to become a reliable starter was Dick Donovan, if only because Donovan's history paralleled Fischer's in some respects. Donovan was a hard-throwing, hometown kid who starred at Quincy High School in the Boston suburbs, at first as a shortstop before showing potenial as a pitcher, and he signed with the Boston Braves for a minimal amount. The Braves seemed to have visions of Donovan swiftly rising through the minors and becoming a Braves Field gate attraction. Only Donovan's career stalled.

For small portions of three seasons starting in 1950 the Braves promoted Donovan to the majors and used him in a limited number of games. After those three tries he was still looking for a major-league win and he had four losses. As the franchise readied for departure to Milwaukee, it lost interest in Donovan. In 1954, under the direction of Atlanta Crackers manager Whitlow Wyatt, a former big leaguer who had played some for the White Sox, Donovan won 18 games and most importantly, he learned how to throw a slider. "That's now my best pitch," Donovan said. "As a matter of fact, I don't believe my stuff is any different from before except for the addition of the slider."[12]

Donovan resurfaced with the Detroit Tigers during the 1954 season, but again failed to win a game. Late that year, Frank Lane acquired Donovan, no longer a young phenom, but an aging hopeful already 27. Donovan had signed out of high school with the Braves, investing 30 cents of his own money for carfare on the subway line to a tryout that resulted in him being paid $125 a month for a minor-league stint in Florida.

When he was picked up by the White Sox, Donovan needed a fresh start, but he also knew that after a decade of bouncing around if he did not make it in Chicago he was never going to cut it in the majors. "I knew it was my last chance," Donovan said. "If I failed I was through with baseball forever. No more minors for me."[13]

In 1955, all of his experience kicked in and Donovan went 15–9 for the White Sox, earning a spot in the team's regular rotation. He won 12 games the next year, went 16–6 in 1957 and won 15 games in 1958.

In 1955, when he got hot, Donovan was a virtual unknown. *New York Times* columnist Arthur Daley took note of what he was doing and said if the White Sox became a pennant winner it would likely because of the addition of Donovan. "Remove him from the roster and the Pale Hose would not even be in contention," Daley wrote.[14]

Donovan revealed that he was grateful to Wyatt, who had also been a late bloomer in his career, indicating he had long wanted to learn how to throw a slider, but couldn't teach himself. "I'd always wanted to have a slider," said Donovan, who ended up winning 122 big-league games, "but I couldn't get the knack of it. No one else could teach it to me, either, but Wyatt taught me in 20 minutes, and that's the pitch that made me."[15]

Donovan was an amiable figure in the White Sox clubhouse — except on the days when he was scheduled to start. He became a recluse of sorts, refusing to talk to anyone, hanging out by his locker lost in his own thoughts. He retreated completely into himself and snubbed the outside world. Teammates learned swiftly not to try to make chit-chat with Donovan when it was his turn in the rotation.

"Donovan was alone in his own world the day he pitched," Billy Pierce said. "Once the game started he sat in the dugout alone, too. If it was a cooler day, or a day you would perspire, he would have a towel with him. He would fold that towel perfectly, lay it on the bench, take his jacket, fold it nicely, and go out to pitch the game. Between innings he would come back in, take out the towel, go to the drinking fountain, have some water, and sit down. Nobody talked to him. Every game, every inning, he had the towel and he folded it the same way each time."[16]

In that era, the White Sox pitchers did their pre-game warming up in foul territory near the home dugout on the third-base side of Comiskey

Park. The gregarious Pierce would talk to the fans who shouted out to him. Donovan would not acknowledge them.

"People would say hello to him, but he would never talk to anybody," Pierce said. "One time, he was having a tough stretch and I happened to be out there and I was talking to somebody sitting in the stands. They were just saying hello and asking you how things were, a normal little bit of conversation. Well, Dick was there and he goes, 'Bill, do you think that helps you?' I said, 'Well, it's relaxing.' For a year or more, he wouldn't talk to anybody at all, but the next time it was his turn to pitch he went out there looking for somebody to talk to. He finally found somebody and was yakkety-yakking a bit. He did it for a little while and then he said to me, 'I'm never going to do that again.' I guess he decided that he had been right all along."[17]

During the 1950s, the White Sox had a pitching coach who hadn't been a pitcher. Ray Berres, who held the job from 1949 to 1966, and for parts of 1968 and 1969, was a master of watching pitchers throw and readily being able to spot if anything was out of synch on mechanics or form. It was important with a team that relied so much on pitching, fielding and baserunning to be able to count on pitchers who recorded low earned run averages and year to year the White Sox staffs did.

In 1955, Pierce led the American League with a 1.97 ERA, if only posting a 15–10 record, and years later, when Berres died at age 99 in 2007, Pierce said the coach was very self-effacing. "He never wanted to take credit for anything," Pierce said.[18]

Several times during Pierce's career he suffered from a back ailment and other shoulder and arm soreness, but through careful Berres nurturing and his own hard work he came back. The White Sox had long before been transformed from the dismal team Pierce feared joining in 1949 and in the mid–1950s he was the ace of the staff, winning 20 games in 1956 and 1957 and 17 in 1958.

Like second baseman Nellie Fox and shortstop Luis Aparicio, Pierce was comparatively undersized, standing just 5-foot-10 and weighing 160 pounds or so. But he always got the job done after some advice from manager Paul Richards, who actually was his catcher when they were both with the Detroit Tigers. "Paul used a mighty simple system for teaching me control," Pierce said. "I was so impatient that I'd fire the ball in as soon as he threw it back to me. I don't know what my hurry was, but I seemed unable to slow down." When Pierce still threw too quickly, Richards added a new tactic. He hung on to the ball, examined it, then pounded his glove and squatted down behind the plate in slow motion, all as a method to break Pierce of his bad habit of rushing. It worked.[19]

Pierce's demeanor was the opposite of Early Wynn's. Maybe because he had to use the guile of a slider more than a smoking fastball to get outs, or maybe just because that was his personality, but Pierce often refused to throw at hitters. On one particular occasion when he was going against the Kansas City Athletics, former White Sox third baseman Cass Michaels came to the plate with the bases loaded. Michaels cracked a single that won the game.

After the game, Frank Lane was in the locker room and he challenged Pierce angrily, saying, "Why the devil didn't you loosen up Michaels with some close ones?" Pierce's reply was a human one, though not what Lane wanted to hear. "I couldn't throw close to Cass," Pierce said. "We're friends. He used to room with me on the Sox and we bowl together during the winter."[20]

That behavior on that occasion seemed to confirm ex–Dodger manager Leo Durocher's proclamation that "Nice guys finish last!" However, Pierce not only won an American League earned run title, he led the league in strikeouts once. He also topped the league in complete games three times and won 211 games in an 18-year career. Pierce just didn't leave as many hitters' bodies strewn in his path.

12

Filling in the Holes

When Jim Landis broke in as the White Sox center fielder in 1957, his fielding was ahead of his hitting. He roamed the outfield pastures of Comiskey Park like a deer, but he looked every bit the youthful rookie he was when at the plate.

Landis hit just .212 and many were of the opinion that he needed more seasoning in the minors. Instead, manager Al Lopez stuck with him, giving him 96 games worth of exposure and permitting him to learn on the job. For a team that ostensibly was going after a pennant, it was a risky move.

The commitment to Landis did pay dividends down the road, however, and being on a team that prized speed and excellence in the field, he was a good fit. Eventually, he even added some of the pop at the plate the White Sox desperately needed. Landis has always recognized Lopez's generosity, but even he concedes that he wasn't ready for the bigs his rookie season.

"In spring training, I had the feeling about what Al Lopez was doing with me, at least as far as spring went," Landis said. "I didn't know for sure he was going to keep me. You sort of have an idea, but I'll be honest, maybe I wasn't quite ready. I was so God-danged nervous it was unbelievable."[1]

Landis' confidence was nearly shattered in his first major-league game against the Cleveland Indians. The Cleveland pitcher was Herb Score, who before he was seriously injured by a line drive, was expected to be the next great American League hurler. Score threw the ball nearly 100 mph and he made even veteran hitters feel like beginners.

First time up, Landis barely got wood on the ball and hit a weak pop-up. Then he struck out. And then he tipped a weak grounder to the infield.

Landis thought he was going to be run out of the league in short order and have to take up a blue collar profession. "I came back to the club house and I said, 'Jesus Christ, if the rest of the pitchers are like this guy, I'd better get my lunch pail.' Right from the beginning, from the first game, I felt overmatched. Then the White Sox moved me from right field to center. I was playing on pins and needles. Finally, they sent me to AAA to get my confidence back. It was about feeling that I belonged. You are reaching your dream and there you are and I wasn't quite ready to handle it."[2]

The interlude in the minors served as an elixir that calmed Landis' nerves. In 1958, he was a full-time starter, playing in 142 games, and his batting average jumped to .277. After that, Landis was a fixture in the White Sox outfield through 1964. There were a fair number of veterans on the 1958 team and Landis was still just 24 at the start of the season. When it came to acting like a big leaguer, he took his cues from Nellie Fox, Billy Pierce, Sherm Lollar, and Minnie Minoso when he was still there.

"Even in little talks with them I call them 'my father,'" Landis said. "They definitely helped me develop. They gave you the feeling that you really belonged with them. The veterans on that ball club were so outstanding to the young guys. There was no jealousy."[3]

Although he rejoined the team in a later trade, Minoso was only there with Landis in 1957, not 1958. He was in the exchange to Cleveland for Early Wynn and Al Smith. Smith was younger than Minoso and could hit. He was excited by his swap to Chicago. He was married to a Chicago woman and had decided to make the city his permanent home, and he had enjoyed playing for Al Lopez before. Just as important, Smith's role in Cleveland had declined and he was being shoved more into a utility role. With the White Sox he regained a starter's spot as a left fielder.

"At Cleveland I played as many as six positions in one season," Smith said. "I was popping from one place to another, sometimes from day to day. I simply complained that I couldn't get going because I was moving around so much. I wanted to play either left field or third base regularly and not be pushed around from one place to another."[4]

The White Sox were in the market for hitters and Smith showed he had the credentials at various times. He hit .306 one season for Cleveland and scored a league-leading 123 runs one year. But the Indians felt he was expendable because in their post–Lopez era Smith's hitting had dropping to the .250 range. His play was rejuvenated when he joined the Sox. Smith's strength was powdering fastballs, but no hitter lasts long in the majors if he can't contend with pitchers' breaking stuff. Smith made himself into a better batter.

"I had to learn how to hit a curveball," Smith said. "You hit the fastball and they're not going to let you see that. They threw me so many breaking balls that I learned how to hit the curveball."[5]

Adding players like Smith, who might beef up the batting order's corps of light hitters, was one of Chuck Comiskey's focuses. Ray Boone was added to the mix in 1958 in the hopes he could slam a few home runs. Boone broke into the majors in 1948 and just prior to joining the Sox was a two-time All-Star who led the American League with 116 RBIs and seemed good for about 20 homers a season. At the time, no one could foresee that he would be the patriarch of one of baseball's all-time popular families, but later his son Bob and grandsons Aaron and Bret made their marks in the majors.

Boone grew up in San Diego and attended Herbert Hoover High School six years behind Ted Williams. He knew him then as everyone in the neighborhood who followed baseball did. Boone had come up to the majors as a shortstop (he committed 33 errors one season), then shifted to third base before moving to first by the time he became a White Sox player. Boone's range became more limited as he battled knee injuries.

He had been with the Indians in the early 1950s and befriended a confused Minnie Minoso when the Cuban player was traded to Chicago. Minoso gained great respect for Boone's sensitivity at that time and praised him for making him feel better when he thought he was just being dumped by Cleveland. "Ray was a class act," Minoso wrote in his autobiography.[6]

Minoso thought he was entrenched in Cleveland, his only major-league organization at the time, and was crushed when he was told he had been traded to the White Sox. Depressed, he retreated to his hotel room and spent lonely hours there. Boone came by to visit and delivered a pep talk. "This is good for you," Boone said. "I hoped if someone would be traded, it would be me. You are going to have a chance to play in Chicago and the people are going to like you right away. You are a very good ballplayer and this is going to help your career."[7]

Minoso was out of Chicago when Boone arrived, but one side benefit for him was that he considered Billy Pierce one of the toughest pitchers to hit. As a teammate he could avoid that challenge, except in batting practice. That bonus did not inflate Boone's stock enough, however. He finished the 1958 season with Chicago, but didn't make it through 1959 with the club.

Shortstop Luis Aparicio and second baseman Nellie Fox were brilliant in the field and could manufacture runs with their savvy singles hitting and baserunning. Jim Landis and Jim Rivera in the outfield were also fast guys, but neither was a home-run hitter. Then, in the days before the designated hitter, the White Sox had the pitcher coming to bat, so that was a soft spot in the lineup. The need for power, for a reliable slugger who could smash doubles and home runs, was acute. Landis proved to be a bit of a surprise in 1958 when he clouted 15 homers to go along with 19 stolen bases. Lollar led the team with 20 homers, but the club smacked just 101 on the year.

In his long career that began with the Boston Braves in 1947, Earl Torgeson, who also carried the nickname of "The Earl of Snohomish," (a reference to his home in Snohomish, Washington) had his moments when he carried a big stick. Torgeson hit as many as 24 home runs for the Braves, but that was 1951, so it wasn't obvious how much Torgeson would produce for the Sox when they traded Dave Philley to the Detroit Tigers for him in June of 1957.

The initial results were promising. Torgeson, a sturdy 6-foot-3 and 190 pounds, clubbed seven home runs and batted .295 in 86 games for Chicago over the second half of the 1957 season. At a time when more subtle baseball statistics were not yet in use, manager Al Lopez was a pathfinder in attempting to discover numbers indicating hitters' true worth beyond their flashy home-run totals. Lopez calculated his own on-base statistics and compiled statistics for advancing the runners. He also kept track of pitches taken. In these areas Torgeson shined.

"The batter must be more selective," Lopez said. "By waiting out the pitcher, forcing him to come in with his pitch, the batter not only does himself a service, but helps the entire ball club. He helps himself because it will make him a better hitter by keeping him from swinging at bad pitches. It helps the team because it forces the pitcher to work harder.

When he becomes weary he loses his stuff and the entire offense picks up."[8]

The studies make Lopez sound like Bill James before Bill James. Rather surprisingly, Lopez's statistics showed that Torgeson was a more patient hitter than even Nellie Fox and Luis Aparicio, much better known as contact hitters. Torgeson had an on-base percentage of .440, compared to Fox's .415. The team leader was the soon-to-depart Minoso at .453. "I definitely believe that by waiting out the pitcher Torgy becomes a better hitter and generally contributes more to our attack," Lopez said.[9]

Torgeson hit 10 homers while batting .266 in 1958. While Lopez would have been happy to see that homer number double, Torgeson was the team's best option at first base. Torgeson was also a good chemistry component in the clubhouse and was praised throughout his career for being a nice guy.

"He had a wonderful baseball mind," said Danny Litwhiler, who played for the Braves with Torgeson. "He was always in shape. He played hard. He never complained. He was a great guy on a ball team. He never had an enemy, not even on the opposing teams."[10]

Al Lopez was not as out-spoken about his team's chances in 1958 as he had been in 1957, though no doubt he believed it was the White Sox' turn to win a pennant. It didn't happen. The White Sox finished second to the Yankees, 10 games behind in the standings. The lineup was not quite perfect yet. A baseball historian looking at the list of players who appeared in games for the White Sox that year would be impressed with the names of up-and-coming talent seemingly ready to bloom.

While the team was searching the nation for veteran ballplayers, the farm system was churning out several young men who would enjoy excellent major-league careers. On the cusp of needing more playing time were cameo players Johnny Callison, Earl Battey, Norm Cash, and Johnny Romano. The White Sox were flush and either didn't really know it, or they were preoccupied with the immediacy of seizing a pennant. None of those players got more than a minimal chance to show off their abilities in 1958. In 1959, they played slightly bigger roles, but all pretty much as part-time fill-ins.

One young hurler who insinuated his way into a handful of opportunities on the mound in 1958 was righty Bob Shaw. Shaw threw 64 innings and had a 4–2 record. Shaw had come up with the Detroit Tigers briefly the year before, but was starting fresh with the White Sox. Shaw was 24 and tired of being shuttled to the minor leagues by a Tigers management that he felt was not giving him a fair shake.

Shaw's loud complaints got him labeled as a clubhouse lawyer in Detroit and he was viewed as a guy with a big mouth who couldn't back up his talk. Shaw felt that he was not being given the chance to show what he could do. When Detroit informed Shaw that he was being sent to Charleston in the American Association for still another apprenticeship in the minors, he told the Tigers he was finished with them. He packed up and went home instead of reporting.

"I went home for a number of reasons," Shaw said. "First, there was a large matter of money. The Tigers had agreed to pay me a big-league salary if I could stick with them until June 15. By sending me down earlier they were costing me $1,500, and to top it off they wouldn't give me the permission to play winter ball and make up the difference. Then, of course, I knew I could pitch in the big leagues. All I wanted was a chance."[11]

That never happened with Detroit. On June 15, instead of being on the Tigers' roster, Shaw was traded to the White Sox with Ray Boone for Bill Fischer and Tito Francona. As soon as Shaw joined the White Sox, both pitching coach Ray Berres and manager Al Lopez worked with him. Lopez urged Shaw to throw all of his pitches with a three-quarter delivery instead of just some of them.

"Ray Berres worked with me a lot on my mechanics," Shaw said. "You don't want to move your hands horizontally. You want to pull that hand out of the glove as soon as possible, as if it's a pendulum. It just swings down, back and up. You don't want to hook behind your body. He helped me tremendously. He simplified my mechanics and with good mechanics your control generally improves. There were things very simple, very basic. Not very confusing, but absolutely dead on and I'd say it will help 90 percent of pitchers."[12]

The form Berres was preaching pushed Shaw into using a figure-eight motion. He practiced it unceasingly. One day Shaw was waiting for a ride outside of Chicago's Piccadilly Hotel and standing in the street kept practicing his pitching motion in the reflection of a plate-glass window. Berres and Lopez drove by and saw him. "I was practicing the mechanics that

Ray Berres taught me and they happen to drive by," Shaw said.[13] Talk about impressing the bosses.

After 40 years without a pennant, and with Fox, Pierce, Rivera and others aging, the White Sox probably could not be blamed for living for the moment and keeping the younger guys on the back burner. Rivera, in fact, thought that the deal that brought Al Smith and Early Wynn to Chicago was the clincher in readying the Sox for a pennant run in 1959.

"Oh, gosh, yes, that solidified the lineup," Rivera said. "Early Wynn was over there with Cleveland and they had a good ball club, but they didn't have a good defensive team like we had. We pulled off a lot of wins for him. I mean Aparicio was the greatest shortstop alive. We knew we were going to be good in 1959, but we didn't necessarily think we were going to win the pennant. We thought we had a good chance. There was that mental thing with the Yankees. You always had to expect that. I give them credit. They were the greatest I ever saw."[14]

Smith and Wynn were part of the 1958 team, too, and did not provide the instant impetus to put the Sox over the top despite Smith's verbal backing of what the old guy could still do. "He'll win at least 17 games and very likely will rack up 20 again," Smith speculated. "That fellow is just a great pitcher no matter whom he may be with. And what a competitor!"[15]

Wynn finished just 14–17 and his performance sent mixed signals. His earned run average was a questionable 4.31, but he led the American League in games started with 37 and with 184 strikeouts, so it didn't seem as if he was wilting. But it was hard to know if age was interfering with the final results and whether or not he would ever be a big winner again.

One of Wynn's problems was that he was gaining weight. He was closer to 225 pounds than his early-in-the-career scale tipper of 200. As a player who had prospered, he ate well. He also was battling gout. When Wynn was still pitching for the Indians and writing his column for a local newspaper, he revealed that the condition was afflicting him. He subsequently received an outpouring of advice from fans.

"Never realized before how many people there are in the 'gout league,'" Wynn wrote. Suggestions for cures and types of medication were proposed, even, he said, "poems to console me. I know they meant well, but whenever I see poetry about someone's ailments, I feel the end is drawing near. Quit scaring me."[16]

Gout is metabolic arthritis characterized by high levels of uric acid in the bloodstream and causes burning pain, swelling and redness in the joints and tendons. The first area affected is often the big toe, but the aches are not limited to that spot. Wynn let the public know he was taking medication and that it had been recommended he bake, broil or stew all of his meals.

Not everyone in the baseball world was sympathetic, however. Hecklers in the stands found something new to shout at Wynn. At a game in Kansas City, Wynn was touched for two home runs by one player and his next time at the plate a spectator yelled, "Throw him your gout ball again, Early!"[17]

The gout did not go away, but neither did Wynn. As the 1959 season loomed Wynn was 39 years old, ancient by baseball standards, and he had the aches and pains accumulated over 20 years in the majors. But he still felt he had enough snap in his arm and wisdom in his brain to be a first-rate big-league pitcher. He planned to show the baseball world that his thoughts were true.

13

The New Guy
Is Different

Bill Veeck was just 11 years old when his father, Bill Veeck Sr., the president of the Chicago Cubs, hired him to perform a plethora of odds and ends for the ball club and Wrigley Field. He sold tickets, sold concessions and even helped out with the groundskeeping.

That was the beginning of his life-long, passionate affair with baseball and his introduction to the inner workings and behind-the-scenes operations of a major-league franchise, a true education from the ground up.

Bill Sr. was a Chicago sportswriter and the family lived in suburban Hinsdale. The elder Veeck did not aspire to a job in baseball management, but he was a strong voice for change in Cubs operations, repeatedly criticizing the Wrigley family for poor judgment and for making unwise deals. One day in 1918 an exasperated William Wrigley confronted Veeck with an ultimatum of sorts. If you are so smart, he said, why don't YOU try to do a better job.

Veeck Sr. took Wrigley up on the offer, but died in 1933 before the Cubs could win another World Series adding to their last victory in 1908. One thing Bill Sr. tried as a promotion that later influenced his son was "Ladies Day," whereupon women were admitted to the ballpark free. Even after Bill Sr. died, Cubs owner P.K. Wrigley (whose own father William had died a couple of years earlier) hired Bill for $18 a week. He put out a fan magazine, worked with the ushers, worked closely with concessionaires and supervised player tryouts. "You would be amazed how much sheer psychology is involved in selling a hot dog and beer," Veeck wrote in his autobiography.[1]

Eventually, Bill became club treasurer. Most famously, the job put Veeck on a collision course with Chicago baseball history. When Wrigley Field was undergoing renovation in 1937, Veeck was assigned by the boss to decorate the green walls with appropriate plant life. Veeck was responsible for installing one of the most venerable and distinguishable traits of Wrigley Field. He supervised the addition of ivy, a popular characteristic of the old ballpark that has endured for decades.

Although by the standards of the many millionaires who bought Major League teams as play things, Veeck was not rich, he still seemed destined to run his own team some day. At the start of his involvement in World War II, in which he lost part of a leg in the fighting, Veeck owned the minor-league Milwaukee Brewers. Veeck had a partnership with former Cub skipper Charlie Grimm, who led the team to three American Association pennants in five years between 1941 and 1946.

One reason Veeck and Grimm could afford to buy the Milwaukee club was that it was failing. When the new co-owners showed up for Boy Scout Day early in their tenure they decided to mingle with the fans. They counted just 22 of them. Fans, not Boy Scouts. "All except three of the Boy Scouts had decided to stay home and tie knots, an undeniable proof that the future of the nation lay in good hands," Veeck observed.[2] He figured out that the team's share of gate receipts was $3.85. Soon enough crowds were pouring out as Veeck dreamed up innovative ways to lure them and entertain them.

Veeck's war wound stemmed from the explosion of an artillery shell that initially required amputation of his right foot. Despite the handicap of at first crutches, then a wooden leg, and numerous surgeries (36 by one estimate over the ensuing years), Veeck the wheeler-dealer put together a coalition of money men and in the late 1940s fulfilled a dream by becoming owner of the Cleveland Indians.

Veeck always thought outside of the box. During the 1940s, he quietly worked to purchase the Philadelphia Phillies. He thought he had a deal, but made the mistake of informing then-commissioner Kenesaw Mountain Landis that he intended to beef up the roster of the pathetic team with many first-rate black players starring in the Negro Leagues. The deal evaporated.

However, as soon as Veeck gained control of the Indians, and just three months after Jackie Robinson had integrated baseball at the start of the 1947 season, he hired Larry Doby as the first African-American in the American League. Before the end of the 1948 season, Veeck also reached out to the aging, but still swift-throwing Satchel Paige, one of the country's most legendary pitchers who had been banned from the majors because of his skin color. Paige was a reliever on the 1948 Indians team that won the World Series (still the last one for Cleveland) and set an attendance record with more than 2.6 million customers.

As good as the Indians were on the diamond, Veeck did not leave attendance to chance. He promoted just as energetically with a winning club as he did with a loser.

"We did not open the ticket windows and expect the citizenry to come rushing up with money in their fists," Veeck wrote. "We have never operated on the theory that a city owes anything to the owner of a baseball franchise out of civic pride, patriotic fervor, or compelling national interest. Baseball has sold itself as a civic monument for so long that it has come to believe its own propaganda. Baseball is a commercial enterprise, operating for a profit." Baseball, he said, had to hustle and promote its product as enthusiastically as General Motors.[3]

In 1951, Veeck took over ownership of the St. Louis Browns, where his most famous stunt was promulgated. Veeck hired a 3-foot, 7-inch tall midget, Eddie Gaedel, to use as a pinch-hitter. Ordered not to swing his bat on penalty of death from Veeck, Gaedel appeared at the plate once, and naturally he walked. When Veeck approached Gaedel, he told him, "Eddie, you'll be immortal." Then he actually measured the crouching Gaedel's strike zone at one-and-a-half inches.[4]

Baseball's straight-laced officials were shocked and immediately implemented rules that would prevent anything like Gaedel's cameo from occurring again. This did help to ensure Gaedel's immortality. Veeck also predicted that he would also be perpetually linked to the maneuver and he was correct about that. The first sentence of a later biography read, "Forever, Bill Veeck and the midget will be joined."[5]

True to his convictions, Veeck never wore a sport jacket and tie, regardless of the occasion and newspapers took to calling him "Sport Shirt" as a nickname in print. A hardcore smoker, Veeck used to flabbergast new acquaintances when he lifted his pants leg and tapped the end of his cigarette against his wooden leg. He had carved an ashtray into the appendage to accommodate the ashes.

Always strapped for money compared to his competitors, Veeck showed off a genius for promotion that enabled his teams (especially in Cleveland) to draw well. Still, he ran short of money (especially in St. Louis where the Browns were in a losing battle with the Cardinals), and had to sell his holdings.

There has never been a more fan-friendly owner than Bill Veeck. Veeck, who owned the Cleveland Indians and the St. Louis Browns, and the White Sox twice, gained control of the Chicago club the first time at the start of the 1959 season. Veeck lost part of a leg in World War II fighting and used a wooden leg with an built-in ashtray. He introduced humorous promotions to boost attendance, never wore a sport coat and tie, and listed his phone number in the telephone book so fans could call him directly. (National Baseball Hall of Fame Library, Cooperstown, New York.)

Constantly out-spoken, even when he was out of the game, Veeck repeatedly ticked off the stuffed-shirt owners. He didn't like them (and said so aloud) and they despised him. Veeck was never shy about letting his thoughts be known publicly, even if it might have benefited him to keep his mouth shut occasionally. Sports writers, who called him "burrhead" for his short, curly hair, lapped up anything Veeck said. In 1958 he authored a massive, six-part, syndicated newspaper series describing what he thought were the ills of the game and how the current owners could save their sport.

The basic theme of his essays was highlighted by a pullout quote: "I Know Who's Killing Baseball." Among Veeck's suggestions was that baseball teams do away with the farm system, implement a universal player draft, ban high bonuses to untried players, limit the number of games televised, boost their public relations and improve their merchandising.

When Veeck wrote his lengthy missive, the Dodgers had just abandoned Brooklyn for Los Angeles and the Giants had fled New York for San Francisco. A few years earlier the Philadelphia Athletics had become the Kansas City Athletics, the Boston Braves had morphed into the Milwaukee Braves, and his old St. Louis Browns had become the Baltimore Orioles. Pro football was also gaining in popularity.

"The time has come to sound the alarm before the National Pastime," Veeck wrote, "as it still calls itself, collapses under the weight of its own archaic rules, mismanagement, lack of leadership and plain stupidity. If this sounds like a harsh indictment of what was once America's 'only game in town,' well, I mean it to be just that. Only a rude awakening, followed by drastic action, can save the sport from oblivion. I'll try to tell you honestly and bluntly — the only way I know how — what I think is wrong with organized baseball."[6]

Veeck did not make new friends in the baseball establishment with his frankness, especially by calling them stupid. Rather predictably, the owners of the richer franchises reacted with disdain to Veeck's comments. Rather humorously, however, he found an ally in an unexpected corner. FBI director J. Edgar Hoover spoke up and said that he agreed with Veeck that baseball should adopt a draft and stop paying extremely high bonuses.

"It makes good, sound sense to me for all of the Major League clubs to pool their resources and have their scouts recommend young baseball talent for a common draft," Hoover, a self-described huge sports fan, said. "Frankly, I don't believe it's good for a boy in his teens to be given a bonus, sometimes around $100,000, just to sign a contract to play baseball. It distorts his sense of values."[7]

Baseball's ownership committee is a very exclusive and tight brotherhood that has the power to deny entry to people who would seem to the public to be very qualified owners. A couple of times they ganged up on Veeck to ensure his bids for teams would not be approved. But in 1959, attuned to the potential opposition, and savvy enough to have learned from his bad experiences, Veeck cobbled together a plan and an ownership group to buy the Chicago White Sox. He wanted back into baseball and Dorothy Comiskey wanted out.

The White Sox had been in the hands of the Comiskey family since Charles Comiskey brought the team into the American League in 1901. When Comiskey presided over the construction of Comiskey Park on the South Side of Chicago in 1910, it was one of baseball's grand palaces. Comiskey died in 1931 at his summer home in Eagle River, Wisconsin.

Son John Louis Comiskey, better known as "Uncle Lou" to his friends, was a sickly man, but ran the team from 1931 to 1939, when he died at 54. Grace Reidy Comiskey was married to John Louis and inherited the team upon his death in 1939. She was the chief executive officer of the White Sox until she died of a heart attack in 1956, though she relied heavily on baseball experts for advice.

"Lou" Comiskey and Grace had three children, but one, also named Grace, died in 1952. That left son Chuck, the team founder's grandson, who had been heavily immersed in daily operations for years, and daughter Dorothy. Dorothy's husband, John Rigney, a one-time pitcher, worked closely with Chuck on team matters. Grace Comiskey had long intended to leave Chuck in charge of the club (and he had been told that from the time he was young), but in 1952 they had a blow-up when he asked for a raise and was refused. Chuck Comiskey had hired Frank Lane, the man who arguably turned the team around, but was blamed by his mother for driving him away. Chuck Comiskey briefly quit the team and his mother and sister forged a new alliance.

"Charles just talks too much," Grace Comiskey said. "When he was younger I could just tell him to keep his mouth shut, but after all, he's 29 now." The testy times proved to be fatal to the future family ownership of the White Sox and to Chuck Comiskey's long-term intentions. When he rejoined the club, his mother wrote her will to leave 54 percent of the shares to Dorothy and 46 percent to Chuck.[8]

Dorothy had always been a White Sox and baseball fan and had also worked for the team, though in less visible roles as a vice president, treasurer, and team secretary. However, after her mother died, when she had the opportunity to become the face of the franchise as principal owner, she declined, avoiding the media spotlight.

Chuck Comiskey felt he should be running the team — it was his birthright, he believed — and in late 1957 he went to court seeking to wrestle a majority interest in the team from his sister. The move backfired. What had been internal dirty laundry because the subject of city-white gossip. Sportswriters chose sides. The unkindest cut might have been the sarcastic labeling of Chuck Comiskey as "the crown prince." The pivotal point in the feud occurred when Dorothy decided to put her share of the team up for sale and Chuck felt she should reduce the price and sell to him.[9]

At the same time, there were two serious outside bidders for the team. One was Bill Veeck and the other, basically unknown to the baseball world at the time, was millionaire Chicago insurance man Charles O. Finley. Finley would ultimately gain control of the Kansas City Athletics, move them to Oakland, win World Series titles, and prove to be almost as much of a maverick as Veeck.

Dorothy chose Veeck's offer of $2.7 million as the best and gave him a 60-day option to buy her stock. Veeck was certain that Chuck Comiskey would match the offer and hang onto the team. Instead, Comiskey countered with an offer roughly $1 million less than Veeck's. Dorothy decided that sibling love went only so far. She agreed to sell to Veeck and an infuriated Chuck Comiskey went to court to try to halt the sale.

"He was basing his action, as near as I could see, upon that ancient doctrine of divine right," Veeck observed in his autobiography. "Charles claimed — and I'm sure this was his honest conviction — that the White Sox belonged to him because his name was Comiskey; that is that his mother had never intended that the club should leave the family."[10]

Veeck won the court's support, but Comiskey immediately appealed.

While this intrigue was playing out, the White Sox were in spring training in Tampa, Florida. Al Lopez, reprising his role as Jeanne Dixon from 1957, once again said that the Yankees were vulnerable and would not win another pennant.

"I meant what I said about the Yankees," Lopez said. "The signs were there last year. They played very little better than .500 the second half after getting off to a commanding lead. This led people to get the idea they were only coasting in the final months. But I knew better. On at least two occasions Casey Stengel was worried in 1958. I knew they were trying their best."[11]

On March 5, the judge in Probate Court turned down two Chuck Comiskey petitions seeking to block the sale of the team and Judge Robert Jerome Dunne even admonished the Comiskey siblings for their fight, saying they should "settle their differences without attendant publicity." Dunne denied one petition asking him to block the sale and a second one that would have removed Dorothy Comiskey as executor of her mother's will.[12]

In mid–March, Frank Lane, the man who helped bring the White Sox back from their period of doom and gloom, and then working as general manager with the Indians made a telling comment. It was not apparent if it was tongue-in-cheek or not, but there was enough seriousness behind it to indicate how messed up Chicago's situation seemed from the outside. "I want to make a deal with the White Sox," Lane said, "but with whom do I make it?" He ticked off a series of names of people who may or may not be in charge of White Sox personnel. "Do I get in touch with Bill Veeck, Chuck Comiskey, Hank Greenberg, John Rigney or traveling secretary Bernie Snyderworth?"[13] It was a fair question.

Right about the same time, Veeck and Chuck Comiskey broke bread together — or at least drank coffee together — with Dorothy Comiskey. A newspaper caption indicated they were toasting to the success of the 1959 White Sox, but it would be hard to imagine they weren't testing the liquids for poison before sipping. Chuck Comiskey's report of what transpired besides caffeine imbibing was as murky as international diplomacy conducted behind closed doors. "I talked to him and he talked to me," Comiskey said. "It was a mutual conversation, with two people talking."[14]

Although Chuck Comiskey was not finished filing appeals, Veeck felt confident enough that he was going to gain control of the team to jet off to spring training to meet some of his employees. However, he did not make a big show of being the new owner, either. Instead, Chuck Comiskey turned up and loudly boasted that he was still in charge. While the courts were sorting through a final disposition of the case, the two protagonists were soaking up the sun and somewhat bizarrely courting public opinion as the team prepared for the season.

Comiskey and Veeck even sat together for a couple of innings during a pre-season game and the joint statement issued was about how good a pitcher Billy Pierce was. When Chuck Comiskey was asked point blank who was running the team he tapped himself on the chest and said, "Me." By then it seemed almost certain that Veeck would be the majority owner, but Comiskey, still retaining 46 percent ownership said, "We're always glad to have stockholders drop in."[15]

As Al Lopez lined up his pitching rotation and his batting order, Bill Veeck lined up his investors and potential members of the board of directors. Even after the courts confirmed the sale, he still needed a majority on the board in order to take care of White Sox business and Comiskey was running around telling everyone he was going to hang on to his 46 percent and would never concede his fight to run the team.

At the end of April, after the season was underway, Circuit Court Judge William J. Tuohy flattened Comiskey's hopes by denying his attempt to derail the sale. The action affirmed the March 10 proposed sale, allowing Dorothy Comiskey to transfer her 54 percent of the stock to Veeck. That at last officially made Veeck the new owner of the White Sox.

Veeck, then 44, may not have been pals with too many other owners, but the sportswriters who had covered his teams in the past always had fond memories of working with him. Veeck made it fun for everyone at the ballpark and he was perhaps the most accessible owner to reporters of any in history. He loved the attention and they loved his witticisms, pronouncements and mad schemes. While not incidental to Veeck, his building a winning team was just a by-product for the entertained writers.

Cleveland sports writer Hal Lebovitz wrote about a spring training experience he had with Veeck in Arizona while Veeck was between owning clubs in the 1950s. While they were sharing a room, Veeck did some scouting for the Indians. Lebovitz said: "He had a briefcase filled with law books and late each night he would sit in the bathtub, soak the stump of his leg and pore over his thick legal texts." Veeck had discovered that in California one did not have to attend law school to become a lawyer, only study for the bar and be sponsored by a genuine attorney. Veeck told him that he was going to become a criminal lawyer. Instead, after striking out in attempts to keep the Browns or buy the Washington Senators, Detroit Tigers or Pittsburgh Pirates, he was the new owner of the White Sox. "This is the legal profession's loss and baseball's gain," Lebovitz noted. "Life with Veeck is never dull."[16]

Veeck's old sportswriter pals popped up writing stories to welcome him back to the majors and inform any readers ignorant of his past that this was a guy who had experience and knew how to have fun. One writer concentrated on how much Veeck had learned working for his father with the Cubs and how that had served him with the Indians and Browns.

"I grew up in that atmosphere of the ballpark," Veeck said. "I grew up with the people in baseball." One day, he said, he was with his father when the day's receipts were being counted. His dad told him to take note of the consistency of the green. "I want you to remember one thing about money," the older Veeck said. "It's all one color — you can't tell who gave it to you." To Veeck that was a message to remember that all people — or customers — were created equal. "That's something I've remembered all my life," the younger Veeck said. "In baseball, you can never say who spent the money at the box office. It can be the richest, the poorest, the whitest, the darkest of people."[17]

Some would have nodded sagely upon hearing the news that Veeck contemplated buying the Ringling Brothers Circus during the 1950s years when he was out of baseball. Yet there was no doubt in his mind that as soon as he exited from baseball with the Browns (primarily because owners would not allow him to make the move to Baltimore, though as soon as he sold, the team did move to Maryland), he plotted a return. In his mind, it was his destiny. "By the time I was 12, I'd decided that I was going to own a baseball team," Veeck said. "My life was going to be centered on baseball. It was inevitable."[18]

Veeck always was a big fan of the circus, even if he never owned one, and his first wife, Eleanor, was actually an elephant trainer with the three-ringed traveling show. She demonstrated her own sense of humor after partnering with Veeck when she said, "When I married, I thought I was through with circuses. I was wrong."[19]

Veeck never minded being compared to P.T. Barnum. While Barnum hustled for every dollar, he made sure his spectators got their money's worth. Veeck hustled to put fannies in the seats, too, but he also tried to build winning baseball teams, a considerably different pressure than that which faced Barnum, who was mostly concerned with making money.

The biggest problem Veeck had each time he became the owner of a baseball team was a lack of cash. He had $11 in his pocket when he bought the Brewers and by the end of the night when he closed the deal after celebrating with friends he had $1 left. "If they'd asked for a $2 deposit on the key at the hotel, I was dead," Veeck said.[20]

He was no multi-millionaire who could raid his bank account and plunk down the payment price without worrying about the long term. He always had to put together a syndicate of money men to supplement his share of the purchase. So he was always beholden to them not to be a reckless spender. But he also never lost sight of the big picture in terms of entertaining the fan. He felt it was his duty to make sure any visitor to the ballpark had a good time. In that sense, in terms of providing the fan with something to talk about when he exited from the field, Veeck was probably the best friend the baseball fan ever had. It is no accident that on Veeck's National Baseball Hall of Fame plaque, the summary of his career ends this way: "A champion of the little guy."

It was always Veeck's dream to run a baseball team. The frosting on the cake for him when he obtained the deed to his third major-league franchise was that it was located in Chicago. He had tried to buy into the White Sox once before, but that idea went nowhere. Now he was king of the castle. "I've come back home," Veeck said. "I first tried to buy the White Sox 20 years ago and now I have 'em. We're going to have lots of fun."[21]

14

Going for It All

For the first half of the twentieth century, with rare exceptions, being assigned to the bullpen was an insult for a major-league pitcher. It meant you weren't good enough to start, or you didn't have the staying power to throw more than four good innings or so. The entire philosophy behind being a member of the four-man pitching rotation was that you were handed the ball by the manager and you went out to pitch nine innings. Failure to make it through all nine and throw a complete game was a sign of weakness.

A hundred years ago pitching staffs were much smaller. None of these 12-man tag-team groups of pitchers for Connie Mack or John McGraw. Not only did the best pitchers start every fourth day, but sometimes they were called upon to relieve if a teammate was in dire need of help.

The first true late-inning relief specialists did not come into vogue until about 1950 and from there the tweaking of the role has continued non-stop. The "closer," the final-out-gathering save man, is now frequently asked to pitch to just one or two batters. The "set-up" man might just throw the eighth inning.

The revolution had begun by 1959. Managers still counted on a four-man rotation, but the philosophy that all of the starters had to go all of the way was fading. Unless they were clobbered, however, they were expected to go after a complete game or to throw into the seventh or eighth. The bullpen was growing in importance, but when the game started there were not as many guys hanging out there as there were in the dugout as now seems to be the case.

If strategy was changing, then the old-fashioned starters still clung to the past. For them it was a sense of responsibility and honor to try to finish every game they started. The current preoccupation with pitch counts baffles old-timers who rarely knew how many pitches they tossed in a game, or they shrugged off the number.

"Pitch counts? I don't believe in pitch counts," said Hall of Famer Bob Feller, star of the 1930s–1950s. "I believe in what's on the ball when you throw it. If they had a pitch count when I was a kid, I never would have got out of the third inning."[1]

In 1956, Billy Pierce started 33 games and completed 21 of them. In 1957, Pierce started 34 games and completed 16 of them. And in 1958, he started 32 games and completed 19 of them. In each season he came out of the bullpen two or three times. More than 50 years later, Pierce views with disdain the current method of running relief pitchers in and out so swiftly their families might miss their appearance in the game. When he makes public appearances Pierce always mentions that he considers it ridiculous that a "quality start" is defined as allowing three runs or less in six innings of throwing. As he points out, that could get you benched in his day. "They gave you the ball and you figured you were going to go nine innings," Pierce said. "And having a 4.50 ERA was not so good."[2]

Bob Gibson, the St. Louis Cardinals' Hall of Fame pitcher often mentioned in the same breath as Early Wynn when it came to brushing batters back, sounds much like Pierce when discussing the modern-day viewpoint of a quality start. "If you pitch five innings, you get a quality something-or-other," Gibson said. "They don't expect you to finish ballgames."[3]

During his first year with the White Sox in 1958, Early Wynn started 34 games and completed 11. That was his lowest total in a decade, but he was 38 at the time. It should be remembered Wynn threw the ball at Lopez once when he relieved him.

Hall of Famer Cy Young threw 749 complete games in his career, a record likely to last forever unless all of the relief pitchers in the world make career changes and become lacrosse players. In 2008, the American League leader in complete games was Toronto's Roy Halladay with nine. Pierce's 19 complete games was tops in the AL in 1958, typical of the era when the league leader recorded about 20 complete games. The outlook was changing by 1959, though. After faltering in one-run games and operating with an aging staff, Lopez wanted to shore up the bullpen.

Left-hander Gary Peters, from Grove City, Pennsylvania, stood 6-foot-2 and weighed 200 pounds. He had a lively fastball and at 21 in spring training was angling to make the White Sox roster any way they would take him. "They had such a good pitching staff," Peters said. "I went to spring training. It was a long battle for me. It took me four years to even get a start in the big leagues."[4]

But Peters got a long look in spring training and he took a long look at Early Wynn, a man who by then had been in the majors for 20 years, and again when Peters had a September call-up as the White Sox were pushing for the pennant.

"He was a battler," Peters said. "Real competitive. Gus pitched differently than almost anybody else. He was behind a lot of hitters. He would be 3-and-1 a lot. It was to where we used to say, 'If he gets them 3-and-1 he's got them right where he wants them.' His breaking ball never hung. He threw a slider and even if he threw it high, it would break good and he would throw that high slider. Normally, nobody ever wants to throw a high slider."

And yes, the young Peters noticed immediately that Wynn employed psychological warfare against batters more than most pitchers. "He was intimidating," Peters said. "I know he hit a few guys. He used to pitch batting practice once in a while and you didn't want to hit one back across that dirt circle when he was on the mound or he would throw at you in batting practice. He did not want that ball back there through the middle. He would throw one over your head or something like that."[5]

Peters did not make the cut out of spring training. Wynn, Pierce and Dick Donovan were the entrenched starters, but the man who beat out Peters to claim the fourth spot in the rotation was Bob Shaw. Shaw had showed well in limited action the year before and much like Peters was tired of being shuttled to the minors. This was his chance.

For the second time in three years Al Lopez told sportswriters that the Yankees could be had. He even had players who were starting to believe the speech that it was their time.

"We had a mixture of veterans and younger players," Shaw said. "The older players were very stable, kind of concrete individuals. You've got Sherm Lollar, Nellie Fox, Billy Pierce, Early Wynn, Dick Donovan, Al Smith, and Earl Torgeson, and some younger guys like Luis Aparicio, Jim

Rivera, Jim Landis, and especially Earl Battey and John Romano. It was a nice mixture there."[6]

The thing that transformed the Go-Go White Sox players into winners who believed they could win the pennant and the World Series, said Shaw, was the way the season evolved. Even in spring training there was much talk about the team lacking home-run power. But as the spring turned to summer and the team kept winning close games with superior fielding and baserunning, that didn't seem to matter as much as baseball observers thought it would. During 1959, the White Sox won 35 out of 50 one-run games.

"I think that as it progressed we got more and more confident," Shaw said. "When we were down by two or three runs we still felt we could win. That feeling sort of radiated and grew. As the season went on our confidence became much stronger."[7]

Shaw began the 1959 season in the bullpen. He got to watch Lopez up close and grew to admire the way the ex-catcher handled pitchers. Lopez also had a built-in winning track record that got players' attention. He led that Cleveland team to the remarkable 111 wins in 1954 and his clubs stayed closer than anybody else to the seemingly invincible Yankees.

"The guy had a quiet demeanor and everybody respected him," Shaw said. "He didn't speak with a loud voice. He was very knowledgeable. He didn't say a lot, but when he spoke you listened and you knew you weren't going to pull anything over his eyes. He really handled the pitching staff well. He didn't overuse us. He didn't abuse the pitchers. I thought his judgment changing pitchers was excellent. I think he was really smart using pitchers over the course of the season, so the pitchers were still capable of doing a good job at the end of the season."[8]

For the first month-and-a-half of the season, Lopez used Shaw primarily in relief before his consistent sharpness convinced the team leadership to try him as a starter. Lopez and pitching coach Ray Berres both liked what they were seeing and there was still a semi-hole in the rotation. The change worked immediately. Shaw was rooming with Early Wynn on the road and he tried to pick up tidbits of advice that could help him adjust to a full-time job in the majors.

At the start of the 1959 season Early Wynn was 39 years old. He had been in the majors since his debut with the Washington Senators in 1939.

Nine times he had won at least 17 games in the majors and his career total was 249 wins. He hadn't really thought about winning 300 games, but it was starting to look possible. The pitcher who had been born into poverty in rural Alabama had a nice home in Florida and enjoyed the spoils of his career. He flew his own plane, owned a boat and off the field he was a fashion plate who took care with his appearance, from his thick head of dark hair to his wardrobe. Shaw was impressionable and thought he could do much worse than have a role model like Wynn. Being Wynn's roommate meant that he spent more time with Gus than anyone else on the team.

"He dressed very well," said Shaw. "He wore mohair suits that he had made in Baltimore. So I got my suits in Baltimore. He bought his shoes in Boston and his underwear and socks in Los Angeles. I followed along the way he dressed. He was business oriented, so he got me thinking that way. He had a pilot's license and I ended up getting a pilot's license."[9]

Wynn influenced Shaw in so many ways and that included soaking up the night life on the road in America's biggest and most exciting cities. The two pals drank wherever they traveled. "We went out a couple of nights and stayed out quite late," Shaw said. "Then I realized I couldn't do it when I came back home. But he went out again. So he had not only stamina on the field, but off the field."[10]

The next morning after a late-nighter, Shaw might be nursing a headache, but Wynn rolled out of bed, pulled on a rubber suit over his clothing and went for a hard run. Wynn sweated heavily as the heat from the baking sun drained the fluids from his body. "He played hard and he worked hard," Shaw said. "But I couldn't keep up with him. I tried, but I knew I couldn't, so I stopped doing it."[11]

Lopez and Berres had given Shaw a considerable amount of individual attention to fine-tune his delivery, but on those nights when he and Wynn went out for some beers, the old pitcher dispensed a different type of wisdom. Wynn talked about the small stuff, the way a pitcher could get an edge, or the way he could hurt himself if he wasn't smart about his behavior on the mound. Naturally enough, Wynn was a proponent of his own style of scaring the bejesus out of batters.

Many teammates took note of Wynn's harsh method of retaliation against hitters who stroked a shot up the middle, but Shaw was one of a smaller group of players that heard Wynn's philosophy on the topic from his own mouth. Essentially, Wynn said that the hitters didn't care about the pitcher's well-being, so why should they care about them? "Do they ever stop if they hit a line drive and they hit you? Do they stop and say they're sorry, or look and see if you're OK?" is the way Shaw paraphrased Wynn. "When you have to go inside, go in hard. Knock them on their ass if you need to do it. Go in on them."[12]

There were other, subtler aspects of pitching Wynn talked about over dinner or at the bar, like ways to save energy. It's often been said that a pitcher's legs go before his arm and as an aging thrower Wynn had given insightful consideration to how he could conserve and preserve what his body could do for as many innings as possible. Shaw had a habit of booting the resin bag out of the way on the mound, practically using it as a soccer ball, so that it was practically out of the dirt and on the grass when he went into his windup. Wynn demanded to know why.

"Dummy," he said. "I don't know why you keep kicking that resin bag down the hill. Why would you walk down and up the hill? That's not very bright." Wynn even suggested foregoing all use of the resin bag. It could change Shaw's grip, he said. "Your hand gets hot," Shaw said. "Now it gets tacky. You've got to wipe your hands off and start all over again. Now everybody uses a resin bag. Everywhere you go, even in Little League, they have a resin bag. But once he taught me that, I never used a resin bag again. I learned things from Early Wynn just by going out and sitting with him. That's when he would teach me something."[13]

Once Shaw settled into the rotation, the bullpen was short-handed. Lopez and Berres consulted and they came up with a plan that served the White Sox well the rest of the season. The concept of a specialist closer who slammed the door on hitters by stomping out of the bullpen and blowing away the last hitter or two in the ninth inning had not yet taken hold. Those finishers had not yet been elevated to the status of savior and pitchers were not as territorial about the role. They just wanted to pitch.

The White Sox had two old pros in the pen that Lopez felt he could rely on in any circumstance at any time of the game. Gerry Staley and Turk Lown were friends and had been around with different teams in different leagues. They had more in common with each other and with Wynn than they did with the young pups on the team because they had seen it all and were not going to face situations that rattled them.

Omar Joseph Lown was known to everyone in baseball as "Turk." The nickname was attributed by some to the player's love of eating turkey. He was born in Brooklyn, New York, in 1924 and broke into the majors with the Chicago Cubs in 1951. He was more starter than reliever for the first three years of his career, but after 1953 he never started another game in his 11-year career. In 1954, Lown appeared in 60 games for the Cubs. In 1957, he appeared in a career-high 67. When Lown joined the White Sox in the latter stages of 1958, the team knew what it was getting. "Rubber armed pitchers have untold value in these days of unlimited master minding by big-league managers," one newspaper story said in 1956, including Lown among those pitchers.[14]

Lown was a late bloomer. He was stuck in the minors until he was 27 partially because he was wild, walking too many men. His control improved with the Cubs, but he was stuck with a weak ball club for most of the 1950s. He was happy to switch from the North Side to the South Side of Chicago near the end of the 1958 season, if only because the White Sox were winners. That laid the predicate for 1959.

"We finished up the '58 season real well," Lown said. "There was no reason not to feel positive about things going into 1959. And we did get a couple of additions to the team that I felt would work out really well. And from my point of view, coming over from the Cubs to the White Sox, I really felt that way."[15]

Lown always considered himself an accidental ballplayer. He was a Brooklyn Dodgers fan and played in the neighborhood, but believed that his older brother Bill was the better player. One of their neighbors knew a Dodger scout and wrangled Bill an invitation to a tryout in 1942. But Bill could not get off work and he couldn't risk getting fired. It was Lown's parents' idea for the younger son to go to Ebbets Field in Bill's place.

"My folks said, 'Well, Junior, why don't you go down?'" recalled Lown, "and I went down out of the clear blue and that's how I got into pro ball. Fortunately, I had a good arm. Actually, I was a catcher when I played with the Queens Alliance team with my brother. He was the pitcher. When I got to Ebbets Field they had about 200 kids there. They went around to each of us asking, 'What do you do? What do you do?' I told them I was a pitcher and that's how I got to be a pitcher."[16]

The tryout camp went on for several days and every day Lown came back to throw. He threw hard each time he showed up so he figured the Dodgers just decided he must have a strong arm. He never imagined that it would take him most of a decade to reach the majors and most of the rest of another decade to play for a top-notch team.

Neither Lown, nor his buddy Gerry Staley (with whom he stayed in touch the rest of his life until Staley died in January of 2008), were specialists. Either one of them could be brought into a ballgame early and be used for several innings, or could be brought into a game late and finish off the opposition. Besides the issue of which one of them was more rested based on recent outings, Lown thinks Lopez chose between him and Staley for an entrance based on a situational circumstance. "Apparently, when he thought we needed a strikeout, he'd bring me in," Lown said, "and when he thought he needed a ground ball for a double play, or something like that, he'd bring Gerry in because he threw sinkers."[17]

Lown's primary weapon was a fastball. Sometimes it seemed to him that Lopez didn't want him to throw anything but fastballs and that if he wanted to throw a curve he almost needed written permission. "It was horrible what I went through," Lown joked, because Lopez was so rigid on the topic. Once in a great while Lopez would relent and let Lown try something different.[18]

The White Sox were playing the Detroit Tigers and coming to the plate was slugger Rocky Colavito. A little bit earlier in the season Colavito had hit a homer off of Lown that was so far up in the upper deck that it couldn't be seen without a telescope. Lown believes he made the mistake of throwing a slider that didn't slide. This at-bat was Lown's first time facing Colavito since the smash that landed closer to Jupiter than the left-field wall.

"I hear a whistle, so I look over to our dugout and they're giving me a sign with the right hand like I should throw a curveball," said Lown. "But slow. That was my change-up and everybody called it a butterfly ball. So I threw it and Colavito just stood there and took it for a strike. I looked over in the dugout and everyone was laughing, including Lopez. They gave me the sign again and I threw it again and struck him out with the same pitch. They were just having a hilarious time on the bench. I threw the ball just like I was throwing a fastball, but then I just let it slip out and it would go in high and come down as a change-up, but I had to get the OK from Al all the time to throw that. He didn't like anything from me except fastballs."[19]

Gerry Staley was the other half of the deadly bullpen duo. Like any self-respecting pitcher coming up through the minors in the 1940s, Staley was focused on becoming a major-league starter. He was born in Brush Prairie, Washington, in 1920 and did not break in with the St. Louis Cardinals until after World War II, where he had served in the Pacific Theatre as an Army sergeant. Another reason that Staley turned 27 before reaching the majors was coming late to the role of pitching. Staley was a high school infielder, but influenced by two older brothers on a semi-pro team he tried twirling and was successful. "Roy and Joe were ambitious for me," Staley said. "They even taught me how to throw a knuckleball. They had been sandlot pitchers who hadn't made the grade."[20]

Staley was 1–0 in 1947 as a rookie, but soon developed into a key man in the Cards' rotation. Between 1951 and 1953, Staley was a first-rate starter, winning 19, 17, and 18 games. He was also an off-season lumberjack, working at the family sawmill to pay his brothers back for their assistance.

A combination of circumstances led to Staley being the Cardinals' Opening Day pitcher in 1950, "opening day" being a slight misnomer because for the first time in major-league history, an opener was played as a night game. St. Louis met the Pirates and Staley won. The victory jump-started a solid career, yet one that drifted to assignments in the bullpen over time and saw Staley become a full-time reliever by 1957. One writer compared him to a decades-earlier Dennis Eckersley.

For a while in the 1950s, Staley did both starting and relieving jobs at the same time because the Cardinals needed his versatility. "I was going good and I was strong, so they used me in both situations," he said. "I had pretty good control and they (batters) were hitting the first or second pitch all the time, which is a great help for any pitcher."[21]

During the early 1950s, the Cardinals were good, but not great, often finishing 12-to-20 games over .500, but never truly threatening for the pennant. They were in the mix for most of the season, but never captured the flag. "There were several years where the Cardinals were just one or two games out of first all of the time," Staley said. "It sure was frustrating."[22]

Staley and Lown were both used to relieving in games, but they did not know that they were part of a revolution that would see the relief pitcher ascend to such an important role in the sport. Likewise, Lopez, assessing the age of his starting staff and being cautious with a ball club that was not high scoring, was ahead of his time in the frequency he employed Staley and Lown. Sportswriters began to notice at mid-season just how often the two were coming in for the starters and wondered how they could keep it up.

"You've got to stay relaxed mentally," Staley said. "We just never let anyone get tense in our bullpen. We insult each other all the time. Nobody ever gets angry. We never give 'em a chance."[23]

It gradually became apparent that the bullpen, previously a weakness for the White Sox in their recent attempts to overtake the Yankees for the American League pennant, had evolved into a strength. The old image of deteriorating pitchers sent to the bullpen in exile was dead. The White Sox were winning games because of Turk Lown and Gerry Staley, not in spite of relievers.

15

Erasing 40 Years
of Bad Luck

Back home in Tampa, when Al Lopez talked baseball, the locals listened. He was the most esteemed and respected baseball man in the city. In White Sox spring training in 1959, in Tampa, Lopez told his team bluntly, "The Yankees can be had."[1] His team set out to prove him right.

"He was serious," said outfielder Jim Rivera. "He got that attitude coming from Cleveland. The ball club he had there, he beat the Yankees. So he figured we could do it. In 1959, you could tell we were motoring. We had not been lower than third since I came over in 1952. We were ready."[2]

The season opened on April 10 at Detroit and it was a long day for the 38,332 fans at Tiger Stadium. It was cold and snow actually fell. Billy Pierce got the Opening Day start for the White Sox, but was removed after five innings. He surrendered four runs. The Tigers' starter was future Hall of Famer Jim Bunning, a right-hander who won more than 100 games in each league and pitched a no-hitter in each league before being elected to the U.S. Senate from Kentucky.

Neither thrower was still around as the 4-hour, 25-minute game dragged well into extra innings. Bunning gave up nine hits and three runs in four and one-third innings before giving way to a reliever. Interestingly, for a team that was supposed to be able to barely scratch out runs, the White Sox put seven runs on the board by the ninth. So did the Tigers. It wasn't until the 14th inning, when Lopez was employing his sixth and seventh pitchers of the day, that Chicago pushed two runs across.

Of all people, second baseman Nellie Fox, about to embark on probably the greatest season of his career, clouted a two-run homer with Sammy

Esposito on base in the top of the 14th off Don Mossi for the winning runs. Fox hit just two home runs all season, but he had a phenomenal day with five hits, two runs scored and three RBIs.

Esposito was a backup infielder who got into one game with the White Sox in 1952 and then returned for good in 1955 after Army service. He never played in more than 98 games for Chicago in one year and his main value was as a utility man who could fill in at third, short and second. When Esposito, who fancied himself a possible starting shortstop, departed for the Army, Chico Carrasquel was the Sox man at short. When he rejoined the organization in 1955 he was assigned to minor-league Memphis and Esposito rushed to catch up to the team on a road trip in Moline, Illinois. Luis Aparicio was on the scene. Before Esposito could even talk to manager Jack Cassini, he saw Aparicio fielding grounders.

"I got out of the Army in '55 and I didn't even go home," Esposito recalled. "I see this little guy bouncing around, making throws and everything. It was Aparicio. And I said to myself, 'Uh, oh, I'm at the wrong place here.'" Compounding Esposito's problem was that Cassini was a player-manager whose spot was second base. When Memphis came off the field and Cassini introduced himself he asked Esposito what position he played. "I immediately said, 'Third base,' Esposito recalled. "I had never played third base in my life. At least I was smart enough to know I wasn't ever going to be the White Sox shortstop — not after seeing Looie play."[3]

Trying to get everyone out of the cold, Lopez pinch-hit the solid swinging Billy Goodman for Aparicio in the top of the seventh, and then inserted Esposito in the field. "I think everybody on both teams was hoping somebody would just win and get it over with, no matter who won, it was so miserable out there," Esposito said. "My thumb was so cold on my throwing hand that when I got a couple of ground balls over there at short, I couldn't feel the ball. I don't know how the hell I got it over to first."[4] Esposito was in the game long enough to bat three times. In the 14th, his single set the stage for Fox's game-winning, two-run shot.

Right from the first game one of the patterns of the season was established. Lopez called on Gerry Staley for long relief. Staley, who hurled four and one-third innings, picked up the win, but Lopez, acting very much like a futuristic manager, called on Don Rudolph to polish off Detroit. Rudolph got the last out. At the time there was no save statis-

tic — an innovation created by Hall of Fame baseball writer Jerome Holtzman soon after — but retroactively, when historians examined game results,
Rudolph was awarded a save.

The White Sox were 1–0 and they never fell back to .500, or below
.500, the entire season.

The White Sox starter for the second game of the season was Early
Wynn. The atmosphere was considerably different at Tiger Stadium.
Despite the game being played on a Saturday, paid attendance was only
5,529. But Wynn was in top form. He pitched a complete game, allowing seven hits and three runs in a 5–3 victory, though only one run was
earned. Whether to illustrate he had not mellowed at age 39 or he was
making a point, in the top of the second inning he hit Detroit lead-off
man Frank Bolling with a pitch. The Tigers did have the audacity to hit
the ball back to the mound in the first inning, but that was Al Kaline at
the plate and Wynn picked up the grounder and started a double play.
Plus, Larry Doby had already come to the plate at the end of the inning
before Bolling got his black-and-blue mark.

More in character with their team personality, the White Sox accumulated their runs by scoring one run in each of five innings. In another
unusual occurrence, Aparicio accounted for one of them, not by stealing
a base and speeding home on a grounder or something, but with a solo
home run. And he hit only six all season.

The starting first baseman that day was Norm Cash. On a veteran
team that was bursting with young talent aching for a chance to play, he
got the start at a position that was still somewhat in flux in Lopez's mind.
Cash was 24 and appeared in 13 games in 1958. He had power and an excellent batting stroke and the White Sox very much wanted him to succeed
in the majors in a hurry.

Nicknamed "Stormin' Norman," Cash had played football at Sul Ross
State College in Texas, where he decided to take up an additional sport —
baseball. Cash was 6 feet tall and weighed 190 pounds, with powerful arms
and he was a left-handed swinger, something somewhat in short supply.
He turned out to be a natural at baseball. That caught the Chicago Bears
off-guard because they spent an 11th round NFL draft pick on him after
Cash gained more than 1,500 yards rushing as a senior.

Cash could have been the White Sox' long-term answer at first base, but they didn't know it. He was raw and lacked experience, something that might be costly in a pennant contending year. Although he inched into the starting lineup in the second game of the season, Cash appeared in just 57 more. He could hit, but not yet as consistently as he thought he could.

"I've never had much trouble hitting," Cash said. "I'm lucky. I swing down on the ball. They say that's the best way to do it. It takes some guys years to learn it. With me it comes natural."[5] Cash got some chances in 1959, but batted .240. He wasn't quite ready for prime-time first-base duty.

The White Sox swept the opening series from Detroit and then won their next game against the Kansas City Athletics to start 4–0. They were in first place in the American League. That didn't last. When they lost their first game to K.C., they fell to second place and did not regain the top spot until May 18, and then only for a day. The Sox were in a pennant race.

It was a pennant race that would energize White Sox fans in a way they hadn't been touched since 1919 when the Black Sox were still the Clean Sox and debates about Shoeless Joe Jackson's abilities were confined to speculation on whether or not he would ever hit .400 again, not whether or not he had been duped into taking part in a scandal by unscrupulous teammates.

One keen observer of the season, with an insider's perch, was young Mike Veeck. Bill Veeck's son, and later a popular minor-league team owner and major-league executive who brought the same sense of joy to a ballpark as his father, fell in love with the White Sox of 1959.

"The Sox represented the South Side," Mike Veeck wrote 40 years later. "They were the South Side. From Hyde Park to South Holland, they represented the working-class city of big shoulders." Veeck said that once, again much later, he was in Las Vegas and was passing a roulette wheel and stopped to make a bet. He put his faith on No. 24. Why that number? Because it was the number Early Wynn wore with the White Sox. "My favorite player of all time," Veeck called the hurler.[6]

Most of the baseball world was still mesmerized by the Yankees. New York was in the middle of a run that would claim 10 pennants in 12 years and few questioned whether or not 1959 would be one of those rare years when the Yanks didn't win. *Chicago Tribune* columnist David Condon picked the White Sox to win the American League pennant, but he did so every year, almost as if he figured he had to be right some day. It was like Ernie Banks on the North Side, every spring suggesting that it was going to be the Cubs' year. However, Richard Dozer, a *Tribune* baseball writer, actually picked the Sox to win the flag based on merit. He factored stats into emotion, noting how well they had played over the second half of the 1958 season. Long-time sports writer Warren Brown was less optimistic. "I don't suppose they will ever get over the blind staggers that seize them every time the Yankees are in sight," he said.[7]

Insanity broke out in an April 22 game at Kansas City. Wynn, who was the loser in a 6–0 defeat to the Athletics on April 16, got another chance to handle the A's. He struggled, giving up six runs in an inning and two-thirds and giving way to Bob Shaw out of the bullpen. Shaw pitched seven and one-third innings of three-hit, six-strikeout relief for the victory after the Sox erupted for 14 more runs in a 20–6 triumph. Fox smacked four hits, Aparicio stroked three and three other White Sox had two hits in a 16-hit attack. In perhaps the most incredible inning in team history, the Sox scored 11 runs in the seventh on just one hit.

At that point Wynn seemed out of sorts. His record was 1–1, but easily could have been 1–2. Shaw long had been confident, but couldn't get the Tigers to believe in him. After his 4–2 showing in 1958 he was impatient for more chances with the White Sox. His year had begun in peculiar fashion. One of Shaw's gripes with the Tigers was that they not only confined him to the minors, but didn't want him to pitch winter ball. Now that Shaw was property of the White Sox that was no longer a prohibition. Shaw had journeyed to Cuba to pitch over the winter and like the many other American ballplayers on hand, had experienced a raucous New Year's Eve.

In December, the long-brewing Cuban revolution was coming to a head. The rebels were working their way to the seat of government in Havana. On December 31, an assault on the Las Villas Province capital of Santa Clara overcame troops loyal to Fulgencio Batista and early the next morning, on the first day of the New Year, he fled into exile. Within days, Castro's army occupied Havana and he took power soon after.

While all of this was going on, however, Cuban baseball continued.

If Early Wynn thought dodging line drives was an occupational hazard, Bob Shaw learned that dodging bullets could come with the territory.

"I was pitching right during the revolution," Shaw said. "I was there in Havana when Castro came into town. So things were different. They had guns, people were shooting at each other. Oh yeah, I mean it was a different ballgame. I remember January 1. I thought there were firecrackers going off, but those weren't firecrackers. They were shooting the guards at the Havana prison. I was sleeping in the bathtub because there was a lot of gunfire and hand grenades and everything going off." At the ballpark, the Cuban guerillas attended fully armed and stood on top of the dugouts. Shaw was pitching one day when he heard some gunshots. "I ran and dove into the dugout," he said.[8]

Shaw lived to tell about it and in spring training he earned Lopez's support. He still wasn't starting, but throwing more than seven innings in relief was just about as good. And after ducking the bombs bursting in air he wasn't going to get flustered by the Kansas City Athletics.

The White Sox floundered a little bit in the early spring, dropping to as low as 11–10 and fourth place on May 6, but that was a temporary condition. Wynn regained his equilibrium and began churning out the wins, a throwback to his old self of five years before. Wynn was not brilliant, but good enough, in a 6–5 win over the Indians on April 26, pitching just five innings, though with eight strikeouts.

As the weather warmed slightly, so did Wynn. On May 1 he pitched one of the best games of his life, blanking the Boston Red Sox 1–0 on one hit while striking out 14 in a complete game. Wynn was 39, he was probably 20 pounds overweight with his belly overhanging his belt a bit despite his hot sun runs in the rubber suit, and he was taking a regular turn in the rotation, pitching every fourth day just like some 22-year-old. If ever a game summed up the potential left in his aging body, this one demonstrated fully what he was still capable of. Even crazier, old Gus hit a home run and a double. Just to show he was human, though, in a close game Wynn walked seven Red Sox batters. Still, the game tape might have been Wynn's all-time highlight reel keepsake.

"He was not a bad hitter," recalled Billy Pierce of Wynn at the plate. "When he first came up he used to pinch-hit for Washington. He was a very good left-handed hitter. Actually, he could hit both ways."[9]

Switch-hitter or not, anything Wynn produced at the plate was a bonus for the White Sox. They wanted him for his arm and by early May he was 3–1 and doing the job. It was becoming apparent to White Sox teammates that Wynn was throwing better than he had the season before when he won 14 games. If he could win 20 again, as he had in the old days, they might be on to something.

"He won a lot of big ballgames for us," Pierce said. "That's where he was at his best. When the competition was strong, he was at his best. No question about it."[10]

After a few days stuck in fourth place in early May, the Sox revved it up again and by May 10 they were back in second place, though their record was only 13–11. The surprise in the baseball world was that the team in front of them was not the New York Yankees, but the Cleveland Indians. The Indians started out hot and stayed hot. They won their first six games and on April 22 they were 10–1.

The magnificent pitching staff of 1954 had dispersed. Wynn was pitching for the White Sox. Bob Feller was retired. Bob Lemon was retired. Art Houtteman was retired. Mike Garcia was hanging around in a spot role (he would go just 3–6 that season). Manager Lopez was in charge of the White Sox. But the Indians had rebuilt. They were managed by former Yankee star second baseman Joe Gordon. The pitching rested on Cal McLish, Gary Bell, Jim Perry, Jim "Mudcat" Grant, and Herb Score, still attempting to regain the sparkle he showed before the line-drive skulling he suffered in 1957.

If there was no one true ace (though McLish was at his best with 19 wins that year), the Indians had a fearsome lineup. The hitters included 42-homer man Rocky Colavito, Tito Francona, Woody Held, Vic Power, Jimmy Piersall, Jim Baxes, Billy Martin and White Sox old friend Minnie Minoso.

Poor Minnie. He put in so much time with the White Sox as they went through their growing pains only to be traded away when the team at last mounted its charge for the pennant. Then, after they won it, he was reacquired. Years into retirement, Minoso remained with the White Sox, working in their community relations department. Minoso says that many fans that were not old enough to be first-hand spectators in 1959 still associate him with the pennant winner. "It is a bit surprising how many people still think I was part of the 1959 championship team," he wrote in his autobiography and has said many times elsewhere.[11]

But that season, Minoso was on the other side. And so was Trader Frank Lane. Lane was the general manager of the Indians, trying to wheel and deal for enough players to hold off the White Sox.

So where were the almighty Yankees while all of this was going on? On May 9, New York's record was 9–13, and the Yankees were in seventh place in the American League. By Memorial Day weekend, they were in eighth place. It would not be until the second half of the season that the Yankees showed signs of rejuvenation. By then it was too late. New York rose to third place, but the summer belonged to the White Sox and Indians.

Comfortable with how the White Sox were doing at season's start, Lopez talked about his hopes with sportswriters. "Why shouldn't I talk pennant?" he said.[12] Why not? Lopez was trying to create a bandwagon for everyone else to jump on.

16

Veeck — As in
What the Heck

The man who brought a midget up to bat in a St. Louis Browns baseball game wasn't going to change his stripes when he took over his third major-league team. Bill Veeck promised the world fun during his tenure as owner of the Chicago White Sox and he did his best to deliver.

Veeck wanted his baseball teams to do well, to win pennants and win World Series. But he also recognized the simple fact that only one team could win the World Series each year. He wanted to hedge his bets by making certain that fans who came to watch his teams play were entertained whether the home team won the game or not, or whether it was in first place or not.

When Veeck wrote his autobiography it was titled *Veeck — As In Wreck*. The point of rhyming his name with wreck was testimony to how many times in his life people had mispronounced Veeck. There must have been thousands of "Veeek" speakers out there for him to make that choice. He probably wanted to steer clear of all potential aspersions potentially cast by a rhyme with "wreak." While fellow owners may have believed Veeck was wreaking havoc with his teams, the vast majority of baseball fans were busy laughing along with him and soaking up the jovial game atmosphere he established.

Although Comiskey Park was not located in the Deep South where heat and humidity would make fans sitting at a ballpark keel over in a faint, Chicago could still get toasty warm in the summer. Veeck had a shower installed in the outfield so fans could cool themselves off at will just by pulling a cord. They were already sweaty, so many didn't mind getting wet all over again if the water was cold. If a member of the staff had walked up to a fan seated in the bleachers and tossed a bucket of water on him, the air coolant would not have been as well received. But by giving permission to the fan to do something almost naughty in public, or at least act out of the norm, the White Sox were complicit in a humorous activity. Fans, as has come to be seen in the ensuing decades, do not possess nearly the amount of modesty they used to (especially after downing a few beers), and also lap up other forms of amusement at the ballpark besides watching the game.

Anything that sounded as if it was halfway upbeat or offbeat was given consideration for fans at the ballpark. Veeck called his events "stunts," but also never forgot that the best entertainment of all is winning.

"Anticipation," Veeck wrote about what the team was selling. "Excitement. Excitement is contagious. It jumps from the fan to the non-fan, and to a degree that is astonishing, it spills over onto the field and infects the players. The first order of business when you take over a franchise that has been in the doldrums is to create the atmosphere that the new order has arrived, that we are living in historic times, that great things are in the air and ultimate triumph inevitable."[1]

Bill Veeck was very, very good at altering atmospheric conditions. Veeck had always been a public relations genius and he was a great cultivator of sportswriters. He did not view them as the enemy, but was wise enough to see them rather as the conduit for his messages. Schmoozing came naturally to Veeck and he actually liked the sportswriters. He was no absentee owner who happened to drop by the ballpark for the occasional game. He was as hands-on as it gets and he was open with the reporters.

Way-back-when Charles A. Comiskey frequently drank with the sportswriters. So did Veeck. Comiskey, who owned a getaway estate in Eagle River, Wisconsin, for hunting and fishing, even invited sportswriters to that home in the off-season. He built a replica lounge of sorts called the Woodlands Bards Room at Comiskey, transplanting the revelry to Chicago. Veeck rejuvenated the room, then known simply as the Bards Room, and he sat around talking baseball and drinking booze with the sportswriters long after games ended. That was one way to make friends and influence people.

The White Sox had essentially been rebuilt by Frank Lane, Chuck Comiskey and John Rigney by the time Veeck arrived. The deadbeat team of the 1920s to 1950 was gone, replaced by an energized group of players and led by a respected manager. Lopez had again predicted the Yankees' demise and he felt certain he had the goods to take the pennant. "We can win it all this year," Lopez said as the season began.[2]

It wasn't as if people weren't listening to Lopez so much as they weren't sure whether or not to believe him. Much of the heavy lifting had been accomplished by the time Veeck took over, but what he did was add a fresh dimension of optimism, humor, and plain old fun, to the mix.

"The players were the players of the previous administration," said Chicago sportswriter Bill Gleason. "But Veeck created a mood. There was never a Chicago team during the Fifties — when they had very good ball clubs — that believed the team could win it. He changed that whole atmosphere, particularly in the clubhouse. For the first time ever I heard a Sox player talk about winning the pennant. Veeck came in and he just excited the entire city."[3]

Veeck remembered that his father pioneered Ladies Day with the Cubs decades earlier and he did him one better. On Mother's Day, as long as any woman showed up with a photograph of her child, she was admitted free to Comiskey Park for a White Sox game against the Cleveland Indians. For a doubleheader, no less.

Free tickets were nice, but Veeck went into the flower delivery business for May 10, as well. He ordered 10,000 miniature orchards to be distributed to picture-toting mommas. "It's not the size of the orchids that counts," Veeck said, "but the sentiment."[4] Critics would be hard-pressed to suggest that the White Sox did not love mothers on their day.

Some of the women went to great lengths to prove their motherhood, too. A woman named Yvonne Miller showed up with a poster-sized photo of two youngsters walking on the beach and ended up posing for a fresh picture with Veeck. More common were the usual wallet-sized photos, but another mom also had her kids' visages tucked away in a locket, so the picture was only slightly larger than a Lincoln penny.

Attendance was 24,346 that day and 3,947 mothers who proved their devotion to raising the next generation got their freebies. They also saw the White Sox sweep the doubleheader, 5–4, with Billy Pierce getting the victory with an 11-inning complete game, and 5–0, with Early Wynn throwing a four-hitter in another complete game.

While Veeck the showman reveled in the publicity garnered through his unique way of celebrating the holiday, Veeck the businessman hoped that the women would have such a good time and look upon him so fondly that they would become regular paying customers. Veeck mingled with the moms at the gate and in the stands and received his share of compliments, enough to allow him to think the ladies might well return for more baseball.

A woman named Antoinette Roberts, of Gary, Indiana, seemed to have an excellent grasp of Veeck's personality and intentions. "He's wonderful, really," she said. "He's promoting and he'll do a good job. I like the things he does for the public. He makes the people come to see what he'll do next. We might get a free car next time." A mother named Pat Howell from the Chicago suburb of Forest Park also praised Veeck. "I love him," she said. "He's a good salesman. He makes you feel like you're welcome. With Bill Veeck we'll go right into first place."[5]

The flowers were only part of the bounty distributed throughout the ballpark that day. Prizes included 1,000 bottles of root beer, 1,000 pies, 1,000 cupcakes, 100 free dinners at a restaurant (as opposed to the concessions stands), 100 cans of beer, and 36 live lobsters delivered to winners' grandstand seats. Oh yeah, tickets for two to the 21 remaining night games, with free babysitting thrown in, were also given away. No wonder the moms loved Veeck, unless they were ones who had to figure out how to get a live lobster safely home (for the lobster and themselves).

"Mother's Day, 1959 in Comiskey Park resembled a mammoth 'Queen For A Day gathering,'" wrote one journalist, referring to the popular television show of the time. Veeck said the White Sox had the lowest number of female patrons in the American League and he wanted to change that. That's why he tried to convince the Commonwealth Edison Company to improve lighting within a four-block radius of the park so women wouldn't be paranoid about walking near Comiskey.[6]

Regardless of occasion, Veeck was visible, at the ballpark and in the press. He had his hair cut short and always wore open-collared shirts. Local newspapers and *The Sporting News*, priding itself on being the "Bible of Baseball," often referred to Veeck not by name, but simply by calling him "Sport Shirt."

Mother's Day was one day and the season was six months long so

Veeck's mind worked overtime to come up with worthy schemes to attract the public through the gates of Comiskey to see his winning ball club on other days.

Veeck threw an unusual parade for National Dairy Week between games of a doubleheader against the Boston Red Sox, with participants including three burros, six cows, pigs, ducks, chickens, and two horses, one of them ridden by a masked figure (could it be the Lone Ranger?). When the mask was removed the mystery man proved to be pitcher Early Wynn.

What followed was a cow milking contest including several of the players who 1) were determined not to get kicked by an irate Bossie and 2) were determined not to get soaked by poorly aimed milk.

Somehow Veeck talked the visiting Red Sox into designating three players to go head to head (or perhaps hand to hand) with his own Wynn, Nellie Fox and Ray Moore. Pete Runnels, Gary Geiger and former White Sox outfielder Jim Busby were the Red Sox milkers. The Red Sox won the competition and one reason was Fox's failure to keep his bucket upright. The cow he was trying to milk kept kicking it over. Though Fox didn't cry over the spilt milk, Veeck was worried that HE might break down in tears if his star got hurt.

"The cow kept kicking and Nellie kept trying and I started writing mental headlines," Veeck said. He envisioned newspapers having a field day with lines like "Fox in Hospital in Critical Condition as Result of Veeck Gag." Veeck said, "I always thought Nellie had a good pair of hands myself. The cow, a more exacting critic, seemed to think otherwise."[7]

On any given day Veeck might do something weird at the park, leaving fans to wonder what was coming next. That was part of his charm and part of his plan. Whereas some teams might provide rather predictable prizes to a person with a lucky seat number, such as a bat, a ball, or a cap, as usual Veeck embraced not only the offbeat idea, but went wholeheartedly for overkill. Among the big prizes a fortunate fan won just for sitting in the right seat at the right time were 22,000 fig bars, 50,000 assorted screws (who said Veeck was screwy?), 1,000 cans of chow mein noodles, and 1,000 cartons of orange juice. There was also the day Veeck gave away 10,000 cupcakes and had them delivered to the winner's home. "Do you have any idea how much room 10,000 cupcakes take up?" Veeck said. "We told the supplier, 'Just keep on moving them in.' He filled the kitchen and the hall and he moved out to the back porch and he was still unloading cupcakes."[8]

But wait, there's more. The baseball season opens in early April and it can still be quite chilly in Chicago. The unprepared that associate baseball with spring can be caught off guard and sit in their seats shivering, so Veeck provided 20,000 pairs of gloves. On a drizzly day he gave out thin plastic rain coats.

To demonstrate solidarity within the team administrative ranks to the public (although it was never very solid), Veeck proposed that he throw Chuck Comiskey the first pitch of a game. Comiskey went along with the show, but Veeck's pitch fell well short of the plate. He didn't care very much. Showmanship was more important than accuracy to Veeck. On a second try he reached Comiskey.

Veeck loved fireworks and he worked hard to integrate star-spangled displays into White Sox games, whether they were set off before or after. Eventually, but not until 1960, his second season in charge of the Sox, Veeck introduced the exploding scoreboard to baseball. A half century later, the White Sox home park still features an exploding scoreboard, where fireworks light the sky after each home run, each victory, and periodically for longer shows throughout the season.

For one game, 20,000 Little League players — in uniform — were allowed free admission to a White Sox game. For another game the first 20,000 women into the game were offered roses.

No promotion was wackier than the day when the Martians landed in the Comiskey outfield and kidnapped Nellie Fox and Luis Aparicio — because they were close to their own size. The mini–Martians were decked out in stereotypical spaceman gear, including the bulbous helmets seen in low-budget movies. Martians Free Admission Day was May 26, and the game was against the Cleveland Indians. A helicopter landed on the field and disgorged four little people dressed as Martians. The ringleader of the band was none other than Eddie Gaedel, the only dwarf to bat in a major-league game when Veeck sent him to the plate for the St. Louis Browns. They had kept in touch. Martians threatened Fox and Aparicio at ray-gun point and "with whom they tried to depart before being convinced that the Sox had greater need of them."[9]

One of colorful White Sox owner Bill Veeck's wild stunts was hiring a group of midgets dressed as Martians to land in the Comiskey Park outfield and attempt to take shortstop Luis Aparicio and second baseman Fox hostage. They relented when they realized the White Sox needed the players more than they did. (National Baseball Hall of Fame Library, Cooperstown, New York.)

One player in whom Veeck took great delight, and who reciprocated those feelings, was Early Wynn. Wynn's and Veeck's acquaintanceship dated back to Cleveland when the pitcher came over from the Washington Senators and Veeck was running the team.

"Early was one of my favorite players and a great personal friend," Veeck wrote. "During the years I was out of baseball I would always run out to his home for barbecued steaks when I was passing through Cleveland." Even Veeck loved to replay the stories of Wynn's likelihood of hitting his mother with a pitch, though he joked that Wynn never even pitched to his mother. But Veeck did note Wynn actually threw at his son and confirmed Wynn's thinking with a direct question. "What else could I do?" Wynn told him. "He had just hit my best curveball against the fence."[10]

Veeck was just about the friendliest owner the players ever met. If a pitcher or hitter had a good day Veeck might spontaneously offer him a $50 bill, or tell him to go to a certain clothing store and buy a suit on him. That would warm a ballplayer's heart. Sometimes players just chuckled at his promotions and sometimes they missed them because the fan treats were taking place while the players were still in the clubhouse.

Pitcher Billy Pierce said he met Veeck when he was running the Indians, but his real first conversation with him didn't take place until Veeck owned the Browns. Veeck had just acquired the solid pitcher, Harry "The Cat" Breechen, and Pierce beat him head-to-head in a 1–0 game. "You dirty dog," Veeck said to Pierce. "What's wrong?" Pierce answered. Veeck said he had hyped Breechen up as the next big winner for St. Louis and "You've taken all my publicity away." That was just business on the field, but Pierce admired Veeck's ability to draw fans. He got a chuckle out of the cow milking. "That was good," Pierce said. The hallmark of good attendance was the one million fan mark in the 1950s and Pierce tipped his hat to Veeck for his creativity. "If the owners don't have any money, you can't get paid," Pierce said. "Some of the promotions were going on when we were changing clothes. Other times we were working out, or after batting or infield practice. The players weren't always involved."[11]

Outfielder Jim Rivera had trouble believing just how many gimmicks and showy ideas Veeck came up with in a short period of time. Sometimes he just shook his head and chuckled about it when Veeck introduced a new stunt that made people laugh or amazed the Comiskey Park audience. "He was a showman," Rivera recalled. "He built it up (attendance). He built the club up. I've got to give him 100 percent credit." Sometimes on a road trip, Veeck might see a player in a clothing store and come up from behind and say, "Go ahead, take it," Rivera said. "Keep it." And Veeck would pay for the item. "Everybody got along with Bill."[12]

Bob Shaw beefed up his wardrobe by following Early Wynn's lead, but he was also cautious in his spending habits because he was far from the best paid player on the White Sox. Veeck became his shirt supplier with little rewards for good games pitched. Once, Veeck was so pleased with a Shaw outing that he gave him $50 to buy a fancy shirt. Shaw was not in the habit of buying $50 shirts. His conservative nature won out at the store and instead he bought five $10 shirts.

"He was annoyed because he wanted me to buy one shirt, an expensive shirt," Shaw said. Another time during the 1959 season Shaw won a big game and Veeck upped the ante. He sent Shaw to a plush Chicago men's clothing store to get a major brand suit. "A handmade suit," Shaw said. "Gray flannel. It was really something. He did that sort of thing and of course that made you feel pretty good."[13]

The White Sox were making themselves feel pretty good early in the 1959 season because of the way they were playing, and Bill Veeck was apparently going to make sure they were the best-dressed team in baseball.

17

Taking a Run at
First Place

On May 18, Early Wynn threw another complete game and the White Sox defeated the Washington Senators, 9–2, at Griffith Stadium. He gave up only five hits and two runs to raise his record to 6–2. Not that many people in Washington, D.C., cared. Paid attendance was only 3,995.

Fans in Chicago were much more interested in the result because the victory moved the White Sox into first place in the American League for the first time since the first week of the season. The ascension didn't last, but it showed that the White Sox might be sticking around for a while near the top of the standings. The Indians reclaimed first place a day later, but the developments to that point in the season certainly indicated that Al Lopez was correct and that the Yankees could be beaten. On May 19, the Yankees were 12–18 and in seventh place.

Wynn was looking like his old, formidable self. Bob Shaw was picking off wins here and there and the bullpen looked tough. Owner Bill Veeck wondered if it was tough enough. He had the fanciful notion of bringing in a free agent to bolster the pen.

One of Wynn's favorite players — and one of the greatest pitchers of all time — was Satchel Paige. Paige had been discriminated against throughout his youth, banned from opportunity in the majors because he was black. He was the best-known African-American player in the country, the star of the Negro Leagues and numerous barnstorming tours, as well as a dominant pitcher in Latin American winter ball.

When Veeck mulled his plan to buy the Philadelphia Phillies and stock the roster with all-star-caliber black players, Paige was at the top of his list. When he bought the Cleveland Indians Veeck signed Paige as a reliever and Paige became the first African-American to pitch in the World Series. When Veeck assumed control of the St. Louis Browns, Veeck hired Paige there, too. With both clubs Paige played excellent ball and made the All-Star team, too.

Now, when the White Sox seemed to need one more bullpen hurler, Veeck thought of Paige again. One problem was that Paige was 53 years old (probably, since his date of birth was always murky). A second problem was that Lopez did want not Paige on his team because he thought he might disrupt chemistry with his habits of turning up late for meetings and buses and disappearing for a day here and there. Veeck told Lopez he was sure Paige would do fine. Lopez told Veeck he would rather not take the chance that Paige would revert to some of his old ways.

Veeck was the boss and he had the power to force Paige on Lopez, but he wouldn't do it. He respected Lopez's authority and judgment and didn't want to rock the boat. "I felt Satch would help us," Veeck said of the seemingly ageless pitcher. "I knew he'd help us at the gate. But Al wants only the players who catch every plane and meet every roll call, and Satch wasn't a particularly good bet to catch the next street car."[1]

Much later Lopez said that just a couple of years earlier, when another close friend, the star player Hank Greenberg, was general manager of the Indians, Greenberg tried to sell him on Paige, too. At the time Veeck was running the Miami Marlins minor-league club and Paige was torching the competition for him. Lopez said he had no doubt at all that Paige could still pitch in 1959 and could help his staff, but he was wary about his individual style. "I can't put up with that stuff where he'll show up whenever he feels like it. You gotta think about the morale on the club."[2]

So Satchel Paige was not riding to the rescue in Chicago, nor, as it turned out, was there any need for a rescue. Bob Shaw, Turk Lown and Gerry Staley had everything under control and when Shaw became a starter Lown and Staley just shouldered the work load.

Shaw was a revelation. After his years of frustration in Detroit, when Shaw got a chance he showed that was worthy of the confidence he had. He got better and better and by the first week in June he had five wins. Shaw had done his homework assigned by Lopez and pitching coach Ray Berres, and when the tutors realized the pupil had soaked up their messages and applied his learning successfully, they turned him loose.

On May 13, Shaw beat the Red Sox, 4–0, on a five-hit shutout. "Bob really showed me something," Lopez said. "He was like an old pro out there. He had wonderful poise and he really convinced me he knows how to pitch."[3] That was the turning point. As soon as he could work it out after that Lopez made Shaw a full-time starter and he kept on winning.

Shaw was happy to be on a team not named Detroit. He was happier still when he became a key cog in the Chicago rotation. As the season wore on it became apparent that although the White Sox had many parts in place to win, they were not going to win with the long ball. All of the talk about relying on pitching, fielding and running was coming true. The summer of 1959 was crammed to overflowing with one-run games for the Sox.

"That was a great bunch of guys and different personalities and I think one of the most exciting parts of it was that every game was exciting because it was either 1–0 or 2–1 or 3–2 or something like that," Shaw said. "So every game was sort of an exciting game because we didn't have much of an attack. We had good pitching and speed, so the games were close...."[4]

Throughout the spring and into the heart of the summer, the White Sox hovered just behind the Indians in the standings. As the schedule flew by it was clear just which team was going to provide the main opposition in 1959 and it was not the Yankees. "Cleveland was a tough team that year," center fielder Jim Landis said.[5]

The Yankees had always terrorized pitchers with the long ball and the Indians had their share of sluggers. The White Sox were slick manufacturers of runs. The Go-Go White Sox identity established years earlier by Minnie Minoso's boldness on the base paths still clung to the White Sox. Shortstop Luis Aparicio was the personification of that in 1959, en route to a league-leading 56 stolen bases.

In other ballparks the loudest cheers were for home runs. At Comiskey Park, the fans lapped up the excitement of the stolen base. The Sox' style of play inspired Al Trace, a former minor-league player, and his friend Walter Jagiello, to write a song that became the White Sox theme. It was called "Let's Go, Go-Go White Sox," and fans sang along for the first time in 1959. The lyrics in part went:

White Sox! White Sox!
Go-Go White Sox!
Let's go, Go-Go White Sox,
We're with you all the way!
You're always in there fighting,
And you do your best.
We're glad to have you out there in the Middle West![6]

Comiskey Park fans came to life when the song was played, often to help spark rallies. Although Bill Veeck didn't have anything to do with the creation of the tune, he knew a good thing when he saw it, recognized the song as free publicity and gave his blessing to it being played at the park.

Sometimes the White Sox positioned themselves for crucial runs after a single and a stolen base by Aparicio. Sometimes they put a man on third because he took an extra base with his speed on a hit to the outfield. One of the team's secret weapons in the effort to make runs out of nothing was third base coach Tony Cuccinello. He was responsible for assessing what was going on in the outfield when a ball was hit and the players relied on his judgment at third to either stop or keep on running. The White Sox philosophy was to keep on running, but it was up to Cuccinello to inform them whether they should keep running home.

In an August game when the White Sox and Indians were still at 0–0, Cuccinello saw Cleveland outfielder Minnie Minoso momentarily bobble a hit by Earl Torgeson. Trying to capitalize on the few-second advantage created, Cuccinello waved Jim Landis to the plate. Landis scored to make it 1–0 in a game that ended 2–0. "It's about time someone gave that guy out on the third base coaching line some credit," said Torgeson. "Tony's the best third-base coach I've ever seen. He's stolen at least three runs for us in recent games. A third-base coach, including Tony, seldom gets any credit. Most folks just think he's a part of the scenery."[7]

Early-season White Sox attendance reflected a certain indifference, with some games attracting less than 10,000 people. When the team began winning and Veeck began promoting, the crowds started showing up. Veeck invited all Chicago bartenders to come to a game for free and attendance was more than 20,000. However, the game against the Tigers was washed out after one inning. Both the Sox and Veeck stayed in there pitching. In 1950, before Frank Lane's rebuilding took hold, the Sox drew

781,330 fans in a 72-game home season. In 1959, the White Sox drew a team record 1,423,144. That was third best in the league. Chicago had something to root for and fans came out to cheer.

"The fans were tremendous," said Turk Lown. "They treated us just fabulous. They were really ready for something special."[8] Forty years of wandering in the desert since the Black Sox scandal had whetted the thirst of White Sox fans.

Lown had been an artist of sorts since he was young. He loved to draw and he kept up the hobby even while making his living as a pitcher. He was fascinated with Early Wynn because of the length of his career and how in 1959 the 39-year-old was ignoring age and recapturing his youth with great efforts. Lown admired Wynn's mean streak, too. He remembers a batter on another team standing in the on-deck circle trying to time Wynn's pitches with the swing of his bat and Wynn frowning on the practice. "He threw the ball at him and tried to knock him down," Lown said.

Wynn's one concession to age was pitching fewer complete games. Even though he led the American League with 37 starts that season he finished just 14. Many times Lown was called from the bullpen for long relief of Wynn. "I drew a picture of Early and he signed it for me," Lown said. "He wrote on it how I helped him with how many games I saved for him. All the other ballplayers signed it, too."[9]

The White Sox stayed right on the Indians' tail as May ran out and June started. On June 3, the White Sox topped the Baltimore Orioles 6–1 and moved into a tie for first place with Cleveland. Billy Pierce got the win. The next day's game, also against Baltimore, was an epic. Attendance was terrible, just 3,514 in the house at Comiskey to watch a first-place club, proving that Veeck had plenty of promotional work still ahead of him.

Dick Donovan got the start for Chicago, but could not hold a 2–0 first-inning lead. The game was knotted at 4–4 after nine innings and then all of the bats shut down until the 13th inning when each side scored one run apiece. When Al Lopez sent Bob Shaw into the game in the 13th, he was on his sixth pitcher. Shaw stayed till the end, hurling five innings in a 17-inning effort that concluded when Earl Torgeson smacked a solo homer in the bottom of the inning.

The win gave the White Sox a half-game lead in first place. Chicago remained in first through June 14, though never by more than one-and-a-half games. On that day, the Sox swept a doubleheader from the Orioles. Wynn upped his record to 9–4 in the opener while cracking four hits and scoring three runs. Chicago was 33–25 and feeling pretty good.

But then the Sox were wiped out by the Yankees in three straight on their way to a five-game losing streak that bunched up the standings and sent them reeling into fourth place briefly. At that moment, the Sox were just 33–30 and did not look like a pennant winner.

Veeck was worried about the hitting and did not believe the team could capture the flag without some slugging help. Veeck had been hot after first baseman Roy Sievers at least since early in the season when a trade offer he made to the Senators' Calvin Griffith became public. Veeck sought to obtain Sievers, pitcher Pedro Ramos and catcher Clint Courtney for $250,000 and players from the White Sox whose names did not leak out. Washington turned him down.

Sievers was an All-Star and a past American League home-run champ, clouting 42 in 1957 when he also led the league in RBIs. But he played in just 115 games that season and had an off year, so it is unclear just how much help he would have provided if Veeck acquired him. Veeck kept sweet-talking Griffith about Sievers, but was not hesitant to look elsewhere. Veeck enjoyed the give-and-take of trading as much as Frank Lane did.

Veeck could live on the telephone for hours at a time. He would have been the first person in the United States to embrace the technological breakthrough of the cell phone. Veeck could talk deals all night long, but he also liked to act in person. At an off-season baseball gathering once he set up a table in the lobby of the hotel and put up an "Open for Business" sign signaling his willingness to trade.

On May 1, less than a month into the season, Veeck swapped pitcher Don Rudolph (he of the strip-teasing wife) and infielder Lou Skizas to the Cincinnati Reds for Del Ennis. This seemed like a good idea at the time. Ennis was acknowledged as an excellent hitter and was a three-time All-Star outfielder with the Philadelphia Phillies. Only Ennis was so close to the end of the line that he stepped over it with the White Sox. Ennis hit .219 in 26 games with Chicago and then retired. Veeck earned points for trying, but he did not truly bolster the team's weak hitting.

Ennis turned 34 on June 8 and Veeck sent him a belated birthday card — and his release notice — a week later. "It wasn't what you would call a surprise," Ennis said. "They were keeping me on the bench and playing a left-hander out there. And there were rumors I was going to be traded to Washington. That would have been the end. I would have quit. There's got to be a limit to handing a man down like he was an old, patched suit."[10] Ennis retired anyway to operate his bowling alley.

On May 3, Veeck swapped Ray Boone to the Kansas City A's for much-traveled and appropriately nicknamed Harry "Suitcase" Simpson. Simpson, who played for five major-league teams in his eight-season career (some of them twice), brought his suitcase and bat to Chicago. In 1956, Simpson's one All-Star season, he led the league with 11 triples. Simpson lasted with the White Sox longer than Ennis, but not that much longer.

Simpson did make a splash on June 27, however, when the Sox broke a four-game losing streak to the Yankees, 5–4. Simpson smashed a grand-slam homer off Bob Turley in the bottom of the eighth inning for the winning runs. The timely blow gave Shaw his sixth victory.

The forever search for more hitting provided occasional opportunities for outfielder Jim McAnany, who did not hit a single home run, but did bat .276 in 67 games. McAnany seemed worth a risk since he had batted .400 at Class A Colorado Springs the season before when he also played a few games for the Sox. The team brought him up from Indianapolis in the American Association in June where he was hitting .315 after Ennis was set free and an ill Johnny Callison was sent down to regain lost weight. McAnany was just shy of 23 and felt very young on a team with many veterans. McAnany made his major-league debut on June 28 in right field. He went 1-for-4 at the plate, but in the second inning, he made a sharp throw to home to nip Bill Skowron. At the time it was 0–0.

"I got off to a good start," McAnany said. "With Al Lopez being the manager, if I didn't get off to a good start, I probably wouldn't have been there much longer. He was a veteran manager with an older group. I'm not sure that he had much patience with younger kids. From what I heard, Chuck Comiskey was my advocate when they were trying to trade for an outfielder. He said, 'Why make a trade? Why don't you go there (Indianapolis)? Let's see what happens.' It was exciting to be there with a contending team, but you know, when you are a young player, you don't think about those things." McAnany was preoccupied with staying on the team.[11]

So was J.C. Martin, at the time a first baseman with some possibilities at third, but he was less successful. Martin was in spring training and he got into three regular-season games, but as a rookie he could not stay in the mix on the field. He was 22, and considered one of the futures, not a guy to be counted on during a pennant race. He did end up as a longer term teammate with most of the '59 regulars before eventually being sent to the minors to learn how to catch.

Martin was more of an outside observer that season. "It was exciting in one way," Martin said of 1959, "but in another way I was far away from it. I was signed with them, but I was not at the party for most of the season. I came up after they clinched the pennant. I got a taste of what the atmosphere was like and what the big leagues were like. I played in Detroit and I got my first Major League hit off Pete Burnside."[12]

Like so many of the other White Sox, Martin reveled in watching Early Wynn on the mound that season, both his success and his demeanor. "He was one rough customer," Martin said. "He hated that (anyone who hit through the middle) with a passion. I hit off him in spring training when he threw batting practice and he would just lay it in there for you to hit. At that time I didn't know the 'Early Rules.' On my last swing I hit a shot back through the middle. Instead of him leaving he pitched all of the way around the group to get to me one more time. Then he just knocked me right down on the ground. As soon as that happened he walked off the mound. He was really one rough dude." Just watching Wynn throw, Martin understood how he lasted so long in the majors. His form put no strain on his body. "He was just so fluid with his motion," Martin said.[13]

The dusting was a welcome-to-the majors moment for the rookie. Later in the season, when the White Sox were visiting Boston, Martin was at his locker in the clubhouse when Wynn trundled in carrying a pile of packages. He had gone clothes shopping and apparently got several bargains. He barely knew Martin, but he immediately offered him gifts.

"I'm sitting there at my locker and he walks over and he goes, 'Hey, you, do you need any clothes?'" Martin recalled. "I said, 'No, I'm OK, Early.' And he goes, 'Well I got some good deals today. Here, take a look at them. If you can use any of this stuff, help yourself.'" Martin was from a small town in Virginia, a Southern boy with a thick accent, and a tendency to wear overalls or shorts rather than formal attire. Wynn began unwrapping packages and he showed Martin some alligator shoes and silk ties. "He said, 'Get two or three of these silk ties.' I said, 'Well, Early, I don't think they'll go with these blue jeans.' He had the same size foot as I did and offered me a pair of shoes. 'You want a pair of these alligator shoes, just help yourself.' What the devil would I do with alligator shoes? I didn't have anything to go with alligator. He was one friendly guy until he got on the field. When he got on the field, he was nasty."[14]

Martin was at the beginning of a 14-year major-league career, but was too raw to help the White Sox much that season.

One player that had grown into his role, overcoming the inexperience of two seasons earlier, was Jim Landis. Lopez had stuck with Landis when he was floundering at the plate and Landis paid him back with a .270s year in 1958 and a similar showing in 1959. He was never going to be a slugger (Landis hit 50 home runs in his 11-year career), but no one ever worried about his defense.

The White Sox battled the Indians and the team made it clear it was going to stay in the hunt for the pennant, but Landis said that the most satisfying thing of all was just how tight the club was. Large groups left the hotel together to eat on the road and families shared time during homestands. The players were friends as well as teammates.

"A great group of guys," Landis said. "Maybe seven or eight guys would go out and have dinner together. Even when we were home at least five couples would go out to eat. It was just tremendous that way. I tell people my greatest feeling in 1959, more than anything else, was the people who played for that ball club. That's my favorite thing."[15]

For Bill Veeck, for Al Lopez, for many players, and for those in the stands, their favorite thing was how the White Sox performed during the second half of the season.

18

The Promised Land
at Last

The White Sox spent 12 days in first place between June 3 and June 14, but then fell behind the Indians again until July 14. On both occasions, Billy Pierce victories pushed the club into the American League lead.

Chicago dropped to second for a couple of days near the end of July, but on July 28 another timely triumph by Pierce, 4–3, over Ralph Terry and the Yankees, shot the White Sox into first once more. New York was always a good draw at Comiskey Park and 43,829 fans showed up that day.

The winning runs scored in the bottom of the eighth when outfielder Al Smith slugged a two-run blast over the left-field wall with Nellie Fox on base. At the end of that day's play, the White Sox record was 57–40, and they had a half-game lead over the Indians in the standings. What no one would have guessed at the time was that the White Sox were in first place to stay and that no AL team would get any closer all season.

The White Sox ended July and began August with a five-game winning streak. The Sox did not go on an unreal tear, but had five different winning streaks of at least three games during that month. A lot had happened during the heat of the summer. If anyone needed one of Bill Veeck's ballpark showers it was the team, but they didn't have any desire to cool off.

Bob Shaw, who began the season in the bullpen, had become the second man in the starting rotation behind Early Wynn. He was on his way to an 18–8 record. The highlight of the regular season for Shaw — and the turning point for Chicago — arrived simultaneously in the closing days of August when the White Sox traveled to Cleveland for a four-game series.

The White Sox arrived for the set in Ohio leading the American League by one and a half games.

Shaw was the winner, 7–3, in the opener. Dick Donovan followed with a 2–0 victory. Wynn captured the next game, 6–3, for his 17th win of the year. And Barry Latman won the fourth game, 9–4. Game, set, match. As August ended, the Sox record was 80–49 overall and they were in first place by five and a half games. The Sox pretty much had drowned the Indians' hopes in Lake Erie.

There were 70,398 fans at Cleveland Stadium for Shaw's game and he loved the atmosphere. "My god, I don't know whatever it was, 70,000 or so," he said. "I started on the Friday night. We won four in a row and that was a really big boost for us. I thought that was the climax of the season. They were kind of chasing us and my game was a big game to win. After that we just kept rolling."[1]

The sweep made a powerful statement, but it clinched nothing for the White Sox. Fans long deprived of a winner, though, were too impatient for a formal pennant clinching to let their heroes know how they felt. On the night of August 30, the White Sox flew back to Chicago ready to continue play with a game against the Detroit Tigers.

To the players' astonishment, they were greeted at Midway Airport by thousands of exuberant fans chanting for them. Some estimates ranged as high as 10,000 as to how many fans overwhelmed the airport. The reception was totally unanticipated. Fans dashed onto the tarmac and circled the plane. One banner read "Welcome Home Champs." "It was a heck of a crowd," outfielder Jim Landis said. "After we got off the plane, we didn't hurry home to our apartments, let's put it that way."[2]

One huge personnel adjustment had occurred just before the start of the Indians' series. Bill Veeck had never ceased searching for a power hitter to complement the Go-Go White Sox. On August 25, the White Sox traded Harry Simpson, whose suitcase was presumably already packed, and a minor leaguer named later, to the Pittsburgh Pirates for first baseman Ted Kluszewski. The White Sox sorely needed the wallop and "Big Klu" advertised his muscles by cutting off the sleeves of his shirt. Big bat, big biceps, that was Ted Kluszewski, who as a bonus was also a local guy from Argo, Illinois.

Kluszewski, about to turn 35, was on the downside of a solid career that saw him lead the National League in home runs (49) and RBIs (141) for the Cincinnati Reds in 1954 and four times be named an All-Star. He had not shined as brightly with the Pirates in recent play, but he seemed like the perfect prescription for the White Sox's only illness. The powerfully built 6-foot-2, 240-pound Kluszewski became an All-Big Ten football end at Indiana University after two years of working at a factory after high school and when he switched to baseball full-time his physique stood out. He joined the Reds in 1947 and various sportswriters or headline writers had called him "Baseball Hercules" or "The Sleeveless Slugger."

In the early 1950s, Leo Durocher, then managing the New York Giants, was raving about how mighty Dodger first baseman Gil Hodges was, calling him the strongest man in the world. Durocher was interrupted by a newsman who said, "What about Ted Kluszewski?" Durocher fired back, "Kluszewski? Well, that's different. Kluszewski ain't human."[3]

Early in his career, Big Klu had been somewhat clueless fielding around the first base bag. Hall of Famer Bill Terry said, "The way that boy fields he'll have to hit .400 to stay in the big leagues."[4] But Kluszewski fielded thousands of grounders hit to him by then-coach Tony Cuccinello and became more graceful. Conveniently, Cuccinello was in the dugout with the 1959 Sox, too, and could speak up for his man.

Evidence that Big Klu was a true Chicagoan was his participation in 16-inch softball as a youth, the most popular type of the game played in the Windy City. His wife Eleanor was a softball player, too, and any time Kluszewski fell into a slump she filmed movies of his stance and they worked on his form together to snap it. "As soon as we ran the movies," Kluszewski said of one early-career hitting funk, "I was able to correct the mistake."[5]

Kluszewski made his White Sox debut on the day of the trade, pinch-hitting in a game against the Boston Red Sox. Ironically, Kluszewski did not record an extra-base hit among his first 13 hits for Chicago, leading him to joke, "What am I, a singles hitter?"[6] Not long after he made the comment, Kluszewski hit a home run against the Kansas City Athletics and drove in five runs.

The main reason Kluszewski had been available to the White Sox was diminished production at the plate stemming from a back injury slow to heal when he was still with the Reds. Off-season swimming helped rebuild his back heading into the 1959 season with the Pirates. But Pittsburgh also had the similarly talented Dick Stuart and they didn't need both Big Klu and Big Stu. "I wound up with the White Sox, which certainly was a break for me," Kluszewski said.[7]

For those who always wondered, Kluszewski did not slice off his sleeves just to be a show off. He said it was all about comfort. "They could never make a uniform for me that would give me enough room," he said. "So one day I just took a pair of scissors and cut the sleeves off."[8]

Kluszewski got rolling in the American League and the White Sox kept rolling. One of the traditional demarcation points of the baseball season has always been where teams stand in the standings on Labor Day with the end of the regular season in sight. On September 7, the day Big Klu exploded, the White Sox swept Kansas City and very much liked their four and a half game lead in first place. "This was a big day for us," outfielder Jim Rivera said. "It puts the pressure on them (the Indians). We don't have to look back over our shoulder and wonder how they're doing. All we've got to do is keep winning and they won't be able to catch us."[9]

The White Sox did keep winning. On September 12, Early Wynn won his 20th game of the season, holding the Orioles to seven hits and one run in a complete-game 6–1 victory in Baltimore. It was Wynn's first 20-game season since 1956 and he was coming off two straight seasons when his record was just under .500. Few would have predicted the level of his dominance in 1959. "In 1959, he just had a great year," Billy Pierce said.[10]

Wynn was on his way to a 22–10 final record with a 3.17 earned run average in 37 starts. He also threw a league-leading 255 and two thirds innings and won the Cy Young Award. "Early would beat you one way or the other," Turk Lown said. "Any way he could beat you, Early would beat you."[11]

As genial as he usually was with his teammates, Wynn could still display signs of grumpiness, especially after a tough loss. Following one of those games, Wynn boarded the team plane in a bad mood. He sat in his seat trying to read a book, but couldn't concentrate. When he noticed players laughing and drinking beer in the rear seats it violated his sense of propriety. He felt they should be mourning.

Wynn arose from his seat, stomped to the rear of the plane, and smacked the beer cups flying. "Dammit," he said. "I'm trying to win a pennant. If you so-and-sos don't give a damn, all right, but don't laugh where I can hear you."[12] The laughter subsided, and dammit, Wynn did pitch them to a pennant.

It was a fabulous season for Wynn, pleasing in its unexpectedness, and it put him in demand among sportswriters. He eventually co-authored a magazine piece with esteemed baseball writer Roger Kahn in which he discussed his "secrets." Perhaps the most telling thing in the story was Wynn saying how after more than 20 years in the majors "it still scares me every time I go to the mound." With 20–20 hindsight Wynn questioned his use of the word "scares," but did not suggest an alternative.

At that point in his career, he threw a knuckleball, a curveball, slider and fastball, Wynn noted. "I try to throw every pitch with the same motion," he wrote. "The curve, the fastball and everything else should look the same until the ball leaves the pitcher's hand. Sometimes when I make a bad pitch — a pitch to the wrong spot — the speed still fools the hitter. He was expecting it to be faster or slower. This is a small edge, but it's important."[13]

Wynn fooled plenty of batters that season, even coming in to hitters with a high slider on 3-and-2, counter to all accepted wisdom. "That's not where you want to pitch it, but that's where Early threw it," J.C. Martin said. "People just swung through it. He was the best pitcher in the world to throw high strikes. But every hitter he went to 3-and-2. I'm telling you, he went the limit every time. It was the craziest thing, but that's how he pitched. There was no working with Early. He threw what he wanted to. He changed signs all the time. If it was one out he went with one pitch and if it was two out he went with another pitch and rubbed his jersey with his glove. If he rubbed his pants, it subtracted the first one. The first game I caught him I had no idea what he was throwing."[14]

Wynn was not above taking advantage of the gullibility of young White Sox players just brought up from the minors, as Martin was in September. Wynn would hang around the batting cage, waving a big bat, spy a potential mark and yell, "Come here, I've got a story I want to tell you!" The player came over, as ordered, Wynn would begin talking, and he punctuated sentences of the story with taps on the player's leg with his big bat. "Everybody would gather around and he would start hitting you on the shin," Martin said. "He was telling this story, but he was beating you to death with the end of the bat on the shin. That was the punch line of the whole thing. He had been telling other people, 'Watch this. Watch this.' I saw guys literally dancing from being hit on the shin bone, but still listening to the story he was telling. It only took one time and you learned very quickly. So he would have to get some other unsuspecting soul. Everybody would be watching and he'd be plink, plink, plink hitting the guy on the shin bone as he listened to this stupid story."[15]

Wynn was always terrific at keeping opposing hitters loose with his Burma shave pitches, but he also contributed to his own team's loose attitude with ploys like that. There was no doubt, however, that his contributions on the field were monumental to the Sox pennant run in 1959. Billy Pierce has no hesitation in saying that if Wynn had merely won the same 14 games he had the two seasons before, the season would have turned out differently. "We probably would have ended up in second place," Pierce said.[16]

Appropriately, the regular season culminated in a Wynn game against the Indians in Cleveland on September 22. Old Gus started for the White Sox against Jim Perry before 54,293 fans. The White Sox scored two runs in the third and two in the sixth in a 4–2 triumph. The key hits in the third were doubles by Luis Aparicio and third baseman Billy Goodman, the one-time American League batting champ for Boston who platooned at third base with Bubba Phillips that season. Al Smith and Jim Rivera each hit a solo homer for the runs in the sixth.

Wynn pitched five and two-thirds innings for the victory, but he needed considerable relief help. Shaw pitched two and two-thirds innings, but when he departed in the ninth he left right-hander Gerry Staley with issues. There was one out, but the Indians had the bases loaded following singles by Jim Baxes, Jack Harshman and Jimmy Piersall when Staley took the mound to face dangerous Vic Power.

It may have been the most critical outing of Staley's career. Like several of the Sox players he had been in the big leagues for a long time while experiencing limited team success. He badly wanted to go to a World Series. The White Sox were holding a three and a half game lead over Cleveland with four games to play. If they lost this game the battle would drag on through the final days of the season. If they won this game they owned the pennant.

170

Staley reared back and fired to the plate. Power swung. He tapped a ground ball to Aparicio. The shortstop fielded it neatly, stepped on second base for one out and threw cleanly to first for a double play. One pitch. Game over. The White Sox win the pennant! There was silence in Cleveland and bedlam in Chicago.

The White Sox hugged and screamed in the visitors' clubhouse. They were as enthusiastic as children, for many realizing a long-held dream. "This is my biggest thrill in 13 years of baseball," Staley said. "This is it. The biggest moment I've ever had. I've never felt better."[17]

Jim McAnany was a rookie surrounded by many long-time major leaguers and he was stuck by how much the moment of clinching the pennant meant to them. "When we wrapped it up in Cleveland that night, that was really excitement," McAnany said. "The veterans really let loose. You could see how happy they were to have played the game for so many years and finally win a pennant, especially since it was the first time in 40 years that the White Sox had won a pennant."[18]

It wasn't only veteran players reveling in the scene and young players marveling over it. Manager Al Lopez had spent the decade of the 1950s chasing the demon Yankees and trying to beat out the best of the American League. He had done it once before with his 1954 Indians team, but despite apparently having the goods, he had been unable to bring the White Sox to the top of the standings. Now it was unreal. After game tries in recent years, the Sox were pennant winners. "We finally won it!" We finally won it!" Lopez repeated in the clubhouse.[19]

The White Sox limited their drinking in Cleveland, but their chartered plane was well-stocked with the champagne champions use to toast one another. During the 400-mile flight home they imbibed, laughing, telling stories, congratulating one another. They still faced a three-game series with the Tigers, but it didn't mean much anymore. If they wanted to stay up all night partying, they could. The players just didn't expect that they would.

Not until they landed in Chicago, that is. The long-deprived fans of the White Sox, tossing off the burden of 40 years of losing, near-misses, and disappointment, had no intention of getting a good night's sleep. As soon as the White Sox clinched in Cleveland, fans poured out of their homes, started dancing in their yards and celebrating with their neighbors. Some made for Midway Airport. Some headed for the downtown Loop. This was to be a shared celebration, not a solitary one. The crowds descending on Midway the first time proved to be a dry run for a second welcome bash. Again, it was estimated that perhaps 10,000 people came out, with another 25,000 downtown. The plane didn't arrive until about 2 A.M. Some players said they heard while on the plane that some people were waiting for them. Others said they had no idea anyone besides family was at the airport for their landing.

The strangest aspect of the entire affair was something that the players missed completely. As their plane was on its descent, the city of Chicago was ordered to set off its air-raid sirens by Fire Commissioner Bob Quinn. Richard J. Daley was mayor and he was a life-long White Sox fan. There was no happier fan than Daley and he wanted to start spreading the news of the Chicago pennant.

Just days earlier, the City Council had passed a resolution in anticipation of the White Sox triumph during which it trumpeted the sounding of all manner of celebratory noise-makers from bells to whistles. Although air-raid sirens were not specifically included, Daley essentially said they were covered. Not everyone responded to the sirens' blare so sanguinely (perhaps they were Chicago Cubs fans irritated because their sleep was interrupted). Citizens by the hundreds telephoned television and radio stations and newspapers to find out if the Soviet Union was invading. They feared that war had been declared by USSR premier Nikita Khrushchev on the U.S., not by the White Sox on the American League. Some were quite angry at the mayor, but he brushed them off.

One of those affected by the sirens when she was 11 years old was future long-time White Sox organist Nancy Faust. She grew up in Chicago and on the night the Sox clinched in 1959, her grandparents, who were from Sweden, were babysitting her. Faust was actually taking a bath when the sirens wailed and her grandparents were not savvy about what they meant.

"They were from a foreign country," Faust said, "and we didn't know what was going on. We had no clue. My folks weren't home. So I called my aunt's and uncle's house. I always had a fear of the Cold War. I used to say, 'Mom, can we move to Sweden so we don't get radiation from being bombed?' I grew up paranoid about that kind of stuff. We had all those drills in school with the duck-and-cover. When I heard those sirens I thought, 'Oh, no, this is the big one.' I called my aunt and uncle and they were White Sox fans and they said, 'Oh, we're over here celebrating because of the White Sox.' Then everything was OK. But my parents always felt so bad that they weren't home to comfort me at a horrible time."[20] Faust ended up working for the White Sox for decades and she later learned it was not a horrible time for White Sox fans.

Warned or not, the players were astounded by the Midway turnout. Jim McAnany said it was overwhelming. "It was hard to believe, you know?" he said. "You dream about those things, but you never think they'll become reality. It was a big deal (to win the pennant). It had been so long. I was just happy to be part of it."[21]

Between enjoying the biggest win of his professional life and drinking champagne on the plane, outfielder Jim Landis felt a bit of a glow from the evening's entertainment. On the flight home he never thought about what was going on in Chicago. "My mind was still in heaven from what happened," he said of beating the Indians. He stepped off the plane and was confronted with a mob scene, Midway flooded with delirious fans. "I definitely was amazed," he said. "I didn't realize any of it was going to happen. I can't remember how long it took to get out of the airport. Honestly, my feeling was, 'I'm staying inside'. To me I was still in heaven."[22]

Thousands and thousands of people filled Midway to bursting, a crowd that actually was bigger than had attended some games at Comiskey Park that season. "We were all excited and exhilarated to see them in the wee hours of the morning," Bob Shaw said. "That was really a big turn-on."[23]

Everyone wanted a piece of the White Sox. The fans wanted to touch their heroes. Newspaper reporters and TV crews wanted to talk to them. Players' families and friends wanted to hug and kiss them. Even if it was for just this one moment in their lives, the players were elevated to pedestals, revered as the most important people in the world. The scene was dizzying, so much so that Jim Rivera, for one, left the airport without remembering to pick up his suitcase. "We took off from the plane and we couldn't get through the fans it was so crowded," Rivera said. "Some of the guys forgot their luggage. I was one of them. We were signing autographs. The newspaper people were there. The photographers."[24]

No one truly knows how many thousands of Chicagoans went public with their partying that night. "I've heard people say 50,000," Billy Pierce said. "But you don't know. I'll tell you, there were people all over the place. There were just people, people, people." There was a plan to take the White Sox players out of Midway by bus, but the bus was surrounded and fans started rocking it. Pierce got off the bus with Earl Torgeson and escaped from the airport by taxi cab. The cab took the players along Garfield Avenue and at 2 A.M. there were people outside on their lawns lighting off flares. "I'll never forget that ride," Pierce said.[25]

Nobody who saw it ever forgot the ride the White Sox took them on in 1959, either. Vindication had been 40 years in the making.

19

Welcome to the World Series

Forty years had passed since the disgrace of the Black Sox scandal. Forty years had passed without a White Sox pennant. The fans, the team, the organization, were all jubilant that the wait was over. Just about everyone in any way connected with the notorious stink of the scandal had passed away and there was no nostalgia to link the 1919 White Sox with the 1959 White Sox.

For most, capturing the pennant was not about exorcising demons, but punctuating the end of a long drought. The White Sox were champions of the American League with a 94–60 record. They had vanquished the Cleveland Indians and New York Yankees and now the World Series was coming to town, the World Series was coming to Comiskey Park. None of the players, not even Early Wynn, had been born the last time the White Sox played in the World Series. "Forty years, you heard that a lot," outfielder Jim Landis said. "About how long it had been."[1]

Many members of the 1959 White Sox had lived through the rebuilding, had rolled with the frustrations of chasing the Yankees. Claiming the pennant and moving on to baseball's biggest stage was a special moment in their careers. "You felt numb and so happy and you said to yourself, 'We worked like hell all year and finally got paid off,'" Jim Rivera said.[2]

While Chicago, from Mayor Richard J. Daley and his air-raid sirens on down, glowed with anticipation, the White Sox did not know who the opponent would be. Their season was finished, but the National League pennant was not decided. In 1957 and 1958, the Milwaukee Braves were kings of the NL. In 1959, the battle for the flag ended in a regular-season tie between the Braves and the Los Angeles Dodgers. Each club was 86–68.

The even finish called for a best-of-three playoff and although the Braves featured Warren Spahn, Lew Burdette, Hank Aaron and Eddie Mathews, the Dodgers swept Milwaukee in two straight.

That showdown postponed the start of the World Series and years later Landis wondered if the White Sox' momentum had been stunted by the forced wait. "We were all hyped up and feeling, 'Let's go get 'em,'" Landis said. "Then we had to wait for the National League playoff. I think it took a little edge off us. I don't want to make an alibi, though."[3]

There isn't much tangible evidence to support Landis' thought, but there is no doubt something else bothered the White Sox a lot. They despised the Los Angeles Memorial Coliseum. Amidst much controversy, the Dodgers abandoned Brooklyn, their long-time home, for the West Coast after the 1957 season. There was no ready-made ballpark for them and during the years Chavez Ravine was under construction they played their home games at the Coliseum.

The Coliseum opened in 1923 and with its nearly 100,000 seats has primarily been a home for football, though it also hosted the opening ceremonies at the 1932 and 1984 Summer Olympics. It was not designed for baseball and to fit a diamond into the building's configuration took Walt Disney–like imagination. As a result, the left-field wall was just 251 feet from home plate. That was so close Little Leaguers could have hit home runs. So Commissioner Ford Frick ordered the Dodgers to add a screen to prevent routine pop-ups from counting as home runs. The screen was 43 feet high. Under the stadium-specific ground rules, cables, girders and towers were in play. And at various times of the day (and World Series games were still played during the day), the sun was brutal on the outfielders. The White Sox wondered if they were playing ball in a fun house.

"That was ridiculous," White Sox pitcher Turk Lown said of the Coliseum. It was also never said of the Coliseum when used for baseball that every seat in the house was a good one. The building was so large that some fans sat more than 700 feet from home plate. Lown said his wife and kids thought of taking in the California games and he said, "Hon, I don't know." When he got home, he told her, "It's a good thing you didn't." Lown said the visiting wives were so far north of the field they might as well have been in the North Pole. "They had the wives up so far they

176

couldn't even see who was playing, or what club was playing. It's huge. It's a football field."[4]

Wherever the Dodgers were playing their home games the 1959 event made history as the first California World Series.

The Dodgers were a formidable team. They had dominated most of the 1950s in Brooklyn and there was still some holdover talent under the direction of veteran manager Walt Alston. A young southpaw named Sandy Koufax was just beginning to come into his own after a few years of wildness. Don Drysdale was an anchor of the rotation. Duke Snider, the power-swinging outfielder, was still in the mix. All four of those men would be inducted into the Hall of Fame. Like the White Sox, the Dodgers also had significant speed on the bases with players like Maury Wills, Jim Gilliam and Charlie Neal and they won 33 out of 55 one-run games, similar to Chicago's 35 out of 50. And there were additional reliable hitters like veteran Gil Hodges, Wally Moon, an All-Star who led the league in triples and hit .302, and Carl Furillo, who dealt with injuries that season, but still batted .290.

This was not a team of no-names, but it was a team in recovery. The Dodgers had plummeted to seventh place in 1958 and they were written off for 1959. Roy Campanella, perhaps the best player in team history, was in a horrific automobile accident, was paralyzed, and never joined the team in Los Angeles. They broke in a new catcher, the fiery and determined Johnny Roseboro, and the pitching staff was in transition.

When the Dodgers out-lasted the Braves, 6–5, in 12 suspenseful innings to clinch the National League pennant the word "Cinderella" was bandied about. "You can win the easy way and you can win 'em the hard way," said Dodger owner Walter O'Malley, "but that doesn't satisfy the Dodgers. They've got to win 'em the Dodger way."[5]

Los Angeles celebrated the unexpected triumph loudly and with great energy. The players had made true believers out of their fans and when the club departed for Chicago to open the Series more than 3,000 saw them off at the airport. The only question despite the euphoria was how much energy the Dodgers had saved for a swift turn-around meeting with the Sox. Were they mentally drained after disposing of the two-time league champ Braves?

It definitely looked it when the Series opened. Chicago was in a festive mood. The Sox were trying to claim their first world championship since 1917. Old Comiskey was dressed up with red, white and blue bunting, and the demand for tickets was off the charts. Paid attendance was 48,013 and the team could have sold twice as many seats. Owner Bill Veeck lamented having to refund $350,000 to ticket-buyers shut out. The atmosphere of a revved-up city infected the players.

"You see all of that going on and it's very exciting," said Billy Pierce, who was not in the starting rotation for the Series. "It's a big thrill for everybody, whether they're in the stands or they're playing on the field."[6]

Al Lopez decided on Early Wynn, Bob Shaw and Dick Donovan as his starters. Ted Kluszewski was the first baseman and Nellie Fox, Luis Aparicio and Billy Goodman rounded out the infield. Sherm Lollar was the catcher. The starting outfielders were Al Smith, Jim Landis and Jim Rivera.

Just hosting a World Series game at Comiskey Park already seemed surreal to White Sox fans after so long, and what happened in the first game on October 1 left them giddy.

Wynn was the ace of the staff after his 22–10 season and the big right-hander got the call for Game 1 against Los Angeles' Roger Craig, who had gone 11–5. At game time the temperature was 63 degrees and anyone in Chicago who did not make it into the ballpark was presumed to be watching the first color television broadcast of a Series with Chicago's Jack Brickhouse and Los Angeles' Vince Scully doing the talking. Businesses allowed employers to set up televisions to watch the games. When it came time for a ceremonial first pitch the team honored two 1917 heroes, pitcher Red Faber and catcher Ray Schalk. When a highlight film was made of the Series, Scully narrated and before play began he said, "It's a great day for White Sox followers whose wonderful loyalty has become a tradition of the game."[7]

The first pitch of the 1959 World Series was a strike to Dodger third baseman Jim Gilliam. Wynn looked big on the mound with his motion that threw both arms extended above his head each pitch. He raised his left foot as he threw, but the kick was not terribly high. The Dodgers did no damage.

The White Sox went ahead 2–0 in the bottom of the first, but exploded for seven runs in the third and added two more in the fourth.

They suffocated the Dodgers with an 11–0 lead that stayed at that score. Wynn got the win, going seven shutout innings and allowing just six hits while striking out six.

The big offensive gun was Kluszewski who hit two home runs and drove in five runs, though Landis had three hits. Kluszewski's was a remarkable slugging performance that brought fans at Comiskey to their feet more than once. It was a magical day for Big Klu, rescued from also-ran Pittsburgh late in the season and smacking the ball around for his hometown team in his first World Series game less than six weeks later. "It was the greatest thrill I ever had," Kluszewski said after the two-homer game. "I wasn't sure about that first one, but I knew I gave that second one a ride."[8]

Alston was caught off-guard by the White Sox' power prowess, expecting more of the station-to-station attack Chicago was famous for. "They told me about how fast the White Sox were," the Dodger manager said of the scouting report, "but they didn't tell me about all that power. They just beat the hell out of us."[9]

It definitely was a thumping, but what did it mean? Unlike National Hockey League playoffs and National Basketball Association playoffs where the teams' lineups are likely to be identical game-to-game, the huge variable in a baseball series is the pitching. The rest of the lineup may be the same, but depending on whom the pitcher is for each side, whether or not he is having a good day or not, whether or not he is a righty or lefty, changes everything.

Still, after clobbering the Dodgers 11–0 and going up a game, the White Sox felt great about themselves and the situation. "We thought we'd knock 'em out four straight," Rivera said.[10] At the least, the thrashing was a terrific confidence booster for the Sox. "Maybe we got too confident, huh?" Landis said. "I don't know really. It was a great moment. I'm proud to say it was my best game.[11] Most assuredly, it was the White Sox' best game of the Series and when it ended they felt they were on their way to the title, sweep or not.

"There's no question that Chicago was ready for that and very happy when that first ball game was so good," Pierce said. "Man alive. That was a crowning blow to win by that score with the home runs. It topped off the whole season. It was just too bad that things didn't progress that way."[12]

Not that the Sox had much time to reflect or celebrate. The second game was the next day, bringing another 47,368 to Comiskey, all hoping that their club could go up 2–0 in the Series. Bob Shaw was the starter for Chicago after his 18–8 season that put him third in the Cy Young Award voting. He went up against southpaw Johnny Podres, who had been the star of the Dodgers' 1955 World Series triumph in Brooklyn.

Nat "King" Cole sang the National Anthem on another 60ish day, but forgot some of the lyrics. U.S. Senator John F. Kennedy, on his way to the presidency the next year, was in attendance, hanging out with Mayor Richard J. Daley, the area's most prominent democrat. In November of 1960 it was said that Daley's "delivery" of Chicago's vote, real or imagined, put Kennedy over the top for his victory. This day, not even Daley could affect the outcome.

With two runs in the bottom of the first inning, Game 2 started much like Game 1. Only the Sox bats stalled there, instead of producing another seven-run rally. It was 2–1 after six innings, but the Dodgers reached Shaw in the top of the seventh. He did not make it out of the inning, replaced by Turk Lown. Los Angeles put up three runs to take the lead. The Sox retaliated with a run in the bottom of the eighth, but could muster no more.

The Sox' undoing was the surprisingly powerful bat of Los Angeles second baseman Charlie Neal. Normally just a so-so hitter, Neal had the best season of his eight-year career in 1959 with 11 triples, 19 home runs and 83 RBIs. The greatest single day of his baseball life, however, was probably October 2, 1959. He smashed two homers off Shaw, who discovered it was not wise to pitch Neal low-and-away. "When I pitched to him in the future," Shaw said, "I got him out consistently. He made himself into a World Series hero that day."[13]

One of the most memorable set of photographs in World Series history accompanied Neal's first home run in the fifth inning. Al Smith retreated to the left-field wall following the path of the ball. He stood at the base of the wall, looking up, as the ball landed barely into the seats. Also tracking the hit was a fan who reached for it while simultaneously hitting a cup of beer. The beer flowed downward in a stream, soaking Smith's head. The incident gained enormous publicity, especially when the Chicago Tribune printed an eight-picture sequence of the event. Initially,

Smith was furious because he thought a fan dumped on him on purpose. "At first I was angry because I thought somebody had thrown the beer at me," Smith said. "I was ticked. But the umpire down the left-field line told me what happened, that a fan had lost it trying to catch the baseball."[14]

The beer bath could have been taken as foreshadowing for what the Sox were about to endure. Their joy ride to the Series title ended in a 4–3 loss capped by the relief showing by the Dodgers' Larry Sherry. Sherry pitched three innings and surrendered one run for the save. Sherry, whose older brother Norm was a catcher with the Dodgers, made a few cameo appearances in 1958, but emerged as a key figure in the Los Angeles bullpen as the season wore on in 1959. Virtually unknown at season's start, Sherry finished 7–2 with seven saves and a 2.19 earned run average and flummoxed the Braves in a playoff game. By the end of the Series he would be one of the best-known players in baseball.

Sherry was born with club feet and as a baby had to undergo surgery, and then wear special orthopedic shoes. He still modified his spikes. Sherry became a better pitcher when he added a slider to his fastball and curve and he said that Norm was his inspiration. "No one worked harder with me than he did," Sherry said in an article he wrote. "Even when we were kids, we'd spend hours working together." Sherry said Norm kept after him to throw "just one more" pitch when he was tired and when he was on the mound against the White Sox when things got tough he heard Norm's voice saying, "just one more."[15]

The World Series makes heroes and creates goats. An even less likely star for the Dodgers was pinch-hitter Chuck Essegian, who hit the game-tying home run off Shaw in the seventh, a shot that was measured at 417 feet. Afterwards, Dodger Ron Fairly said, "The last time I saw Essegian hit a ball that far was a driving range."[16]

The Series moved to Los Angeles for the third game. Although no serious baseball fan was a fan of the Coliseum, its spacious interior allowed the championship-hungry Los Angeles ticket-buyers a better opportunity than would have been available anywhere else. Game 3, pitting Dick Donovan against the Dodgers' Don Drysdale on October 4, attracted an all-time Series record 92,394 spectators.

Donovan authored fine work, going six and two-thirds innings with just two runs allowed before being relieved by Turk Lown in a 3–1 loss. Drysdale pitched himself in and out of trouble constantly, giving up 11 hits and four walks in seven innings, but just a single run before Larry Sherry came in again. Sherry notched his second save of the Series, permitting one hit in two innings. The number of hits was testimony to the concentration of the hitters because they faced a sea of white shirts behind the pitcher on a sunny day. Perpetual squinting was necessary. Famed sports columnist Red Smith wrote about the difficulty of seeing balls hit in the air and Pierce said in warm-ups he was struck by how tough it was to keep your eye on the ball.

"I was out there shagging flies and you noticed it right away," Pierce said. "The sun was out and all of the people wearing white shirts made it very hard to pick up the ball in center field."[17]

The game was scoreless until the seventh inning, partially because Landis made a diving catch off a Gilliam swipe in the first. The White Sox left 13 men on base and Sherry induced Sammy Esposito to hit into a double play in the seventh with the bases loaded.

So the White Sox trailed two games to one, all of the confidence built in the first-game landslide dissipated. Game 4 was also in Los Angeles and it was an important one for Chicago. They sought to tie the Series and essentially start over. Early Wynn, it became known, had left Game 1 with a twinge in his throwing arm, but he pooh-poohed any effects before lining up to throw against Roger Craig again. "I can still feel the elbow," Wynn said, "but it's nothing. I've had this several times during the season, but never missed a start because of it. Old age, you could call it."[18]

The crowd of 92,650 broke the earlier-in-the-Series attendance record while watching the Wynn-Craig rematch. But Wynn did not have his usual stuff. His elbow might well have been bothering him. Wynn was hit hard, surrendering four runs on eight hits in two and two-thirds innings. Al Lopez had to sort out his pitching by committee the rest of the game. Pierce's showing was critical, hurling three innings of no-hit, no-run relief. Craig was just sharp enough to hang around a little longer than Wynn, through the seventh, but he also allowed four runs.

After Pierce's three-inning stint, Lopez called on Gerry Staley. In the bottom of the eighth inning, muscular Dodger first baseman Gil Hodges swatted a solo homer on a Staley sinker for the go-ahead run. "I knew it was gone when I hit it," Hodges said.[19] Sherry, relieving again, had taken over in the top of the inning. When he handcuffed the White Sox in the ninth, he and the Dodgers had a 5–4 victory. Sherry had two saves and a win as the Dodgers led by a demoralizing 3–1 count in games.

The fans just kept coming. Somehow the Dodgers figured out a way to cram a few more into the Coliseum each game. For Game 5, a chance to see Los Angeles become the first California team to clinch a World Series was part of the attraction and attendance hit 92,706. Strangely, in what was termed an effort to change their luck, the White Sox actually donned the black socks worn during regular-season play. The symbolism was intriguing, that they were casting doubt on any residual

An aerial view of the Los Angeles Coliseum during Game 5 of the 1959 World Series between the Los Angeles Dodgers and the Chicago White Sox. Built as a football stadium, the field was a temporary home for the Dodgers after their move West from Brooklyn. Its one major benefit was an ability to attract all-time Series record crowds of 92,000-plus fans. (National Baseball Hall of Fame Library, Cooperstown, New York.)

curse from the Black Sox scandal. "We thought we'd change the script," Lopez said.[20]

The pitching match-up was Bob Shaw against Sandy Koufax. Koufax was a bonus baby who had been trying to harness his blinding fastball and spike his wildness for a few seasons. No one realized that in seven years he would be acclaimed as one of the greatest pitchers of all time and retired at only age 30 because of elbow inflammation.

In 1959, Koufax was a periodic starter who recorded an 8–6 mark with a 4.05 earned run average. He was not yet the Sandy Koufax he would become, but in the World Series he was that future star, engaging in a compelling duel with Shaw. The Dodgers were out to win a championship. The White Sox were trying to survive. Both starters were dazzling. Shaw scattered nine hits over seven and one-third innings, yielded to Pierce for one batter, and watched Donovan finish up over one and two-thirds. Koufax went nine innings, struck out six, and gave up one run on five hits. The one run was just enough to beat him. It wasn't as if he was clobbered, either. Nellie Fox singled to right, went to third on a Landis single, and scored on a Sherm Lollar double-play ball. That was the day's offense, never enough to make the Sox feel comfortable.

There were times it seemed the White Sox might not make it beyond sundown. In the eighth inning, Landis, who hated the Coliseum, lost a ball in the sun. At the last second, he dropped into a squat, threw his glove up in front of his face, and had the ball land a couple of feet in front of him. Later he said the ball actually hit his toe.

"I had never played in a tougher ballpark," Landis said. "Both ways, especially for hitting and playing center field. Visualize, say, some 50 rows up and all you see is white shirts. It was so tough to pick up a ball. Plus the sun. I dropped that one in the sun."[21] But the miscue did not harm the White Sox.

In the Dodger seventh, Lopez made a strategic move in the field. He moved right-fielder Al Smith to left, removed rookie Jim McAnany, and inserted speedy Jim Rivera in right. Playing percentages, Lopez thought Charlie Neal might pull the ball to left. Instead, Neal nailed a pitch that sailed to deep right. Rivera turned and ran toward the Coliseum fence and willed the ball over his shoulder and into his glove. That preserved the Sox shutout.

Jungle Jim had survived the jungle of the Coliseum. Rivera remembered that when he played winter ball in Puerto Rico that Neal hit a lot of balls to right-center, so he shaded Neal a little towards center. "Sure enough he hit the ball where I was, but it was far and I had to run like hell to get it," Rivera said. "I didn't think I'd get it at first, but I finally did get it."[22]

The Dodgers still led 3–2 in games, but the White Sox were happy for the new life, particularly since they were headed back to Comiskey Park — and away from the Coliseum. "We're glad we're taking the Dodgers back to a legitimate ballpark," Wynn said.[23]

He was not alone in his analysis of the playing field. "Here (Chicago) the weather may be worse and the dough less, but the ballpark is built for baseball, not track and football," said St. Louis sports writer Bob Broeg. And certainly the confidence of the White Sox was higher, with Lopez saying, "We'll win now."[24]

Comiskey was not friendly enough and Lopez was wrong. The Sox did not win. They trotted out Gus one more time — he deserved it as the season-long ace — but Wynn's age or elbow or just the Dodger bats caught up to him. So clutch all season, Wynn could not perform one more time to keep the Sox alive to even the World Series. If Shaw-Koufax was a pitcher's duel, Game 6 was a hitter's duel.

Wynn was gone after three and one-third and surrendering five runs. A two-run homer by Duke Snider didn't help. When Lopez came to the mound to remove Wynn and send him to the dugout, the manager clapped his season's most reliable pitcher on the shoulder.

Donovan, the first reliever, didn't get an out and gave up three runs. Lown, Staley, Pierce and Ray Moore all did fine, but it was too late, despite the weak start for Los Angeles lefty Johnny Podres. Podres, who gave up three runs, and was also showering after three and one-third innings. The difference maker — once more — was Larry Sherry. Sherry pitched five and two-thirds innings, permitted four hits and no runs and earned his second win of the Series. He was chosen the Most Valuable Player and soon after the Series ended was appearing as a guest on the popular nationally televised variety show hosted by Ed Sullivan.

The final score was 9–3, despite the heartfelt swinging by Ted Kluszewski, who hit another home run and knocked in 10 runs in the series. When the field had cleared and the fans filed out of Comiskey Park quietly, the White Sox players lingered in the clubhouse. Wynn was forthright about his role in the loss. "I goofed it up good," he said. "I was trying to baffle 'em and it didn't work."[25]

In some ways, it was the greatest season of Early Wynn's career. He led a team all of the way to October, but in the end the White Sox couldn't overcome the best week of Larry Sherry's life. Still, the White Sox won a pennant, played in a World Series, and became one of the franchise's most popular teams of all time. They didn't so much erase haunting memories of the Black Sox scandal as they manufactured fresh, feel-good memories that endured in the hearts and minds of their fans.

20

Too Late for Early
and the Sox

The honors and respect Early Wynn earned in 1959 added a special glow to the sunset of his career. Wynn was the Cy Young Award winner when just one award was presented to the premier pitcher in baseball, not one Cy Young trophy to a player in each league. There was no reason, he thought, that 1960 shouldn't be the same, that as a 40-year-old he couldn't keep winning.

The White Sox, too. They captured that elusive pennant. Why couldn't they do it again a year later?

Old Gus was a year older, but maybe, just maybe, he was just as good. At the end of the 1959 season, Wynn had banked 271 wins. He began thinking he might be able to reach the magic number of 300. Yet the end was approaching faster than Wynn anticipated. The 22–10 triumph of 1959 signaled not that Wynn could last forever, but that he had had one last great year in his right arm.

In 1960, Wynn finished 13–12 with a 3.49 earned run average. Not bad. But by 1961, the sportswriters were saying that he was washed up and must retire. Wynn went 8–2 in limited action because of an elbow injury that truncated his season in July. "He says he'll be all right and I believe he will," White Sox manager Al Lopez said at the start of the 1962 season.[1] A solid victory in May was Wynn's first win in 10 months and when asked how he felt, he said, "Well, just say the old man isn't going to quit."[2] And then Wynn struggled to a 7–15 finish.

Time to go! Everyone shouted it. Wynn might have agreed this time, might have been willing to put his pitching career to rest, except for one factor. He owned 299 victories and he wanted one more. One loss charged to Wynn in 1962 occurred when the Red Sox' Bill Monbouquette beat him 1–0 on a no-hitter. Three times near the end of the season, Wynn went for the big one and did not get the win. One win for 300 — he had to have it.

On April 2, 1963, as the exhibition season was coming to a close, the White Sox made the unsentimental, harsh decision to cut Wynn loose one victory shy of the win total that would ensure baseball immortality. General Manager Ed Short made the call, telling Wynn, then 43, that the team had to go with young pitching and that he was free to make a deal for himself with another team. The announcement was made just after Wynn, who had a solid spring, pitched two-hit, shutout ball for four innings.[3] "The White Sox had promised me the chance to win the 300th," a disgruntled Wynn recalled years later."[4]

A month after his release, Wynn was still unemployed, waiting for a team in need of a pitcher to hire him. He threw batting practice and ran near his home in Venice, Florida, and hung out at the Early Wynn Steak House and Bowling Lanes. He was concerned that his long career would end on a sour note. "I'm thinking about going fishing," Wynn said.[5]

It took another month, but Wynn signed with the Cleveland Indians, his old team, on June 7. He worked out hard for two weeks and then manager Birdie Tebbetts gave him a start — against the White Sox. Chicago won, 3–0. "That was the one I would have liked to win it on," Wynn said.[6]

Wynn claimed his 300th victory on July 13, in the second game of a doubleheader in Kansas City. The Indians beat the A's, 7–4, before 13,565 fans. Wynn threw five innings and gave up six hits and four runs. He even had a hit in the game. At the end of the contest his record was 1–1 and his earned run average was 2.89. Wynn spent most of the rest of the season working in relief and retired at the end of the year with a mark of 300–244 spread over 23 years of big-league pitching.

"I thought I'd never win it," Wynn said of the 300th victory. "I made about seven or eight starts and was even used in relief, but somehow it always escaped me. I was ready to give up the chase, but Lefty Grove, who won 300 himself, urged me to keep trying. That figure 300 seems to be something special, and now that I have it, it is."[7]

There was no repeat American League pennant for the White Sox in

1960. In perhaps the biggest misjudgment of his career, owner Bill Veeck traded away most of his young talent to try to win immediately. The move backfired with an 87–67 third-place finish. The Yankees won the pennant again and the Baltimore Orioles took second.

Veeck bargained away the White Sox' future in a series of trades between December 1959 and April 1960. He sent Norm Cash, Johnny Romano and Bubba Phillips to the Indians, reacquiring Minnie Minoso. He sent Johnny Callison to the Phillies for Gene Freese. He traded Earl Battey and Don Mincher to Washington for Roy Sievers. And he shipped Barry Latman to the Indians for Herb Score.

Cash won the American League batting title for Detroit in 1961. Romano was a two-time All-Star for Cleveland. Callison played 16 years and was a three-time All-Star. Battey played 13 years and was a four-time All-Star. Mincher played 13 years and was a two-time All-Star. Latman had a 13-win season for the Indians, but Score never really recovered from his devastating injury when hit by a line drive.

The holdover veterans could not understand what Veeck was doing. "We lost a lot," pitcher Billy Pierce said. "It just didn't make sense to us. We couldn't figure it out. The team was getting older and the trades made us even older."[8]

In 1964, the White Sox won 98 games and finished one game behind the Yankees in the American League standings. One by one, the figures from 1959 retired or were traded.

Suffering from poor health, Veeck sold the team to a partner in 1961, but shocked the baseball world when he bought the team again in 1976 and kept it until 1980. Nancy Faust, the team organist since 1970, said she was anxious to meet Veeck when he assumed command again. "I knew of his reputation as being flamboyant and unconventional and I hoped that he felt I was unconventional enough to keep me," she said. "He was colorful. You never knew what to expect. There was always the surprise element that you never knew what the next promotion would be. I think he entertained himself with creating wacky entertainment. The fan came first. He was in the Chicago phone book and you could reach him at any hour at his home."[9] Faust was unconventional enough and Veeck did not trade her to Cleveland.

Al Lopez stepped down as manager in 1965, but returned for the 1968 and 1969 seasons before retiring to Tampa.

By January of 1965 when he was traded to Kansas City, Jim Landis was the only regular on the 1959 pennant winner still playing for the White Sox. A few players who made cameos during the championship season — J. C. Martin, Gary Peters, and Romano, who was reacquired — still wore White Sox uniforms. That was all.

For four seasons between 1959 and 1962, Peters was a yo-yo, pitching well for White Sox minor-league affiliates, going through spring training, being cut, and then being brought up at the end of the year for a very few appearances. During his September call-up of 1959, Peters felt a bit out of his depth. "I thought, 'I'll never make this club,'" he said. "It was like a big party all the time, though. The players, the people, the Sox fans, everybody was excited."[10]

It all changed for Peters in 1963. When the White Sox cut Wynn at the last minute in April of that year, they kept Peters for good. The southpaw compiled a 19–8 record and was Rookie of the Year.

At the end of the 1990 baseball season Comiskey Park closed after 80 years as the home of the White Sox. The next spring, a new, modern Comiskey Park (later called U.S. Cellular Field) opened across the street. Old memories were interred and new memories were created.

In 2005, the White Sox returned to the World Series for the first time since 1959. When the team won the championship it marked the first World Series triumph by the venerable franchise in 88 years, or since 1917. Al Lopez lived to see it. He was 97 years old and days after his old team defeated the Houston Astros for the title, he passed away.

In the 2000s, the White Sox retired several jersey numbers and stenciled pictures of some of their most famous and popular players on the left-field wall. Included among those players are Billy Pierce (No. 19), Luis Aparicio (No. 11), Minnie Minoso (No. 9) and Nellie Fox (No. 2). The club also began commissioning statues commemorating some of the team greats. Among those honored with statues of their likeness displayed on the center-field concourse are Pierce and Minoso, who in his 80s still works as a team ambassador, still dresses with the wardrobe flair he adopted in the 1950s and still drives a Cadillac. An action statue of Aparicio and Fox together, completing a double play, was also unveiled.

Veeck, Lopez, Aparicio, and Fox are all members of the Baseball Hall of Fame. So is Early Wynn, who was selected in 1972. His Cooperstown classmates were Yogi Berra, Sandy Koufax, Josh Gibson, Buck Leonard, Lefty Gomez, Will Harridge, and Ross Youngs.

As the years passed, more and more of the players who carried the White Sox to their 1959 pennant died, some well before their time. The White Sox were perhaps most shaken by the death from skin cancer at age 47 of Fox in 1975. "The docs had given up hope, but we were still wishing for a miracle," said Pierce when Fox died.[11] Fox was the American League Most Valuable Player in 1959, and thus, along with Wynn, the most recognized leader of the pennant-winner.

Catcher Sherm Lollar was just 53 when he died of a heart attack in 1977. By the time the 2009 season began, 50 years after the pennant celebration, Bill Veeck, Al Lopez, coaches Ray Berres and Tony Cuccinello, Ted Kluszewski, Al Smith, Billy Goodman, Norm Cash, Dick Donovan, Gerry Staley, Earl Torgeson, Bubba Phillips, Ron Jackson, Sammy Esposito, Ray Boone, Del Ennis, Johnny Callison, Don Rudolph, Ray Moore, Harry Simpson, Larry Doby, and Earl Battey also had died.

Billy Pierce still lived in the suburbs of Chicago. Jim Rivera was living in Indiana. Jim Landis and Jim McAnany were residents of California. J.C. Martin lived in North Carolina. Gary Peters and Bob Shaw were living in Florida. Turk Lown was living in Colorado.

Early Wynn threw no more after the 1963 season when he won his 300th game. In the following years he maintained a home in Florida where he kept his boat and a plane. He became the pitching coach for the Minnesota Twins and served as a broadcaster for the Toronto Blue Jays at a time in their history when the franchise had fewer wins than he did. He also lobbied vigorously for improved pensions for old-timers who made much less money than their modern-day counterparts.

During his Blue Jays radio days, Wynn offered some revisionist history about his reputation as a hard guy. "I wasn't really as mean as people made out to be," he said. Wynn also said it was a great pleasure to play for Bill Veeck and Al Lopez. "They were two of the most wonderful people I ever associated with in baseball and I was able to pitch for them twice (in Cleveland and Chicago)," he said.[12]

Wynn recalled what the evening was like after he notched his long-sought-after 300th win. It was the second game of a doubleheader in Kansas City and the Indians had a flight immediately after the series ended

In the summer of 2007, the White Sox unveiled a statue of Billy Pierce, the way the young pitcher looked when he was throwing for them in the 1950s. (Author's collection.)

that Sunday. Their next opponent was the Minnesota Twins and with a few days off guaranteed Wynn thought he would celebrate his achievement. Much to his surprise and dismay, finding a drink on a Sunday night in Minnesota was a tougher challenge than beating the Athletics.

"They had some sort of blue law in Minnesota that closed all the bars and liquor stores," Wynn said. "If there was ever a time a guy wanted to celebrate something over a couple of beers, that was it. I had waited so long to win my 300th game and now I had to wait another day to celebrate it, too."[13]

At the end of his life, Wynn was residing in an assisted living center in Venice, Florida. He suffered a stroke and died on April 4, 1999. He was 79 years old and a million miles in accomplishment from his days of picking cotton as an Alabama youth. The memorial service at the Ewing Funeral Home in Venice included The 23rd Psalm in the program honoring Wynn's life.

There is no statute of Early Wynn in Chicago. Nor is his White Sox jersey number retired. He did not have the length of service with the franchise that others did on that 1959 team.

But in a Hall of Fame career notable for victories and for longevity both, the greatest of Wynn's seasons was spent in a White Sox uniform. In 1959, he lifted the White Sox to their first pennant in 40 years and for that long, hot summer he was the most impressive pitcher in the world.

Epilogue
Fifty Years Later

On a cold January day in a downtown Chicago hotel function room, Billy Pierce, Jim Landis, Jim Rivera and Bob Shaw gathered to talk over old times before talking over old times with the media and the public.

The 2009 off-season event was called Sox Fest and the quartet was on hand as living symbols of the 1959 pennant-winning club. Most of the action focused on present-day players and the upcoming season, but this group's area of expertise was the one season between the two World Series champs of 1917 and 2005 that was nearly as beloved by White Sox fans.

They were glad to be present. Pierce lived only about 20 miles away, but the others traveled some distance for the shared remembrance, happy the team and its fans remembered them.

"The fans make you feel terrific," said Shaw, then 75, who was nursing a knee injury and came in a wheelchair from Florida. "It does make you feel old, though. It's scary because there are fewer and fewer of us."[1]

Jim Rivera, 86, from Fort Wayne, Indiana, said it was good to be a part of the event and still feel connected to the White Sox, but thinking back and realizing how many years had passed since he joined the team and played in the World Series for Chicago was a bit overwhelming. "It's good to see all the guys," Rivera said. "I love it (being back)."[2]

All of the players, whether that day in small forums or large, or in advance of the event, praised their absent friends, those who had died and could not relive any 50th anniversary reunions, especially Cy Young Award winner Early Wynn and MVP Nellie Fox.

"That's the toughest part," said Pierce, who turned 82 a couple of months later. "Earl Torgeson is gone, Ted Kluszewski's gone, Nellie's gone,

Bubba Phillips, Billy Goodman, Earl Battey, Sherm Lollar. That's a little bit sad for me. Some of them passed away way too young. When you talk about the White Sox in '59 you've got to talk about Luis (Aparicio), Nellie and Early. They were the stars of our team that year and Nellie and Early are gone and Luis is in Venezuela."[3]

Aparicio rarely ventures to Chicago, though he did attend the ceremonies when the statue of he and Fox together was unveiled.

Shaw remained grateful for the top-notch fielding by Fox, Aparicio and Landis. As a sinker-ball specialist, batters hit the ball on the ground quite often to second and short. "All those guys came out and worked hard every day and played hard every day," Shaw said. "It really helped me."[4]

"Luis," Rivera chimed in, "was a wizard."[5]

The former players kept marveling at the passage of time. How long it had been between the 1917 pennant and the 1959 pennant, how long it was between the 1959 pennant and the 2005 World Series crown, how long it had been since they helped bring that 1959 pennant to Chicago.

"Fifty years ago," said Landis, then 74, who lived in Northern California. "It's unbelievable that it's that long ago. To be remembered, what a feeling it is for us. Most of my baseball memories are here in Chicago. We're so glad we can come back."[6]

Remembered they were. The 1959 players were cheered and applauded and signed autographs for the thousands of White Sox fans that passed through the event.

"We were very proud to win in 1959," Pierce said.[7]

After the weekend the players went their own ways again. They returned to their corners of the country, from there planning to follow the White Sox' fresh quest for pennants and World Series titles. A couple of months later, on April 7, Pierce was at U.S. Cellular Field to start the new season by throwing out the first pitch. Wearing a White Sox cap and a No. 19 jersey, Pierce moved halfway between the mound and the plate. He just didn't have that old arm strength.

So many years had passed.

Chapter Notes

Chapter 1

1. Billy Pierce, personal interview, December 17, 2008.
2. Ibid.
3. "Shoeless Joe Dead at 63; Always Denied 'Fix' Guilt," *The Sporting News*, December 12, 1951.
4. Richard C. Lindberg, *The White Sox Encyclopedia* (Philadelphia: Temple University Press, 1997), p. 291.

Chapter 2

1. Harry T. Paxton, "Baseball's Human Hurricane," *Saturday Evening Post*, May 30, 1953.
2. Ibid.
3. Pierce interview.
4. Paxton, "Baseball's Human Hurricane."
5. Frank Graham, "Is Frank Lane Crazy?" *Sport Magazine*, January 1957.
6. Paxton, "Baseball's Human Hurricane."
7. William Leonard, "Trader Lane of the White Sox!" *Chicago Tribune*, March 6, 1955.
8. Jim Rivera, personal interview, December 16, 2008.
9. Ibid.
10. Paxton, "Baseball's Human Hurricane."
11. Pierce interview.
12. Ibid.
13. Lindberg, *The White Sox Encyclopedia*, p. 294.
14. Paxton, "Baseball's Human Hurricane."

15. Lindberg, *The White Sox Encyclopedia*, p. 294.
16. Pierce interview.

Chapter 3

1. Kenneth T. Jackson, Arnie Markoe and Karen Markoe, *The Scribner Encyclopedia of American Lives* (Farmington Hills, Michigan: Cengage Gale Publishing, 1998), pp. 639–640.
2. Joe Beckham, "Early Wynn: More Than A Hall of Famer," *Grassroots South*, July/August 1976.
3. Ibid.
4. Ibid.
5. "Early Wynn: The Professionals' Pitcher," *Sport Magazine*, July 1960.
6. "Early Wynn Trades and Transactions," *Baseball Almanac*, www.baseball-almanac.com.
7. "Early Wynn Quotes," *Baseball Almanac*, www.baseball-almanac.com.
8. Ibid.
9. Ibid.
10. Ibid.
11. Ibid.
12. Ibid.
13. "Early Wynn," *Answers.com*, www.answers.com.
14. Ibid.

Chapter 4

1. Lew Freedman, *Game of My Life: Chicago White Sox* (Champaign, Illinois: Sports Publishing, 2008), p. 124.
2. Ibid.

3. Pierce interview.
4. Rivera interview.
5. Ibid.
6. Ibid.
7. Rich Marazzi, "Chico Carrasquel: The Father of Venezuelan Shortstops," *Sports Collectors Digest*, July 29, 1994.
8. John C. Hoffman, "Chicago's Nuts About Chico!" *Chicago Sun–Times* (Reprinted in *Baseball Digest*, 1950).
9. Bob Vanderberg, "Venezuelan Was at Team's Core of 1950s Standouts," *Chicago Tribune*, May 26, 2005.
10. Marazzi, "Chico Carrasquel: The Father of Venezuelan Shortstops."
11. Vanderberg, "Venezuelan Was at Team's Core of 1950s Standouts."
12. John C. Hoffman, "Baseball's New Mr. Shortstop," *Collier's*, April 28, 1951.
13. Vanderberg, "Venezuelan Was at Team's Core of 1950s Standouts."
14. Ibid.
15. Minnie Minoso and Herb Fagen, *Just Call Me Minnie* (Champaign, Illinois: Sports Publishing, 1994), p. 115.
16. Ibid.

Chapter 5

1. Pierce interview.
2. Ibid.
3. Ibid.
4. Bob Lutz, "The Rope Delighted in Fooling Pitchers," *Wichita Eagle*, September 9, 2004.
5. Rob Neyer, "Lou Kretlow's Big Week," *ESPN*, August 5, 2002, www.espn.com.
6. *Detroit News*, March 11, 1983.
7. Rick Van Blair, "Bob Keegan Packed a Lot into a Brief Career," *Sports Collectors Digest*, January 27, 1995.
8. Gene Kessler, "Keegan Resembles Ruffing — and Can Hit Like Red, Too," *Chicago Sun–Times*, June 10, 1954.
9. Ibid.
10. Van Blair, "Bob Keegan Packed a Lot into a Brief Career."
11. Ibid.
12. Rich Marazzi, "Like Babe Ruth in Reverse, Former Slugger Jack Harshman

Switched to the Mound," *Sports Collectors Digest*, February 21, 1997.
13. Fred Russell and George Leonard, "The Ballplayer and the Lady," *Saturday Evening Post*, March 24, 1956.
14. Marazzi, "Like Babe Ruth in Reverse, Former Slugger Jack Harshman Switched to the Mound."
15. Bob Vanderberg, "A Fond Adios to Sandy Consuegra," *Chicago Tribune*, December 29, 2005.
16. Howard Roberts, "He's a Baseball Hero Again ... And It's Costing Him $2,000," *Chicago Daily News*, August 15, 1954.
17. Harold Rosenthal, "Fain, of A's, Traded to White Sox for Robinson," *New York Herald–Tribune*, January 28, 1953.
18. Ibid.
19. Ralph Bernstein, "Fain's on First," *Collier's*, February 14, 1953.
20. Ibid.

Chapter 6

1. Lindberg, *The White Sox Encyclopedia*, p. 64.
2. Keith Niebuhr, "He's the Hall's Senior Citizen," *St. Petersburg Times*, July 25, 2005.
3. Harry T. Brundidge, "Caught First Pitch on Nose; Now He's Star as Dodger," *St. Louis Star–Chronicle*, February 16, 1933.
4. Niebuhr, "He's the Hall's Senior Citizen."
5. Brundidge, "Caught First Pitch on Nose; Now He's Star as Dodger."
6. Keith Niebuhr, "Al Lopez Reaction from the Baseball World," *St. Petersburg Times*, October 31, 2005.
7. Ibid.
8. Frank (Buck) O'Neill, "Wynn, Nats Scalp 'Em," *Washington Times–Herald*, May 14, 1942.
9. Ibid.
10. Bob Dolgan, "Legendary Indians Pitcher, Coach Dies," *Cleveland Plain-Dealer*, October 21, 2002.
11. Ibid.
12. "Wynn Was Known as Fierce Competitor," Associated Press, April 6, 1999.

13. "Early Wynn," *Answers.com.*
14. Bob Broeg, "A Blue Ribbon Battler," *The Sporting News,* July 25, 1981.
15. Shirley Povich, "If Wynn Doesn't Belong in Hall of Fame, Who Does?" *The Sporting News,* January 16, 1971.
16. Jim Murray, "The Eyes Have It," *Los Angeles Times,* August 25, 1964.
17. "Early Wynn," *Answers.com.*
18. Art Rosenbaum, "How Early Wynn Made DiMaggio Quit," *The Best of Baseball Digest* (Chicago: Ivan R. Dee Publishers, 2006).
19. Povich, "If Wynn Doesn't Belong in Hall of Fame, Who Does?"
20. Murray, "The Eyes Have It."
21. Arthur Daley, "Nothing Done," *New York Times,* January 24, 1971.
22. "Mike Garcia," *Onpedia Encyclopedia,* www.onpedia.com.
23. "Wynn Was Known as Fierce Competitor."
24. "100 Years of the World Series: Greatest Moments," *Time Magazine,* www.time.com.
25. John P. Carmichael, notebook item, *Baseball Digest,* September 1971.

Chapter 7

1. *Baseball Digest,* 1955.
2. "Sherman Lollar, an Ex-Catcher For White Sox, Is Dead at 53," United Press International, September 26, 1977.
3. Brent Musberger, "Lollar Seeking Minor League Manager's Job," *Chicago American,* September 30, 1963.
4. Pierce interview.
5. Frank Monardo, "Northey, A.L. King at .385, 'Just Meets Ball,'" *The Sporting News,* February 20, 1957.
6. Robert Cromie, "When a Critical Situation Arises, So Does Sox' Ron Northey!" *Chicago Tribune,* September 18, 1956.
7. Monardo, "Northey, A.L. King at .385, 'Just Meets Ball.'"
8. Ibid.
9. Bob Vanderberg, "Sox Ride the Wind to Spot in History," *Chicago Tribune,* April 22, 2005.
10. Virgil O. Trucks, Ronnie Joyner and

Bill Bozman, *Throwing Heat: The Life and Times of Virgil 'Fire' Trucks* (Dunkirk, Maryland: Pepperpot, 2004), p. 180.
11. Ibid., p. 193.
12. Ibid., p. 199.
13. Ibid., pp. 203–204.
14. Lindberg, *The White Sox Encyclopedia,* p. 64.
15. Lindberg, ibid.
16. Ira Berkow, "He Crossed Color Barrier, But In Another's Shadow," *New York Times,* February 23, 1997.
17. Ibid.
18. "Doby Now Tonic to Old Foe," *New York World–Telegram and Sun,* May 5, 1956.
19. Chuck Murr, "His Legend Will Live Forever: Larry Doby," *Indians Ink,* July 8, 2003.
20. Jerome Holtzman, "Doby's Rightful Recognition," *Chicago Tribune,* March 4, 1998.

Chapter 8

1. William Barry Furlong, "Ain't Big, But He's All Fire," *Saturday Evening Post,* May 14, 1955.
2. Ibid.
3. Ibid.
4. Ibid.
5. Edgar Munzel, "They Call Fox 'Biggest Little Guy in Game,'" *The Sporting News,* September 4, 1957.
6. Ibid.
7. Furlong, "Ain't Big, But He's All Fire."
8. David Gough and Jim Bard, *Little Nel, The Nellie Fox Story: An Up Close and Personal Look At Baseball's Mighty Mite* (Alexandria, Virginia: D.L. Megbec, 2000), p. 194.
9. Letter from Ty Cobb to Nellie Fox dated November 14, 1959. National Baseball Hall of Fame Library.
10. Roger Kahn, "Little Nellie's A Man Now," *Sport Magazine,* April 1958.
11. Ibid.
12. Ibid.
13. Pierce interview.
14. Glen Rosenbaum, personal interview, December 19, 2008.
15. Ibid.

16. Kahn, "Little Nellie's A Man Now."
17. Jerry Holtzman, "Little Nell and Enos Among All-Stars as Tobacco Chawers," *The Sporting News*, September 2, 1959.

Chapter 9

1. Jim Landis, personal interview, December 19, 2008.
2. Ross Forman, "Little Looie," *Sports Collectors Digest*, June 28, 1991.
3. Rosenbaum interview.
4. Ibid.
5. Bob Vanderberg, "Modest Start to Hall of Fame Story," *Chicago Tribune*, April 16, 2006.
6. Gilbert Rogin, "Happy Little Luis," *Sports Illustrated*, May 9, 1960.
7. Ibid.
8. Ibid.
9. Forman, "Little Looie."
10. Ed Prell, "Senor Shortstop of the White Sox," *Saturday Evening Post*, August 16, 1958.
11. Ed Prell, "Mr. Shortstop? Aparicio, Of Course!" *Chicago Tribune*, September 13, 1959.
12. Ibid.
13. Wendell Smith, "Luis' Greatest Day Knots Sox for Lead," *Chicago American*, August 15, 1960.
14. Ibid.
15. Ed Prell, "Fox, Aparicio Challenge Great DP Duos," *The Sporting News*, October 7, 1959.
16. Ibid.
17. Pierce interview.
18. Ibid.

Chapter 10

1. "Early Wynn Quotes," *Baseball Almanac*.
2. Joe King, "Burly Early Bellows Warning to Bombers," *New York World–Telegram and Sun*, August 31, 1960.
3. Jerome Holtzman, "Early Wynn: Fierce Foe, Nice Guy," *Chicago Tribune*, April 6, 1999.
4. Early Wynn, "Trade Talk Irks Wynn, Says Lane Made Mistake," *Cleveland News*, December 4, 1957.
5. Early Wynn, "Swap or Cut Talk — Wynn Gets Action," *Cleveland News*, December 11, 1957.
6. Minoso and Fagen, *Just Call Me Minnie*, p. 113.
7. Wynn, "Swap or Cut Talk — Wynn Gets Action."
8. Pierce interview.
9. Holtzman, "Early Wynn: Fierce Foe, Nice Guy."
10. Ibid.
11. Landis interview.
12. Ibid.
13. Ibid.
14. *Baseball Digest*, July 1965.
15. Rosenbaum interview.
16. Pierce interview.
17. Landis interview.
18. Rivera interview.

Chapter 11

1. Al Lopez and Milton Richman, "Who's Afraid of the Big Bad Yankees?" *Saturday Evening Post*, July 13, 1957.
2. Ibid.
3. Ibid.
4. Bob Vanderberg, *Minnie and the Mick* (South Bend, Indiana: Diamond Communications, 1996), p. 87.
5. Edgar Munzel, "White Sox Were Stopped Only by Lack of a Stopper — Senor," *Chicago Sun–Times*, October 2, 1957.
6. Pierce interview.
7. Bill Hageman and Bob Vanderberg, "Cubs Tales, Sox Yarns," *Chicago Tribune*, June 30, 2004.
8. Braven Dyer, "Barry Quick to See Funny Side — But Not When He's on Mound," *The Sporting News*, March 7, 1964.
9. David Condon, "Latman Says He Can Win For White Sox," *Chicago Tribune*, March 18, 1959.
10. Tom Mortenson, "Bill Fischer: M.L. Record-Holder to Begin 44th Year in Pro Ball," *Sports Collectors Digest*, November 29, 1991.
11. "Pitching Mentor Marks 50th Year," *USA TODAY*, August 4, 1997.

12. Edgar Munzel, "Dick Donovan," *Chicago Sun–Times*, May 18, 1955.
13. "Donovan on Verge of Retiring in '55," *Chicago Daily News*, October 7, 1959.
14. Arthur Daley, "Patience Pays Off," *New York Times*, September 5, 1955.
15. Ibid.
16. Pierce interview.
17. Ibid.
18. Bob Vanderberg, "Ex-Sox Pitching Coach Berres Dies," *Chicago Tribune*, February 2, 2007.
19. Arthur Daley, "The Hardluck Kid," *New York Times*, March 15, 1956.
20. David Condon, "In the Wake of the News," *Chicago Tribune*, August 4, 1957.

Chapter 12

1. Landis interview.
2. Ibid.
3. Ibid.
4. Edgar Munzel, "Smith 'At Home' on White Sox as Chi Resident and Left Fielder," *Chicago Sun–Times*, December 25, 1957.
5. Rick Hines, "Al Smith: He Took a Beer Bath in the '59 Series," *Sports Collectors Digest*, June 21, 1991.
6. Minoso and Fagen, *Just Call Me Minnie*, p. 51.
7. Ibid.
8. Edgar Munzel, "Torgy Rates Added Salvo from Senor for Batting Extras," *Chicago Sun–Times*, November 13, 1957.
9. Ibid.
10. Craig Basse, "Earl Torgeson, Major League First Baseman in the 1950s," *St. Petersburg Times*, November 10, 1990.
11. Stan Isaacs, "Nobody Laughs At Bob Shaw Now," *Sport Magazine*, July, 1960.
12. Bob Shaw, personal interview, December, 18, 2008
13. Ibid.
14. Rivera interview.
15. Munzel, "Smith 'At Home' on White Sox as Chi Resident and Left Fielder."
16. Early Wynn, "Well-Wishers Tag All Bags on Wynn," *Cleveland News*, September 4, 1957.
17. Ibid.

Chapter 13

1. Bill Veeck and Ed Linn, *Veeck — As In Wreck* (Chicago: University of Chicago Press, 2001), p. 37.
2. Ibid., p. 49.
3. Ibid., p. 104.
4. Ibid., p. 13.
5. Gerald Eskenazi, *Bill Veeck: A Baseball Legend* (New York: McGraw-Hill, 1988), p. 1.
6. Bill Veeck, "I Know Who's Killing Baseball: Drastic Action Can Save 'National Pastime,'" *Cincinnati Post &Times-Star*, August 11, 1958.
7. George T. Davis, "Hoover Agrees With Veeck On Baseball, Bonus, Draft," *Los Angeles Herald–Examiner*, August 4, 1958.
8. Lindberg, *The White Sox Encyclopedia*, pp. 314–315.
9. Ibid., p. 316.
10. Veeck and Linn, *Veeck — As In Wreck*, p. 323.
11. Ed Prell, "Lopez Wrecks Yankee Dynasty — and Twice!" *Chicago Tribune*, September 20, 1959.
12. Robert Cromie, "Chuck Loses Plea To Halt Sox Sale," *Chicago Tribune*, March 6, 1959.
13. "Finally! Veeck Meets Chuck," *Chicago Tribune*, March 13, 1959.
14. Ibid.
15. "I'm Running Sox: Comiskey," March 23, 1959.
16. Hal Lebovitz, "Roller-Coaster Veeck Off on Another Ride," *The Sporting News*, March 4, 1959.
17. Bill Furlong, "Dad's Work Rubbed Off on Veeck," *Chicago Daily News*, February 19, 1959.
18. David Condon, "Something New in Chicago Baseball: Bill Veeck," *Chicago Tribune*, March 3, 1959.
19. Ibid.
20. Furlong, "Dad's Work Rubbed Off on Veeck."
21. Condon, "Something New in Chicago Baseball: Bill Veeck."

Chapter 14

1. Mike Berardino, "Counting Concerns," *Sporting News Baseball Yearbook*, 2009.
2. Pierce interview.
3. Berardino, "Counting Concerns."
4. Gary Peters, personal interview, December 18, 2008.
5. Ibid.
6. Shaw interview.
7. Ibid.
8. Ibid.
9. Ibid.
10. Ibid.
11. Ibid.
12. Ibid.
13. Ibid.
14. Irving Vaughan, "Rubber Armed Lown Rescues Almost Daily," *Chicago Tribune*, September 16, 1956.
15. Turk Lown, personal interview, December 18, 2008.
16. Ibid.
17. Ibid.
18. Ibid.
19. Ibid.
20. Bob Broeg, "Staley and the Opening Day Jinx," *Complete Baseball Magazine*, Winter 1950.
21. Brent Kelley, "Gerry Staley: Forerunner to Today's Dennis Eckersley," *Sports Collectors Digest*, July 12, 1991.
22. Gerry Staley, personal interview, summer 2007.
23. Richard Dozer, "Gerry Staley — Game," *Chicago Tribune*, July 19, 1959.

Chapter 15

1. Lindberg, *The White Sox Encyclopedia*, p. 69.
2. Rivera interview.
3. Bob Vanderberg, "Modest Start to Hall of Fame Story," *Chicago Tribune*, April 16, 2006.
4. Bob Vanderberg, *'59: Summer of the Sox* (Champaign, Illinois: Sports Publishing, 1999), p. 35.
5. Joe Falls, "Detroit's Ready Cash," *Saturday Evening Post*, May 19, 1962.

6. Vanderberg, *'59: Summer of the Sox*, p. VII.
7. Ibid., p. 33.
8. Ibid., pp. 26–27.
9. Pierce interview.
10. Ibid.
11. Minoso and Fagen, *Just Call Me Minnie*, p. 121.
12. Vanderberg, *'59: Summer of the Sox*, p. 37.

Chapter 16

1. Veeck and Linn, *Veeck — As In Wreck*, pp. 332–333.
2. Eskenazi, *Bill Veeck: A Baseball Legend*, p. 124.
3. Ibid., p. 124.
4. "Whatta Day! Moms at Sox Game Agree," *Chicago Daily News*, May 11, 1959.
5. Ibid.
6. Harvey Duck, "Veeck Dreams Up New Gimmicks To Lure Fans," *Chicago Daily News*, June 28, 1959.
7. Veeck and Linn, *Veeck — As In Wreck*, p. 342.
8. Veeck and Linn, *Veeck — As In Wreck*, p. 341.
9. Vanderberg, *'59: Summer of the Sox*.
10. Veeck and Linn, *Veeck — As In Wreck*, p. 346.
11. Pierce interview.
12. Rivera interview.
13. Shaw interview.

Chapter 17

1. Vanderberg, *'59: Summer of the Sox*, p. 38.
2. Ibid.
3. Edgar Munzel, "Bob Shaw Shines Up Senor's Magic Wand," *The Sporting News*, May 27, 1959.
4. Rick Hines, "Bob Shaw Was a Big Man for '59 ChiSox," *Sports Collectors Digest*, March 8, 1991.
5. Landis interview.
6. "Let's Go, Go-Go White Sox," *Wikipedia, The Free Encyclopedia*.
7. Ed Prell, "Coach Tony Cuccinello

Helps Go-Go White Sox 'Steal' Runs," *Chicago Tribune*, August 30, 1959.
8. Lown interview.
9. Ibid.
10. Hugh Brown, "Del Canned, But Can Still Can-Can," *Philadelphia Bulletin*, June 18, 1959.
11. Jim McAnany, personal interview, December 19, 2008.
12. J.C. Martin, personal interview, December 18, 2008.
13. Ibid.
14. Ibid.
15. Landis interview.

Chapter 18

1. Shaw interview.
2. Vanderberg, *'59: Summer of the Sox*, p. 122.
3. Tom Meany, "Baseball Hercules," *Collier's*, May 26, 1951.
4. Ibid.
5. Ibid.
6. Jerry Holtzman, "Big Crasher Klu Gives Go-Go Sox Boom-Boom Bat," *The Sporting News*, September 16, 1959.
7. Edgar Munzel, "Klu Takes Cue — Fills Bill as Sox Socker," *The Sporting News*, September 23, 1959.
8. Paul M. Anderson, "Ted Kluszewski Dead at Age 63," *Des Plaines Valley News*, April 1, 1988.
9. Holtzman, "Big Crasher Klu Gives Go-Go Sox Boom-Boom Bat."
10. Pierce interview.
11. Lown interview.
12. Bob Broeg, "A Blue-Ribbon Battler," *The Sporting News*, July 25, 1981.
13. Early Wynn and Roger Kahn, "My Pitching Secrets," *Saturday Evening Post*, April 9, 1960.
14. Martin interview.
15. Ibid.
16. Pierce interview.
17. Jerry Holtzman, "Staley Threw Just One Pitch — and Sox' 40-Year Wait Ended," *The Sporting News*, September 30, 1959.
18. Jim McAnany, personal interview, December 19, 2008.

19. Holtzman, "Staley Threw Just One Pitch — and Sox' 40-Year Wait Ended."
20. Nancy Faust, personal interview, December 16, 2008.
21. McAnany interview.
22. Landis interview.
23. Shaw interview.
24. Rivera interview.
25. Pierce interview.

Chapter 19

1. Landis interview.
2. Rivera interview.
3. Landis interview.
4. Lown interview.
5. Braven Dyer, "Rags to Riches for Cinderella Team," *Los Angeles Times*, September 30, 1959.
6. Pierce interview.
7. *Baseball Classics: 1959 World Series*, Rare Sportsfilms, 2000.
8. "'Greatest Day,' Says Big Klu," Associated Press, October 2, 1959.
9. "Alston Moans: 'Didn't Tell us About Power,'" Associated Press, October 2, 1959.
10. Rivera interview.
11. Landis interview.
12. Pierce interview.
13. Shaw interview.
14. Vanderberg, *'59: Summer of the Sox*, p. 155.
15. Larry Sherry, "Sherry Credits Brother," United Press International, October 9, 1959.
16. Vanderberg, *'59: Summer of the Sox*, p. 155.
17. Pierce interview.
18. Richard Dozer, "It's Wynn vs. Craig Again Today In No. 4," *Chicago Tribune*, October 5, 1959.
19. "Hit Home Run on Sinker: Hodges," Associated Press, October 6, 1959.
20. "Sox Change Socks, Script," *Chicago Tribune*, October 7, 1959.
21. Landis interview.
22. Rivera interview.
23. Lester J. Biederman, "Revived Sox Bring Series Home," *Pittsburgh Press*, October 7, 1959.
24. Bob Broeg, "'We'll Win Now,'" *St. Louis Post–Dispatch*, October 7, 1959.

25. Robert Cromie, "World Championship to Los Angeles," *Chicago Tribune*, October 9, 1959.

Chapter 20

1. Jerry Holtzman, "Gaffer Wynn Spikes 'Washed Up' Report," *Chicago Sun–Times*, May 9, 1962.
2. Ibid.
3. Edgar Munzel, "Wynn Glances for Signal — Sees 'No Vacancy' Sign," *The Sporting News*, April 13, 1963.
4. Early Wynn, "Wynn's Better-Late-Than-Never 300th," *New York Times*, May 9, 1982.
5. Richard Dozer, "Worried Wynn Tunes Flipper, Waits by Phone," *Chicago Tribune*, "May 11, 1963.
6. Wynn, "Wynn's Better-Late-Than-Never 300th."
7. Lester J. Biederman, "Early Wynn Happy He Remained Active For 300th Victory," *Pittsburgh Press*, February 14, 1964.

8. Pierce interview.
9. Faust interview.
10. Peters interview.
11. "'We Were All Wishing for a Miracle,' Says Former Teammate," Associated Press, December 2, 1975.
12. "Wynn Recalls 'Mean' Old Days," United Press International, April 2, 1978.
13. Ibid.

Epilogue

1. Bob Shaw, public appearance, Chicago, January 30, 2009.
2. Jim Rivera, public appearance, Chicago, January 30, 2009.
3. Pierce interview.
4. Shaw public appearance.
5. Rivera public appearance.
6. Jim Landis, public appearance, Chicago, January 30, 2009.
7. Pierce interview.

Bibliography

Books

Eskenazi, Gerald. *Bill Veeck: A Baseball Legend*. New York: McGraw-Hill, 1988.

Freedman, Lew. *Game of My Life: Chicago White Sox*. Champaign, Illinois: Sports Publishing, 2008.

Gough, David, and Bard, Jim. *Little Nel, The Nellie Fox Story: An Up Close and Personal Look at Baseball's Mighty Mite*. Alexandria, Virginia: D.L. Megbec, 2000.

Jackson, Kenneth T., Arnie Markoe, and Karen Markoe. *The Scribner Encyclopedia of American Lives*. Farmington Hills, Michigan: Cengage Gale Publishing, 1998.

Kuenster, John, ed. *Best of Baseball Digest*. Chicago: Ivan R. Dee, 2006.

Lindberg, Richard C. *The White Sox Encyclopedia*. Philadelphia: Temple University Press, 1997.

Minoso, Minnie, and Herb Fagen. *Just Call Me Minnie*. Champaign, Illinois: Sports Publishing, 1994.

Trucks, Virgil, Ronnie Joyner, and Bill Bozman. *Throwing Heat: The Life and Times of Virgil "Fire" Trucks*. Dunkirk, Maryland: Pepperpot, 2004.

Vanderberg, Bob. *'59: Summer of the Sox*. Champaign, Illinois: Sports Publishing, 1999.

_____. *Minnie and the Mick*. South Bend, Indiana: Diamond Communications, 1996.

Veeck, Bill, and Ed Linn. *Veeck—As in Wreck*. University of Chicago Press, 2001.

Newspaper Articles

"Alston Moans: Didn't Tell Us About Power." Associated Press, October 2, 1959.

Anderson, Paul M. "Ted Kluszewski Dead at Age 63." *Des Plaines Valley News*, April 1, 1988.

Basse, Craig. "Earl Torgeson, Major League First Baseman in the 1950s." *St. Petersburg Times*, November 10, 1990.

Berkow, Ira. "He Crossed Color Barrier, but in Another's Shadow." *New York Times*, February 23, 1997.

Biederman Lester J. "Early Wynn Happy He Remained Active for 300th Victory." *Pittsburgh Press*, February 14, 1964.

_____. "Revived Sox Bring Series Home." *Pittsburgh Press*, October 7, 1959.

Broeg, Bob. "We'll Win Now." *St. Louis Post-Dispatch*, October 7, 1959.

Brown, Hugh. "Del Canned, but Can Still Can-Can." *Philadelphia Bulletin*, June 18, 1959.

Brundidge, Harry T. "Caught First Pitch on Nose; Now He's Star as Dodger." *St. Louis Star-Chronicle*, February 16, 1933.

Condon, David. "In the Wake of the News." *Chicago Tribune*, August 4, 1957.

_____. "Latman Says He Can Win for White Sox." *Chicago Tribune*, March 18, 1959.

_____. "Something New in Chicago Base-
ball: Bill Veeck." *Chicago Tribune*,
March 3, 1959.
Cromie, Robert. "Chuck Loses Plea to
Halt Sox' Sale." *Chicago Tribune*, March
6, 1959.
_____. "When a Critical Situation Arises,
So Does Sox' Ron Northey!" *Chicago
Tribune*, September 18, 1956.
_____. "World Championship to Los An-
geles." *Chicago Tribune*, October 9, 1959.
Daley, Arthur. "The Hardluck Kid." *New
York Times*, March 15, 1956.
_____. "Nothing Done." *New York Times*,
January 24, 1971.
_____. "Patience Pays Off." *New York
Times*, September 5, 1955.
Davis, George T. "Hoover Agrees with
Veeck on Baseball, Bonus, Draft." *Los
Angeles Herald–Examiner*, August 4,
1958.
"Doby Now Tonic to Old Foe." *New York
World–Telegram and Sun*, May 5, 1956.
Dolgan, Bob. "Legendary Indians Pitcher,
Coach Dies." *Cleveland Plain–Dealer*,
October 21, 2002.
"Donovan on Verge of Retiring in '55."
Chicago Daily News, October 7, 1959.
Dozer, Richard. "Gerry Staley — Game."
Chicago Tribune, July 19, 1959.
_____. "It's Wynn vs. Craig Again Today in
No. 4." *Chicago Tribune*, October 5,
1959.
_____. "Worried Wynn Tunes Flipper,
Waits by Phone." *Chicago Tribune*, May
11, 1963.
Duck, Harvey. "Veeck Dreams Up New
Gimmicks to Lure Fans." *Chicago Daily
News*, June 28, 1959.
Dyer, Braven. "Rags to Riches for Cin-
derella Team." *Los Angeles Times*, Sep-
tember 30, 1959.
"Finally! Veeck Meets Chuck." *Chicago
Tribune*, March 13, 1959.
Furlong, Bill. "Dad's Work Rubbed Off on
Veeck." *Chicago Daily News*, February
19, 1959.

"Greatest Day, Says Big Klu." Associated
Press, October 2, 1959.
Hageman, Bill, and Bob Vanderberg.
"Cubs Tales, Sox Yarns." *Chicago Tri-
bune*, June 30, 2004.
"Hit Home Run on Sinker: Hodges." As-
sociated Press, October 6, 1959.
Holtzman, Jerome. "Doby's Rightful Recog-
nition." *Chicago Tribune*, March 4, 1998.
_____. "Early Wynn: Fierce Foe, Nice
Guy." *Chicago Tribune*, April 6, 1999.
_____[Jerry]. "Gaffer Wynn Spikes
'Washed Up' Report." *Chicago Sun–
Times*, May 9, 1962.
"I'm Running Sox: Comiskey." *Chicago
Tribune*, March 23, 1959.
Kessler, Gene. "Keegan Resembles
Ruffing — and Can Hit Like Red, Too."
Chicago Sun–Times, June 10, 1954.
King, Joe. "Burly Early Bellows Warning
to Bombers." *New York World–Telegram
and Sun*, August 31, 1960.
Leonard, William. "Trader Lane of the
White Sox!" *Chicago Tribune*, March 6,
1955.
Lutz, Bob. "The Rope Delighted in Fool-
ing Pitchers." *Wichita Eagle*, September
9, 2004.
Munzel, Edgar. "Dick Donovan." *Chicago
Sun–Times*, May 18, 1955.
_____. "Smith 'At Home' on White Sox as
Chi Resident and Left Fielder." *Chicago
Sun–Times*, December 25, 1957.
_____. "Torgy Rates Added Salvo from
Senor for Batting Extras." *Chicago
Sun–Times*, November 13, 1957.
_____. "White Sox Were Stopped Only by
Lack of a Stopper — Senor." *Chicago
Sun–Times*, October 2, 1957.
Murray, Jim. "The Eyes Have It." *Los An-
geles Times*, August 25, 1964.
Musberger, Brent. "Lollar Seeking Minor
League Manager's Job." *Chicago Ameri-
can*, September 30, 1963.
Niebuhr, Keith. "Al Lopez Reaction from
the Baseball World." *St. Petersburg
Times*, October 31, 2005.

_____. "He's the Hall's Senior Citizen." *St. Petersburg Times*, July 25, 2005.

O'Neill, Frank (Buck). "Wynn, Nats Scalp 'Em." *Washington Times–Herald*, May 14, 1942.

"Pitching Mentor Marks 50th Year." *USA TODAY*, August 4, 1997.

Prell, Ed. "Coach Tony Cucinello Helps Go-Go White Sox 'Steal' Runs." *Chicago Tribune*, August 30, 1959.

_____. "Lopez Wrecks Yankee Dynasty — and Twice!" *Chicago Tribune*, September 20, 1959.

_____. "Mr. Shortstop? Aparicio, of Course!" *Chicago Tribune*, September 13, 1959.

Roberts, Howard. "He's a Baseball Hero Again ... and It's Costing Him $2,000." *Chicago Daily News*, August 15, 1954.

Rosenthal, Harold. "Fain, of A's, Traded to White Sox for Robinson." *New York Herald–Tribune*, January 28, 1953.

"Sherman Lollar, an Ex-Catcher for White Sox, Is Dead at 53." United Press International, September 26, 1977.

Sherry, Larry. "Sherry Credits Brother." United Press International, October 9, 1959.

Smith, Wendell. "Luis' Greatest Day Knots Sox for Lead." *Chicago American*, August 15, 1960.

"Sox Change Socks, Script." *Chicago Tribune*, October 7, 1959.

Vanderberg, Bob. "A Fond Adios to Sandy Consuegra." *Chicago Tribune*, December 29, 2005.

_____. "Ex-Sox Pitching Coach Berres Dies." *Chicago Tribune*, February 2, 2007.

_____. "Modest Start to Hall of Fame Story." *Chicago Tribune*, April 16, 2006.

_____. "Sox Ride Wind to Spot in History." *Chicago Tribune*, April 22, 2005.

_____. "Venezuelan Was at Team's Core of 1950s Standouts." *Chicago Tribune*, May 26, 2005.

Vaughan, Irving. "Rubber Armed Lown Rescues Almost Daily." *Chicago Tribune*, September 16, 1956.

Veeck, Bill. "I Know Who's Killing Baseball: Drastic Action Can Save 'National Pastime.'" *Cincinnati Post & Times–Star*, August 11, 1958.

"We Were All Wishing for a Miracle, Says Former Teammate." Associated Press, December 2, 1975.

"Whatta Day! Moms at Sox Game Agree." *Chicago Daily News*, May 11, 1959.

Wynn, Early. "Swap or Cut Talk — Wynn Gets Action." *Cleveland News*, December 11, 1957.

_____. "Trade Talks Irk Wynn, Says Lane Made Mistake." *Cleveland News*, December 4, 1957.

_____. "Well-Wishers Tag All Bags on Wynn." *Cleveland News*, September 4, 1957.

_____. "Wynn's Better-Late-Than-Never 300th." *New York Times*, May 9, 1982.

"Wynn Recalls 'Mean' Old Days." United Press International, April 2, 1978.

"Wynn Was Known as Fierce Competitor." Associated Press, April 6, 1999.

Magazine Articles

Beckham, Joe. "Early Wynn: More Than a Hall of Famer." *Grassroots South*, July/August 1976.

Berardino, Mike. "Counting Concerns." *Sporting News Baseball Yearbook,* 2009.

Bernstein, Ralph. "Fain's on First." *Collier's*, February 14, 1953.

Broeg, Bob. "A Blue Ribbon Battler." *The Sporting News*, July 25, 1981.

_____. "Staley and the Opening Day Jinx." *Complete Baseball Magazine*, Winter 1950.

Dyer, Braven. "Barry Quick to See Funny Side — But Not When He's on Mound." *The Sporting News*, March 7, 1964.

"Early Wynn: The Professionals' Pitcher." *Sport Magazine*, July 1960.

Falls, Joe. "Detroit's Ready Cash." *Saturday Evening Post*, May 19, 1962.

Forman, Ross. "Little Looie." *Sports Collectors Digest*, June 28, 1991.

Furlong, William Barry. "Ain't Big, but He's All Fire." *Saturday Evening Post*, May 14, 1955.

Graham, Frank. "Is Frank Lane Crazy?" *Sport Magazine*, January 1957.

Hines, Rick. "Al Smith: He Took a Beer Bath in the '59 Series." *Sports Collectors Digest*, June 21, 1991.

_____. "Bob Shaw Was a Big Man for '59 ChiSox." *Sports Collectors Digest*, March 8, 1991.

Hoffman, John C. "Baseball's New Mr. Shortstop." *Collier's*, April 28, 1951.

Holtzman, Jerry. "Big Crasher Klu Gives Go-Go Sox Boom-Boom Bat." *The Sporting News*, September 16, 1959.

_____. "Little Nell and Enos Among All-Stars as Tobacco Chawers." *The Sporting News*, September 2, 1959.

_____. "Staley Threw Just One Pitch — and Sox' 40-Year Wait Ended." *The Sporting News*, September 30, 1959.

Issacs, Stan. "Nobody Laughs at Bob Shaw Now." *Sport Magazine*, July 1960.

Kahn, Roger. "Little Nellie's a Man Now." *Sport Magazine*, April 1958.

Kelley, Brent. "Gerry Staley: Forerunner to Today's Dennis Eckersley." *Sports Collectors Digest*, July 12, 1991.

Lebovitz, Hal. "Roller-Coaster Veeck Off on Another Ride." *The Sporting News*, March 4, 1959.

Lopez, Al, and Milton Richman. "Who's Afraid of the Big Bad Yankees?" *Saturday Evening Post*, July 13, 1957.

Marazzi, Rich. "Chico Carrasquel: The Father of Venezuelan Shortstops." *Sports Collectors Digest*, July 29, 1994.

_____. "Like Babe Ruth in Reverse, Former Slugger Jack Harshman Switched to the Mound." *Sports Collectors Digest*, February 21, 1997.

Meany, Tom. "Baseball Hercules." *Collier's*, May 26, 1951.

Monardo, Frank. "Northey, A.L. King at .385, 'Just Meets Ball.'" *The Sporting News*, February 20, 1957.

Mortenson, Tom. "Bill Fischer: M.L. Record-Holder to Begin 44th Year in Pro Ball." *Sports Collectors Digest*, November 29, 1991.

Munzel, Edgar. "Bob Shaw Shines Up Senor's Magic Wand." *The Sporting News*, May 27, 1959.

_____. "Klu Takes Cue — Fills Bill as Sox Socker." *The Sporting News*, September 23, 1959.

_____. "They Call Fox 'Biggest Little Guy in Game.'" *The Sporting News*, September 4, 1957.

_____. "Wynn Glances for Signal — Sees 'No Vacancy' Sign." *The Sporting News*, April 13, 1963.

Murr, Chuck. "His Legend Will Live Forever: Larry Doby." *Indians Ink*, July 8, 2003.

Paxton, Harry T. "Baseball's Human Hurricane." *Saturday Evening Post*, May 30, 1953.

Povich, Shirley. "If Wynn Doesn't Belong in Hall of Fame, Who Does?" *The Sporting News*, January 16, 1971.

Prell, Ed. "Fox, Aparicio Challenge Great DP Duos." *The Sporting News*, October 7, 1959.

_____. "Senor Shortstop of the White Sox." *Saturday Evening Post*, August 16, 1958.

Rogin, Gil. "Happy Little Luis." *Sports Illustrated*, May 9, 1960.

Russell, Fred, and George Leonard. "The Ballplayer and the Lady." *Saturday Evening Post*, March 24, 1956.

"Shoeless Joe Dead at 63; Always Denied 'Fix' Guilt." *The Sporting News*, December 12, 1951.

Van Blair, Rick. "Bob Keegan Packed a Lot into a Brief Career." *Sports Collectors Digest*, January 27, 1995.

Wynn, Early, and Roger Kahn. "My Pitching Secrets." *Saturday Evening Post,* April 9, 1960.

Interviews

Faust, Nancy. Telephone interview with author, December 16, 2008.
Landis, Jim. Telephone interview with author, December 19, 2008; personal interview at public appearance, Chicago, January 30, 2009.
Lown, Turk. Telephone interview with author, December 18, 2008.
Martin, J.C. Telephone interview with author, December 18, 2008.
McAnany, Jim. Telephone interview with author, December 19, 2008.
Peters, Gary. Telephone interview with author, December 18, 2008.
Pierce, Billy. Telephone interview with author, December 17, 2008; personal interview at public appearance, Chicago, January 30, 2009.
Rivera, Jim. Telephone interview with author, December 16, 2008; personal interview at public appearance, Chicago, January 30, 2009.
Rosenbaum, Glen. Telephone interview with author, December 19, 2008.
Shaw, Bob. Telephone interview with author, December 18, 2008; personal interview at public appearance, Chicago, January 30, 2009.
Staley, Gerry. Telephone interview with author, summer 2007.

Web Sites

"Early Wynn." *Answers.com.* www.answers.com
"Early Wynn Quotes" and "Early Wynn Trades and Transactions." *Baseball Almanac.* www.baseball-almanac.com
"Let's Go, Go-Go White Sox." *Wikipedia*
"Mike Garcia." *Onpedia Encyclopedia.* www.onpedia.com
Neyer, Rob. "Lou Kretlow's Big Week." *ESPN,* August 2, 2002. www.espn.com
"100 Years of the World Series: Greatest Moments." *Time Magazine,* www.time.com

Archives

Letter from Ty Cobb to Nellie Fox dated November 14, 1959. National Baseball Hall of Fame Library.

Video

Baseball Classics: 1959 World Series, Rare Sportsfilms, 2000.

Index

Aaron, Hank 176
Alabama 5, 29, 35, 63, 133, 193
All Star teams 36, 39, 41, 42, 47, 50, 52, 53, 54, 56, 58, 59, 62, 66, 71, 72, 73, 84, 88, 89, 90, 93, 112, 157, 161, 162, 167, 177, 189
Alston, Walt 177, 179
American Association 19, 69, 115, 119, 162
American League 1, 6, 11, 12, 14, 21, 25, 30, 32, 39, 41, 43, 44, 46, 47, 48, 53, 55, 57, 61, 62, 66, 68, 70, 72, 73, 77, 82, 86, 88, 100, 101, 102, 108, 109, 110, 112, 116, 120, 123, 130, 138, 142, 143, 146, 150, 152, 156, 160, 161, 165, 166, 168, 170, 171, 188, 189, 191
American Legion 65
Aparicio, Ernesto 84
Aparicio, Luis 1, 2, 3, 41, 43, 73, 84, 85, 86, 88, 89, 90, 91, 108, 113, 114, 116, 131, 140, 141, 143, 158, 159, 170, 171, 178, 190, 195
Aparicio, Luis, Sr. 84
Appling, Luke 16, 41, 42, 43
The Apprentice 19
Argo, Ill. 166
Arizona 126
Arkansas 65
Atlanta Braves 106
Atlanta Crackers 106
Avila, Bobby 62

Baltimore 66, 133, 168
Baltimore Orioles 24, 48, 49, 52, 71, 89, 122, 127, 160, 161, 189
Banks, Ernie 143
Bards Room 148
Barnum, P.T. 128
Baseball Almanac 38
Baseball Encyclopedia 38
Baseball Hall of Fame 1, 2, 3, 16, 21, 23, 27, 30, 32, 41, 43, 56, 74, 79, 128, 141, 177, 190, 193
Batista, Fulgencio 143
Battey, Earl 114, 132, 189, 191, 194
Baxes, Jim 145, 170
Bell, Gary 145
Bender, Chief 58
Berra, Yogi 55, 66, 88, 101, 103, 191
Berres, Ray 25, 52, 93, 108, 115, 116, 132, 133, 134, 157, 191
Bevans, Floyd 23
Big Ten 20, 167
Black Sox scandal 1, 8, 11, 13, 14, 15, 18, 142, 160, 175, 184, 186
Blackburne, Lena 82, 83
Bolling, Frank 141
Boone, Aaron 112
Boone, Bob 112
Boone, Bret 112
Boone, Ray 112, 113, 115, 162, 191
Boston 13, 46, 106, 133, 163
Boston Braves 106, 113, 114, 122
Boston Red Sox 49, 52, 57, 62, 69, 144, 151, 158, 167, 188
Boudreau, Lou 57, 73
Boyd, Bob 48
Breechen, Harry 154
Brickhouse, Jack 178
Briggs Stadium 11
Brissie, Lou 37
Broeg, Bob 185
Brooklyn 3, 10, 135
Brooklyn Dodgers 27, 38, 41, 56, 62, 72, 109, 122, 135, 167, 180
Brown, Warren 143
Brush Prairie, Wash. 137
Bucknell University 50
Buffalo 23
Bunning, Jim 139
Burdette, Lew 176

Burnside, Pete 163
Busby, Jim 39, 73, 151

California 3, 10, 54, 127, 177, 191, 195
Callison, Johnny 114, 162, 189, 191
Campanella, Roy 38, 177
Caracas 85
Carrasquel, Chico 23, 41, 42, 43, 44, 73, 76, 84, 85, 88, 89, 90, 91, 140
Cash, Norm 114, 141, 142, 189, 191
Cassini, Jack 140
Castro, Fidel 143, 144
Cavaretta, Phil 52, 53
Chapman, Ben 35
Charleston 115
Chase Hotel 48, 49
Chavez, Hugo 43
Chavez Ravine 176
Chicago 1, 2, 6, 7, 8, 13, 16, 21, 22, 23, 25, 26, 39, 42, 43, 46, 47, 52, 53, 63, 66, 70, 73, 76, 84, 91, 94, 102, 112, 113, 116, 123, 124, 128, 140, 147, 148, 150, 152, 155, 156, 157, 159, 162, 166, 167, 171, 172, 173, 175, 177, 178, 180, 189, 191, 193, 194, 195
Chicago American 19
Chicago Bears 69, 141
Chicago City Council 172
Chicago Cubs 11, 52, 53, 57, 118, 119, 127, 135, 143, 172
Chicago Sun Times 41, 81, 83
Chicago Tribune 19, 143, 180
Chicago White Sox 1, 2, 3, 6, 7, 8, 10, 11, 12, 13, 14, 15, 16, 17, 18, 19, 20, 21, 22, 23, 24, 25, 26, 27, 28, 37, 38, 39, 40, 41, 42, 43, 44, 45, 46, 47, 48, 49, 50, 51, 52, 53, 54, 55, 63, 64, 65, 66, 67, 68, 69, 70, 71, 72, 73, 74, 75, 78, 79, 81, 82, 83, 84, 86, 88, 89, 90, 91, 92, 93, 94, 95, 97, 98, 99, 100, 101, 102, 103, 104, 105, 106, 107, 108, 110, 111, 112, 113, 114, 115, 116, 123, 124, 125, 126, 127, 128, 130, 131, 134, 135, 136, 138, 139, 140, 141, 142, 143, 145, 146, 147, 148, 150, 152, 154, 155, 156, 157, 158, 159, 160, 161, 162, 163, 164, 165, 166, 167, 168, 169, 170, 171, 172, 173, 174, 175, 176, 177, 178, 179, 180, 181, 182, 183, 184, 186, 187, 188, 189, 190, 191, 193, 194
Cicotte, Ed 14, 15
Cincinnati Reds 7, 11, 14, 15, 19, 103, 161, 167
Clemens, Roger 106

Cleveland 8, 13, 43, 73, 94, 101, 111, 112, 116, 121, 126, 139, 153, 165, 170, 171, 189
Cleveland Indians 1, 6, 8, 14, 24, 25, 35, 36, 38, 44, 45, 55, 57, 58, 59, 62, 63, 64, 66, 73, 81, 85, 86, 93, 100, 101, 110, 111, 119, 120, 127, 132, 145, 146, 149, 152, 156, 157, 158, 159, 160, 164, 165, 166, 170, 173, 175, 188, 189, 191
Cleveland News 93
Cleveland Stadium 166
Coan, Gil 67
Coates, Jim 93
Cobb, Ty 3, 59, 79, 81
Colavito, Rocky 136, 145
Cole, Nat "King" 180
Collins, Eddie 14, 90
Colorado 191
Colorado Springs 162
Comiskey, Charles 16, 17, 18, 123, 148
Comiskey Charles, II 7
Comiskey, Chuck 20, 25, 26, 44, 100, 103, 112, 123, 124, 125, 126, 148, 152, 162
Comiskey, Dorothy 123, 124, 125, 126
Comiskey, Grace Reidy 18, 20, 26, 71, 123
Comiskey, John Louis 17, 123
Comiskey family 1, 20, 123
Comiskey Park 2, 3, 8, 13, 22, 38, 47, 50, 53, 90, 101, 108, 110, 123, 147, 148, 149, 150, 152, 154, 158, 159, 160, 165, 173, 175, 178, 179, 180, 185, 186, 190
Commonwealth Edison Company 150
Concepcion, Davey 43
Condon, David 143
Connecticut 69
Connie Mack Stadium 13
Consuegra, Sandy 52
Cooperstown 190
Corriden, John 26
Courtney, Clint 161
Craig, Roger 178, 182
Crosman Pellguns 81
Cuba 37, 55, 143, 144
Cuccinello, Tony 102, 159, 167, 191
Cunningham, Joe 95
Cy Young Award 2, 168, 180, 187, 194

Daley, Arthur 107
Daley, Richard J. 25, 172, 175, 180
Dallas 53
Dean, Dizzy 49
DeMaestri, Joe 53
Detroit 11, 12, 13, 21, 46, 49, 70, 115, 139, 140, 141, 142, 157, 158, 163, 189

Detroit Tigers 11, 13, 51, 63, 70, 79, 106, 108, 113, 115, 127, 136, 139, 143, 159, 166, 171
Dickey, Bill 66
DiMaggio, Joe 5, 61
Ditmar, Art 73, 74
Dixon, Jeanne 125
Doby, Larry 62, 63, 72, 73, 74, 102, 120, 141, 191
Donovan, Dick 104, 106, 107, 108, 131, 160, 166, 178, 181, 184, 185, 191
Dothan, Ala. 29
Dozer, Richard 143
Dracula 20
Dropo, Walt 69, 73
Drysdale, Don 177, 181, 182
Dunne, Robert Jerome 125
Durocher, Leo 109, 167
Dykes, Jimmy 16, 26

Eagle River 123, 148
"Earl of Snowhomish" 113
Early Wynn Steakhouse and Bowling Lanes 188
Eastern League 31
Ebbets Field 135
Eckersley, Dennis 137
Einstein, Albert 98
Eisenmann, Charles 23
Elliott, Bob 70
Elson, Bob 41
Ennis, Del 161, 162, 191
Esposito, Sammy 140, 182, 191
Essegian, Chuck 181

Faber, Red 16, 178
Fain, Ferris 53, 54
Fairly, Ron 181
Farrell, James 14
Faust, Nancy 172, 189
Fayetteville 65
Feller, Bob 11, 57, 130, 145
Felsch, Happy 15
Finley, Charles O. 124
Fischer, Bill 105, 106, 115
Florida 30, 49, 55, 93, 105, 106, 133, 188, 191, 193, 194
Florida State League 31, 56
Ford, Whitey 6, 55, 101, 102, 103
Forest Park 150
Fort Wayne 194
Fort Worth 42
Fox, Joanne 77

Fox, Nellie 1, 2, 21, 25, 27, 28, 75, 76, 77, 78, 79, 81, 82, 83, 90, 91, 97, 108, 111, 113, 114, 116, 131, 139, 151, 152, 165, 178, 184, 190, 191, 194
Francona, Tito 115, 145
Freese, Gene 90, 189
Frick, Ford 176
Friend, Owen 70
Fullerton, Hugh 14
Furillo, Carl 177

Gaedel, Eddie 120, 152
Gandil, Chick 15
Garcia, Mike 57, 62, 145
Gary, Ind. 150
Geiger, Gary 151
Geneva County High School 29
Gibson, Bob 95, 130
Gibson, Josh 37, 191
Gilbert, Larry 51
Gilliam, Jim 10, 177, 178, 182
Gleason, Bill 149
Gleason, Kid 7, 14
"Go Go White Sox" 39, 44, 79, 86, 88, 101, 132, 158, 159, 166
Gomez, Lefty 191
Goodman, Billy 140, 170, 178, 191
Gordon, Joe 90, 145
Grabiner, Harry 18
Grant, Jim "Mudcat" 145
Great Depression 18, 35
Greenberg, Hank 85, 125, 157
Greenville 15
Griffith, Calvin 161
Griffith Stadium 156
Grim, Bob 44, 55
Grimm, Charlie 119
Groth, Johnny 70
Grove, Lefty 188
Grove City 131
Guillen, Ozzie 41, 43

Haas, George 26
Halladay, Roy 130
Hancock, Fred 23
Harder, Mel 58, 59, 94
Harridge, Will 73, 191
Harris, Bucky 35
Harshman, Jack 42, 43, 51, 52, 170
Hartford, Ala. 29, 30, 58
Hatfield, Fred 44, 94
Hatton, Brady 49
Havana 37, 143, 144

Hawaii 78
Haynes, Joe 36
Held, Woody 145
Herbert Hoover High School 112
Herzog, Whitey 90
Hoderlein, Mel 39
Hodges, Gil 167, 177, 182, 183
Holtzman, Jerome 74, 141
Hoover, J. Edgar 122, 123
Hornsby, Rogers 23
Houtteman, Art 57, 145
Howard, Elston 101, 103
Howell, Pat 150

Illinois 24, 140, 166
Indiana 150, 191, 194
Indiana University 167
Indianapolis 103, 162
International League 66, 76

Jackson, Ron 68, 191
Jackson, Shoeless Joe 7, 14, 15, 64, 142
Jagiello, Walter 158
James, Bill 114
Johnson, Darrell 70
Johnson, Walter 56

Kahn, Roger 79, 169
Kaline, Al 141
Kansas 66
Kansas City 19, 117, 143
Kansas City Athletics 90, 109, 122, 124,
    142, 143, 144, 162, 167, 188, 190, 193
Keegan, Bob 50, 51
Kell, George 49
Kennedy, John F. 180
Khrushchev, Nikita 172
Kielman, Ed 36
Kiner, Ralph 78, 90
Kluszewski, Eleanor 167
Kluszewski, Ted 166, 167, 168, 178, 179,
    185, 191, 194
Korean War 105
Koufax, Sandy 177, 184, 185
Kress, Red 85
Kretlow, Lou 49, 70
Krsnich, Rocky 49
Kubek, Tony 101

Ladies Day 2, 118, 149
Lake Erie 166
LaLanne, Jack 20
Lancaster 82

Landis, Jim 84, 95, 97, 98, 110, 111, 113,
    132, 158, 159, 164, 166, 173, 175, 176,
    178, 179, 182, 184, 190, 191, 194, 195
Landis, Kenesaw Mountain 7, 15, 16, 119
Lane, Frank 7, 11, 12, 14, 18, 19, 20, 21, 22,
    23, 24, 25, 26, 27, 28, 37, 39, 41, 43,
    44, 45, 46, 47, 49, 50, 52, 53, 55, 63,
    64, 65, 66, 69, 70, 71, 75, 76, 84, 93,
    100, 103, 106, 109, 125, 146, 148, 159, 161
Las Vegas 142
Las Villas Province 143
Latin American winter ball 156
Latman, Barry 104, 105, 166, 189
Lebovitz, Hal 126, 127
Lemon, Bob 57, 62, 92, 145
Leonard, Buck 37, 191
Liston, Sonny 8
Litwhiler, Danny 114
Lollar, Sherman 23, 65, 66, 67, 86, 102,
    105, 111, 113, 131, 178, 184, 191, 194
Lopat, Ed 101
Lopez, Al 2, 3, 6, 8, 27, 50, 51, 55, 56,
    57, 66, 72, 81, 89, 93, 94, 100, 101, 102,
    103, 104, 105, 110, 111, 112, 113, 114, 115,
    125, 126, 130, 131, 132, 133, 134, 136,
    137, 138, 139, 140, 145, 146, 149, 156,
    157, 158, 164, 171, 178, 182, 184, 185, 187,
    189, 190, 191
Los Angels 133, 181
Los Angeles Dodgers 3, 10, 175, 176, 177,
    178, 179, 180, 181, 182, 183, 184, 185
Los Angeles Memorial Coliseum 3, 176,
    181, 183, 184, 185
Los Angeles Times 62
Louisville Slugger 81
Lown, Bill 135
Lown, Turk 134, 135, 136, 138, 157, 160,
    168, 176, 180, 182, 185, 191
Lyons, Ted 16, 26, 50

Mack, Connie 17, 54, 75, 76, 129
MacPhail, Larry 19
Mantle, Mickey 6, 33, 38, 55, 101, 104,
    105
Maracaibo, Venezuela 84
Marion, Marty 52, 68, 71, 72, 73, 76, 81,
    100
Martians Free Admission Day 152
Martin, Billy 73, 74, 145
Martin, J.C. 163, 164, 169, 190, 191
Maryland 127
Mathews, Eddie 176
Mattoon, Ill. 24

Mays, Willie 63
McAnany, Jim 162, 163, 171, 173, 184, 191
McDougald, Gil 60
McGhee, Ed 53
McGraw, John 129
McLish, Cal 145
McMullin, Fred 15
Mele, Sam 39
Memphis 140
Meyers, Chief John Tortes 58
Miami Marlins 157
Michaels, Cass 76, 109
Michigan 11
Midway Airport 8, 166, 172, 173, 174
Milan, Clyde 30, 31
Miller, Yvonne 149
Milwaukee 106
Milwaukee Braves 10, 122, 175, 176, 177
Milwaukee Brewers (minors) 119, 128
Mincher, Don 189
Minnesota Twins 191, 193
Minoso, Minnie 25, 37, 38, 39, 41, 43, 44, 45, 48, 52, 82, 90, 94, 111, 112, 113, 114, 145, 158, 159, 189, 190
Miranda, Willie 24, 25
Mississippi 48
Mississippi River 25
Missouri 48
Moline, Ill. 140
Monbouquette, Bill 188
Montreal 23
Moon, Wally 177
Moore, Ray 151, 185, 191
Moosup, Conn. 69
Mossi, Don 140
Murray, Jim 62
Murray, Ray 37

Naimoli, Vince 57
Nashville 51
National Basketball Association 179
National Dairy Week 151
National Football League 19
National Hockey League 179
National League 10, 14, 53, 71, 79, 167, 175, 176, 177
Neal, Charlie 177, 180, 184
Nebraska 76
Negro Leagues 38, 72, 119, 156
New York 7, 13, 40, 46, 47, 50, 55, 102
New York Cubans 38
New York Giants, 51, 63, 122, 167

New York Times 107
New York Yankees 2, 6, 19, 23, 43, 44, 49, 50, 53, 54, 55, 57, 61, 66, 70, 71, 89, 92, 100, 101, 102, 103, 104, 105, 114, 116, 125, 132, 138, 142, 143, 146, 156, 158, 161, 162, 171, 175, 189
Newcombe, Don 38, 41
Newhouser, Hal 11, 60, 62
Nieman, Bob 22, 23, 70
Nokomis 93
North Carolina 191
Northey, Ron 67, 68

Oakland 124
O'Connor, Les 18, 20
Ohio 19, 166
O'Malley, Walter 177
Onslow, Jack 26, 75

Pacific Coast League 23, 38, 90
Paige, Satchel 37, 70, 120, 156, 157
Pennsylvania 50, 75, 78, 131
Perry, Jim 145, 170
Peters, Gary 131, 190, 191
Philadelphia 13, 53, 54
Philadelphia Athletics 17, 25, 52, 53, 69, 75, 76, 122
Philadelphia Phillies 119, 156, 161, 189
Philley, Dave 49, 113
Phillips, Bubba 170, 189, 191, 194
Piccadilly Hotel 115
Piedmont League 31
Pierce, Billy 1, 7, 11, 12, 13, 21, 24, 25, 26, 27, 39, 42, 44, 47, 48, 50, 66, 81, 91, 94, 95, 97, 98, 102, 103, 107, 108, 109, 111, 113, 116, 126, 130, 131, 144, 145, 154, 160, 165, 168, 170, 174, 178, 179, 182, 184, 185, 189, 191, 194, 195
Piersall, Jimmy 145, 170, 190
Piniella, Lou 57
Pittsburgh Pirates 78, 127, 137, 166, 168, 179
Podres, Johnny 180, 185
Polo Grounds 63
Porter, J.W. 70
Power, Vic 145, 170, 171

Quincy High School 106
Quinn, Bob 172

Ramos, Pedro 161
Raschi, Vic 101
Reese, Pee Wee 90

Reynolds, Allie 55, 101
Richards, Paul 27, 28, 38, 41, 42, 43, 46, 47, 50, 55, 65, 70, 71, 76, 77, 78, 79, 81, 89, 108, 109
Richardson, Bobby 101
Rickey, Branch 38, 41, 72
Rigney, John 7, 44, 103, 123, 125, 148
Ringling Brothers Circus 127
Risberg, Swede 15
Rivera, Jim 23, 24, 39, 40, 41, 99, 101, 102, 116, 132, 139, 154, 168, 170, 173, 175, 178, 179, 184, 185, 191, 194, 195
Rizzuto, Phil 90
Roberts, Antoinette 150
Robinson, Aaron 13
Robinson, Eddie 36, 53
Robinson, Jackie 38, 48, 62, 72, 73, 90, 120
Rochester, N.Y. 50
Romano, Johnny 114, 132, 189, 190
Roosevelt, Teddy 85
Roseboro, Johnny 177
Rosen, Al 62, 63
Rosenbaum, Glen 81, 82, 85, 98
Rothstein, Arnold 15
Rudolph, Don 103, 104, 140, 141, 161, 191
Runnels, Pete 151
Ruth, Babe 7

St. Louis 13, 25, 48, 72
St. Louis Browns 23, 24, 40, 48, 66, 69, 70, 71, 120, 121, 122, 127, 147, 152, 154, 157
St. Louis Cardinals 22, 44, 63, 68, 71, 95, 121, 137
St. Thomas 75
San Diego 112
Sanford, Fla. 30, 31
Santa Clara, Cuba 143
Saturday Evening Post 19
Schalk, Ray 178
Score, Herb 81, 110, 145, 189
Scully, Vince 178
Seattle 23
Seattle Mariners 57
Seaver, Tom 106
Shantz, Bobby 101, 102
Shaw, Bob 114, 115, 131, 132, 133, 134, 143, 144, 154, 155, 156, 157, 158, 160, 162, 165, 173, 178, 180, 184, 191, 194
Sherry, Larry 181, 182, 183, 185, 186
Sherry, Norm 181
Short, Ed 188

Sievers, Roy 161, 189
Simpson, Harry "Suitcase" 162, 166, 191
Skizas, Lou 161
Skowron, Bill 101, 162
Slaughter, Enos 73
Smith, Al 7, 45, 94, 95, 111, 112, 116, 131, 165, 178, 180, 181, 184, 191
Smith, Red 182
Snider, Duke 177, 185
Snyderworth, Bernie 125
Sockalaxie, Louis 58
South Carolina 15
South Grand Forks 79
Southeastern Conference 20
Southern League 51
Spahn, Warren 176
Spain 55
Sport magazine 19
"Sport Shirt" 150
The Sporting News 150
Staley, Gerry 134, 136, 137, 138, 140, 157, 170, 171, 182, 185, 191
Staley, Joe 137
Staley, Roy 137
Stengel, Casey 6, 43, 55, 89, 102, 125
Strickland, Dr. Hubert 30
Stuart, Dick 168
Sul Ross State College 141
Sullivan, Ed 185
Summer Olympics 176
Syracuse 50

Tampa 3, 7, 55, 57, 105, 125, 139, 189
Tampa Bay Devil Rays 57
Tampa Smokers 56
Tebbetts, Birdie 188
Terry, Bill 167
Terry, Ralph 165
Texas 27, 141
Thorpe, Jim 58
Thurston, Hollis 90
Tiger Stadium 139, 141
Tipton, Joe 21, 75
Torgeson, Earl 113, 114, 159, 160, 174, 191, 194
Toronto Blue Jays 191
Trace, Al 158
Trout, Dizzy 11
Trucks, Virgil 70, 71
Trump, Donald 19
Tuohy, William J. 126
Turley, Bob 162

Union Stock Yard 13
U.S. Army 31, 76, 137, 140
U.S. Cellular Field 1, 190, 195
U.S. Congress 32
U.S. Marines 105
U.S. Navy 19
University of Connecticut 69

Valdivielso, Jose 60
Vancouver, B.C. 69
Veeck, Bill 1, 2, 3, 23, 24, 44, 57, 69, 70,
  72, 73, 74, 78, 86, 103, 104, 118, 119,
  120, 121, 122, 123, 124, 125, 126, 127,
  128, 142, 147, 148, 149, 150, 151, 152,
  153, 154, 155, 156, 157, 159, 161, 162,
  164, 165, 166, 178, 189, 191
Veeck, Bill, Sr. 118
Veeck, Eleanor 127, 128
Veeck, Mike 44, 142
Venezuela 41, 43, 84, 86, 195
Venice 188, 193
Vernon, Mickey 32, 33, 35, 61
Vero Beach 41
Viceroy 81
Virginia 164
Vizquel, Omar 43

Washington D.C. 13, 54, 156, 162
Washington Senators 1, 5, 30, 31, 32, 35,
  36, 39, 51, 52, 56, 57, 58, 60, 61, 84,
  93, 127, 132, 144, 153, 156, 161, 189
Washington state 137
Wausau, Wis. 105
Waxahachie, Tex. 27
Weaver, Buck 14, 15, 16, 90
Wertz, Vic 62, 63
White, Hal 70
Wichita Eagle 48

Williams, Lefty 15
Williams, Ted 62, 112
Wills, Maury 177
Wilson, Bob 53
Wilson, Jim 49
Wilson baseball gloves 81
Wisconsin 25, 105, 123, 148
World Series 1, 2, 3, 6, 7, 8, 10, 11, 13, 14,
  21, 43, 57, 63, 65, 89, 118, 120, 124, 132,
  147, 157, 175, 176, 178, 179, 180, 181, 183,
  184, 185, 186, 190, 195
World War II 5, 18, 19, 35, 54, 66, 75,
  119, 137
Wrigley, P.K. 118
Wrigley, William 118
Wrigley Field 53, 118, 119
Wyatt, Whitlow 106, 107
Wynn, Blanche 29
Wynn, Early 1, 2, 5, 6, 7, 8, 10, 29, 30, 31,
  32, 33, 34, 35, 36, 45, 50, 57, 58, 59,
  60, 61, 62, 63, 64, 92, 93, 94, 95, 97,
  98, 99, 109, 111, 116, 117, 130, 131, 132,
  133, 134, 141, 143, 144, 145, 149, 153,
  154, 156, 160, 161, 163, 164, 165, 168,
  169, 170, 175, 178, 179, 182, 185, 186,
  187, 188, 190, 191, 193, 194, 195
Wynn, Early, Sr. 29, 30
Wynn, Joe 31, 98
Wynn, Loraine 31
Wynn, Mabel 31
Wynn, Sherry 31

Yankee Stadium 60
Ybor City 55
Young, Cy 130
Youngs, Ross 191

Zoldak, Sam 37